# Monstrous Bodies

# Monstrous Bodies

*Feminine Power in
Young Adult Horror Fiction*

JUNE PULLIAM

McFarland & Company, Inc., Publishers
*Jefferson, North Carolina*

LIBRARY OF CONGRESS CATALOGUING-IN-PUBLICATION DATA

Pulliam, June Michele.
    Monstrous bodies : feminine power in young adult horror fiction / June Pulliam.
        p.    cm.
    Includes bibliographical references and index.

    ISBN 978-0-7864-7543-8 (softcover : acid free paper) ∞
    ISBN 978-1-4766-1663-6 (ebook)

    1. Young adult literature—History and criticism.
2. Other (Philosophy) in literature.   3. Women in literature.
4. Horror in literature.   5. Young adults—Books and reading.   I. Title.
PN1009.A1P86 2014
809.3'8738082—dc23                    2014020399

BRITISH LIBRARY CATALOGUING DATA ARE AVAILABLE

© 2014 June Pulliam. All rights reserved

*No part of this book may be reproduced or transmitted in any form or by any means, electronic or mechanical, including photocopying or recording, or by any information storage and retrieval system, without permission in writing from the publisher.*

Cover images © Arman Zhenikeyev/Thinkstock

Printed in the United States of America

*McFarland & Company, Inc., Publishers*
  *Box 611, Jefferson, North Carolina 28640*
  *www.mcfarlandpub.com*

For Rosa

# *Acknowledgments*

My name on the cover of this book is deceptive in that might cause you to believe that I am the only person responsible for producing this work. Indeed, that couldn't be further from the truth. A book is always a collective effort, and various people have officially and unofficially helped me write this one, and I would like to acknowledge them here.

I am deeply grateful to my editor, Colleen Fava, as well as my research assistant, Josh Hamburg, for patiently reading the manuscript several times and giving me their feedback. I am also grateful to Robin Roberts, who, as my dissertation director, was the patient midwife of the original version that I labored to produce. I would also like to express my appreciation to my adolescent literature and horror fiction students, who helped me think through this project when they discussed this fiction with me in my classes.

Finally, I would like to thank the proprietors of Highland Coffees in Baton Rouge, Louisiana, and the Globe Café in Prague, the Czech Republic, who let me nurse a cup of coffee for hours on end while occupying a comfy chair and working on this project.

# Table of Contents

*Acknowledgments* 7
*Introduction* 11

CHAPTER 1
Subversive Spirits: Resistance and the Uncanny
in the Young Adult Ghost Story  21

CHAPTER 2
Blood and Bitches: Sexual Politics and
the Female Lycanthrope in Young Adult Fiction  73

CHAPTER 3
"An ye harm none, do as ye will": Magic, Gender and
Agency in Young Adult Narratives of Witchcraft  123

*Conclusion* 173
*Chapter Notes* 179
*Bibliography* 183
*Index* 189

# *Introduction*

YOUNG ADULT HORROR FICTION is uniquely able to examine the challenges facing young women, who even today are encouraged to embrace restrictive gender roles. Examining these roles is an important first step in resisting them. Both horror and Young Adult fiction are genres that have received little critical attention. Critics and academics frequently disdain genre fiction as a whole, viewing it as material whose alleged adherence to conventions necessarily bars it from having artistic merit or the ability to engage in useful social commentary. Yet both genres merit critical analysis. Young Adult horror fiction in particular deserves feminist scholarly inquiry because it uniquely explores the process by which teen girls become gendered subjects.

Young Adult horror fiction does not simply reproduce through the form of the monstrous Other sexist ideas about women; rather, it uses the tropes horror to deconstruct sexist ideas about women's supposed essential nature, which have been used to justify their subordination. In this way, Young Adult horror fiction differs from mainstream horror fiction, which is as likely to affirm sexist ideas about women (as well as racist ideas about non-whites) as it is to challenge these beliefs.

Horror fiction has its roots in the Gothic, a type of fiction characterized by an atmosphere of mystery and terror. However, the horror genre with its pantheon of monsters would not emerge in its contemporary form until the 1930s, where it flourished in pulp magazines, film and horror comics. A defining quality of the horror genre has been its emphasis on difference, specifically sexual difference. For example, the werewolf as a type of monster is masculine in that the creature's hirsutism and appetites for sex, food and violence are all extreme versions of normative masculinity. The witch as

# Introduction

type of monster, on the other hand, is feminine, as her connection to the natural world links her to some traits of stereotypical femininity. Also, most witches are represented as female. In his introduction to *The Dread of Difference: Gender and the Horror Film*, Barry Keith Grant argues that horror film is always "preoccupied with issues of sexual difference and gender" (1). Grant's observations about the horror film also apply to the wider category of horror fiction, which includes films and graphic novels as well as literary texts. In horror, specific types of monsters are gendered, though the individual monsters may be male or female.

Young Adult literature is a much newer genre than horror fiction, emerging in the late 1960s or early 1970s. Like horror fiction, Young Adult literature is broadly defined. Young Adult fiction is nearly always a type of *Bildungsroman* in which teen protagonists negotiate the familiar problems of adolescence in order to answer the question "Who am I and what am I going to do about it?" (Campbell 485). Because Young Adult fiction is concerned with development, it necessarily ponders the effects of power and subjectivity.[1]

Young Adult horror fiction exists at the intersection of these two genres. Young Adult horror fiction contains a monstrous Other and a teen protagonist (who are sometimes the same character) and explores issues that are of interest to adolescents such as sexuality and concerns about belonging. The monstrous Other is nearly always a sympathetic character in Young Adult horror fiction. The reverse is true in horror fiction in general, which has its share of sympathetic monsters, but is still dominated by unsympathetic ones.[2]

In her book *Disturbing the Universe*, Roberta Seelinger Trites's describes Young Adult fiction as a genre that necessarily explores issues of power and subjectivity. While Trites' work is concerned with representations of power and subjectivity in Young Adult fiction, its main focus is not on how gender affects this equation. It is assumed in Young Adult fiction that *male* protagonists (white ones, anyway) will emerge from adolescence with adult senses of self grounded in the expectation that they will eventually have a great deal of autonomy. However, female protagonists face a more complicated situation. To develop similarly autonomous identities, young adult females must fight against cultural and institutional expectations which would deprive them of agency. Any simple efforts to move easily into the dominant

## Introduction

culture thus falter, as girls confront the incompatibility between femininity and the "normal" course of adolescence. Only feminist analysis can fully explain the situation of Young Adult female characters. This book explores how Young Adult horror fiction represents teen girls as struggling with institutional forces that attempt to coerce them into various feminine subject positions that set them up for an adulthood devoid of autonomy.

For actual teen girls, the transition into adulthood is particularly difficult since the institutions that shape them into young women, such as the school, the family, organized religion and consumer culture, often accomplish this goal by limiting girls' mobility, silencing their voices and contorting their psyches. In 1949, Simone de Beauvoir's book *The Second Sex* described adolescence as the time when girls come to understand their relative lack of power in relation to boys. de Beauvoir's assessment of adolescent women still holds true: psychologist Mary Pipher observes that "girls are expected to sacrifice parts of themselves that our culture considers masculine on the altar of social acceptability and to shrink their souls down to a petite size" (39).

Other authors have recently documented the myriad ways in which teen girls are still expected to diminish themselves in order to "become women." In 1980, psychologist Carol Gilligan described how girls are encultured to value relationships over rules (*In a Different Voice: Psychological Theory and Women's Development* [1982]). Gilligan built upon these ideas with Lyn Mikel Brown in *Meeting at the Crossroads* (1992), a book which illustrates how girls go from being confident and outspoken children to timid and silent adolescents. In the same year, the American Association of University Women published its report *How Schools Shortchange Girls* (1992), which documented how girls' self-esteem plummets during adolescence. Peggy Orenstein's ethnography *Schoolgirls: Young Women, Self-Esteem and the Confidence Gap* (1994) reproduces the AAUP's findings about the oppression of teen and tween girls.

While Gilligan, Brown, Orenstein and the AAUP document how girls' self-esteem is diminished during adolescence, other authors focus on the cultural factors behind girls' plummeting self-esteem. Lyn Mikel Brown's study *Girlfighting: Betrayal and Rejection Among Girls* (2003) explores how relational violence hidden in girls' peer groups does the work of patriarchy by policing the borders of femininity in order to coerce girls into subordinate

## Introduction

feminine subject positions. Joan Brumberg's *The Body Project: an Intimate History of American Girls* (1997) considers how over the past 150 years girls have been increasingly encouraged to focus on manipulating their physical appearance as the fundamental way of improving themselves. Like the girlfighting phenomena, the body project that Brumburg describes ratifies the interests of patriarchy by diverting girls' energy into obsessing over the minutia of their appearance, rather than cultivating skills that would make them strong and autonomous. Lynn Phillips's *Flirting with Danger: Young Women's Reflections on Sexuality and Domination* (2000) analyzes how popular magazines disseminate normative discourses of gender that perpetuate sexist stereotypes about men and women, sometimes while appearing to represent "post-feminist" and therefore liberated models of masculinity and femininity. Sharon Lamb and Lyn Mikel Brown's *Packaging Girlhood* (2006) evaluates how twenty-first century mass culture for girls similarly reproduces sexist stereotypes under the guise of promoting "girl power." And Catherine Driscoll's *Girls: Feminine Adolescence in Popular Culture and Cultural Theory* maps how girls experience themselves in relation to contemporary discourses of girlhood.

These studies of popular culture show not only how girls are pressured into subordinate gender roles, but how they resist these pressures and their understandable anger about the limited role they are being coerced into occupying. Lyn Mikel Brown describes early adolescence as a time when girls "see the cultural framework, and girls' and women's subordinate place in it, for the first time" and the understandable "shock, sadness, anger, and a sense of betrayal" that they experience after this realization (Brown *Raising* 16). Moreover, girls begin to be encultured at this time to disavow their anger as illegitimate, as a personal problem that has the potential to make them unfeminine and therefore liable to rejection by their peers. Brown observes that "since these strong feelings emerge just as girls move into the dominant culture, at the very moment when their anger is most disruptive to the social order, proponents of the status quo have much invested in covering or pushing these feelings out of public view" (*Raising* 16). As Elizabeth Spelman argues,

> the expression of anger is intimately tied to self-respect, to the capacity to realize and author one's life fully. For this reason, women's anger is often considered not only inappropriate but also an act of insubordination [qtd. in Brown *Raising* 11].

## Introduction

So part of a girl's education in how to be a woman includes swallowing anger over the restrictive gender roles she is expected to occupy. Trites observes that cultural silencing "is one of the dominant forces that shape female growth" (Trites *Waking* 47). Teen girls have difficulty later reclaiming their silenced voices not only because we live in a sexist culture, but also because the institutional forces that oppress girls are invisible, or presented as natural, making it seem that the resulting subordination of their sex is the product of an irresistible biological imperative rather than an effect of power which can be reversed.

The genre of horror presents the possibility for resistance to these seemingly untraceable institutional forces that oppress girls. The genre's conventions permit it to reveal the genealogy of gender by exposing what is most disturbing to hegemonic culture. Isabel Pinedo views horror as something that denaturalizes "the repressed by transmuting the 'natural' elements of everyday life into the unnatural form of the monster" (39) which makes the terrors of daily life emotionally accessible. In this way, horror is similar to dreams, which "are unconscious attempts to express conflicts and resolve tensions" (Pinedo 40). Similarly, Barbara Creed sees horror as a process by which we can purify the abject and so redraw the boundaries between the ego and what threatens it ("Horror"). Creed interprets Julia Kristeva's theory of the abject in *The Powers of Horror* as descriptive in how it attempts "to explain the origins of patriarchal culture" ("Horror" 47). Pinedo's and Creed's observations also pertain to Young Adult horror fiction. Horror as a genre of cinematic and literary texts "redraws the boundaries between the human and non-human" (Creed "Horror" 46). Yet this redrawing of the boundaries does more than merely perpetuate the structures of patriarchal culture. The process itself exposes these boundaries as constructed rather than natural, suggesting the possibility of resistance.

Horror redraws the boundaries between the abject and the subject, between human and nonhuman, through the figure of the monster, a type of Other and a double. Teen girls have firsthand experience with the Other: in a patriarchal culture, they *are* the Other, even when they successfully contort themselves into a restrictive normative femininity. The Other in its various forms is always a double. Robyn McCallum sees the figure of the double as useful in revealing how subjectivity is constructed dialogically. Because "an individual's identity is formed in dialogue with others and with social discourses, ideologies and practices," we "can never see ourselves directly." Instead, "we construct a sense of ourselves by appropriating the position of the other, outside the self. This means that subjectivity is grounded in an internal fragmentation and multiplicity" (McCallum "Other Selves" 17–18). It is fairly easy to understand the monstrous Other as double in Young Adult horror fiction since this character is nearly always sympathetic, and is frequently the protagonist.[3] Thus, while the monstrous Other is represented as horrifying in the eyes of others, readers or viewers can identify with the monster and see how this creature is similar to themselves.

In *Gender Trouble*, Judith Butler argues that not just gender, but sex, is the result of disciplinary practices whose origins are rooted so deeply in the unconscious that they take on the appearance of nature. According to Butler, "gender is an identity tenuously constituted in time, instituted in an exterior space through a *stylized repetition of acts*" and so it "ought not to be construed as a stable identity or locus of agency from which various acts follow" (Butler *Gender* 140). The subsequent silencing of women is an effect of these stylized repetitions of acts by which gender and sex are naturalized. Because the genealogy of these acts is obscured, resistance to this silencing initially appears to be futile.

This double and monstrous Other also suggests possibilities for resistance because it is a reiteration of the original, but with a difference. Butler observes that "there is the potential for subversiveness in repetition, which has the potential to call into question the regulatory practice of identity itself" (*Gender* 32). By way of example, Butler cites the ability of drag to destabilize the boundaries between male and female and expose the artificiality of sex. As a performative activity, drag reveals that "the possibilities of gender transformation are to be found precisely in the arbitrary relation between such acts, in the possibility of a failure to repeat, a de-formity, or a parodic repetition that exposes the phantasmic effect of abiding identity as a politically tenuous construction" (*Gender* 141). Because "genders can be neither true nor false, neither real nor apparent, neither original nor derived" (Butler *Gender* 141), their genealogy can be exposed through repetition which reveals that they are not natural and inevitable, but constructed and therefore open to reinterpretation.

If iterations of the monstrous feminine then can be understood as a purification of the abject that breaks down boundaries and calls their naturalness into question rather than reinforcing these boundaries, then horror is rife with subversive potential. Horror can thwart the ability of various institutional discourses about sex and gender to individualize and totalize subjects in order to more easily control them. Monsters were originally thought of as divine warnings: "the word 'monster' derives from the Latin *monere*, meaning 'to show'" (Fonseca and Pulliam *Hooked on Horror, Volume III* 155). In horror fiction, the monstrous Other reveals that gender, and even sex, are constructed categories rather than immutable biological truths. This revelation is powerful because what can be done can also be undone. In *The Psychic Life of Power*, Butler muses that rather than laboring to discover *what* we are, we should *refuse* what we are, a condition that is the result of how we have been individualized and totalized by the institutional discourses that enact our subjectivities. Instead, "we have to promote new forms of subjectivity thorough the refusal of this kind of individuality which has been imposed on us for several centuries" (Butler *Psychic* 101). The monstrous Other then points to ways we can "refuse what we are."

This book examines horror fiction populated by teen female characters with supernatural abilities. The texts I examine are feminist either in that the main character transcends conventional gender roles while "embrac[ing] and celebrat[ing] certain characteristics traditionally linked to femininity" (Trites *Waking* 4–5), or in that the main character demonstrates what happens when women are unwilling or unable to transcend conventional gender roles.

Because Butler sees both sex and gender as constructed through subjectivity, I pay particular attention to how each protagonist's body is the site of her struggle against being relegated to a confining gender role. Many feminist theorists have observed how control of the body is at the center of women's oppression. These theorists are particularly indebted to Foucault's genealogical works such as *Discipline and Punish* and *The History of Sexuality* to describe how the regulation of the body through various disciplinary techniques produces subjects. Lois McNay, for example, sees Foucault's theories of power and the body as useful to feminists for "placing a notion of the body at the center of explanations of women's oppression that does not fall back into essentialism or biologism" (11). For these reasons, I too rely on feminist interpretations of Foucault to explore subjectivity and gender in Young Adult horror fiction.

## Introduction

The definitions of Young Adult literature and horror fiction that I will be using in this study are based on critical traditions and marketing categories. In *Disturbing the Universe*, Trites defines Young Adult literature as fiction "with adolescent protagonists who strive to understand their own power by struggling with the various institutions in their lives" (8). This is the definition I employ to describe Young Adult fiction. My definition of horror fiction builds upon Kristeva's idea of the abject in *Powers of Horror*. Horror always includes a monstrous Other whose existence precipitates a redrawing of the boundaries between human and monster, ego and abject (Creed "Horror"). My definition of horror is as expansive as my definition of Young Adult fiction, allowing the inclusion in my survey of works of dark fantasy, contemporary Gothic fiction and paranormal romance with substantial horror elements. After all, dark fantasy, paranormal romance and horror fiction are all born of the much older Gothic tradition.[4]

Because the purpose of this book is to consider gender and power in this type of fiction, I examine horror texts containing female protagonists with supernatural abilities or paranormal experiences, features common to many Young Adult works of horror. These texts show female characters at their most monstrous and powerful. Also, the protagonists in the texts I examine are all white, and the majority of them are middle class as well. While both Young Adult fiction and horror fiction deal with identity politics and anxieties about racial difference, Young Adult horror fiction to date is still populated overwhelmingly by white protagonists.[5]

Finally, my study includes cinematic as well as literary works of Young Adult horror, as film is a central medium of the horror genre. In fact, in some subgenres of horror fiction such as the werewolf narrative, contemporary representations of the creature are derived equally from literary and filmic texts. More recent and expansive definitions of Young Adult fiction such as the one put forth by the Young Adult Library Services Association view the genre as one that is not limited to literary texts, but includes films marketed to adolescents with teen protagonists who deal with issues of growth and maturity (Cart "The Value of Young Adult Literature").

This book is divided into three chapters, each examining a different subgenre of Young Adult horror including the ghost story, the werewolf narrative, and stories about witches. I consider each type of monster in ascending order of how it represents teen girls negotiating subjectivities in which

## Introduction

they are increasingly empowered. Each subgenre of horror such as werewolf fiction and the ghost story has its own type of monster, and organizing each chapter around specific types of monsters enables me to evaluate common themes. Furthermore, though most monsters can be either male or female, our common idea of each is usually gendered. For example, the werewolf is generally thought of as representing an extreme iteration of normative masculinity, whereas the witch embodies negative qualities associated with women and femininity. Thus, in every chapter I consider how representations of each particular monster in Young Adult fiction either reproduces or inverts the more usual gendered representations of them.

I selected these three subgenres of horror fiction after making a broader survey of works of literature and film that can be defined as both Young Adult fiction and horror fiction. That investigation revealed the prevalence of three primary subgenres of Young Adult horror fiction with female protagonists: the ghost story, the werewolf narrative and stories about witches. While there are a number of Young Adult vampire novels with female protagonists, I have not included this subgenre in my study as these texts often lack female protagonists who are either monsters with supernatural abilities of their own or who are sufficiently affected by the work's supernatural characters that they too become monstrous. Rather, they are nearly always focused on a mortal girl's relationship with a much more powerful vampire. For most of Stephenie Meyer's Twilight Saga, for example, the protagonist Bella lacks supernatural powers of her own. Furthermore, her relationship with Edward does not make her monstrous in the way that the haunted girl is affected through the spirit who possesses her.

Finally, I have organized my chapters in ascending order of how each type of monster represents teen girls as negotiating subjectivities in which they become increasingly empowered. The girls in Chapter 1 who are haunted by spirits appear to outsiders as unproblematic models of white, middle class girlhood. Each girl has repressed feelings and behaviors that are incompatible with conventional femininity. As result, she can be more easily manipulated by others. The ghost returns to the girl it haunts what she has repressed, which permits her to become a strong and autonomous woman. However, the ghost is able to help the haunted girl reincorporate the repressed in such a way that the change to her is not immediately obvious to those who at present still have the right to control her. In this way, the ghost enables the haunted girl to nurture her strengths in stealth to avoid being punished for stepping outside of her proscribed gender role. In Chapter 2, I examine teen female werewolves whose lycanthropy makes them unable to appear conventionally feminine. Instead of being smooth, weak, silent, and asexual, the teen female werewolf is hairy, strong and able to express her anger and sexual desire. In this way, she is more empowered than the haunted girls of Chapter 1, but she fears serious repercussions for not being both normatively feminine and normatively human. Chapter 3 investigates the figure of the teen witch, whose epistemological perspective is more threatening than her body or even her magical powers. Because the teen witch understands that all knowledge is constructed and the knower is an intimate part of the known, she is able to challenge patriarchal authority and encourage other women to do likewise.

The tropes of horror express how teen girls feel in a culture where women are still considered radically Other. More than realistic fiction, Young Adult horror fiction allows a coded exploration of issues of gender, sexuality and agency. This coded exploration is particularly important for teen readers who do not have sufficient experience to be able to describe the incongruity between their own feelings and pressures to be "normal" girls in the way represented through contemporary discourses of gender. In his book *The Uses of Enchantment and Magic*, psychologist Bruno Bettelheim sees the unrealistic nature of fairy tales as an important literary device which makes it obvious that the story's concern is not to convey useful information about the external world, but about the inner processes that take place within an individual (25). In this way, the fairy tale permits the reader to find her own solutions within the story. Bettelheim's observation about the value of unrealistic literature can also be applied to horror fiction. The figure of the monstrous female Other, with its supernatural abilities, similarly enable the reader to resolve the incongruity between "what she is" and "what she ought to be," as represented to her by her culture. The monster, like the drag king or queen, is an iteration with a difference, and that difference calls into question the naturalness of gender, and even biological sex.

CHAPTER 1

# *Subversive Spirits: Resistance and the Uncanny in the Young Adult Ghost Story*

IN THE YA GHOST STORY, teen girls have a unique relationship with the spirits who haunt them. Instead of being menaced by the spirits of the dead, these girls are protected by them from representatives of a wider patriarchal culture that would coerce them into a subordinate feminine subjectivity where their voices go unheard and they are deprived of the ability to control their lives.

The figure of the ghost is ancient and common to most cultures. It can be loosely defined as a disembodied spirit of someone who has died, but who is unwilling or unable to quit this world. The ghost is characterized by its relationship with the living as much as by what it is. A ghost does not truly "exist" unless it haunts someone, and it passes among the living because it has unfinished business in our world. The ghost might be unable to rest in its grave until it first rights a wrong, as is the case with Hamlet's father, or it must stop the subject of its haunting from committing a serious error, as the spirit of Jacob Marley must do to Ebenezer Scrooge in Dickens' *A Christmas Carol*. Some ghosts do not realize that they are dead, such as the wraiths that Cole Sear glimpses in M. Night Shyamalyn's film *The Sixth Sense* (1999) or the spirits in Alejandro Amenábar's film *The Others* (2001). Nevertheless, the ghost is anxious about wandering among the living, and it requires the assistance of the human it haunts to complete its business and pass into the next world. Therefore, ghost stories are as much about those who are haunted and who bear witness to the its presence as they are about the ghost.

## Monstrous Bodies

While accounts of ghosts are estimated to be as old as human civilization, the ghost story emerged as a distinctive genre in the mid–nineteenth century, evolving from the Gothic novel of the late eighteenth century. The ghost story enjoyed wide popularity in the nineteenth century, and even beyond the late Victorian and Edwardian period, if one takes into account the work of women authors of these stories whose writings had wide audiences, but who have received scant critical attention (Carpenter and Kolmar 6). Ghost stories continue to be popular today, with the 1970s and 1980s not only witnessing "the resurgence of ghosts in popular genres such as in film and television, but the reentry of the supernatural into mainstream literature" (Carpenter and Kolmar 9–10) such as Toni Morrison's *Beloved* (1987) or Maxine Hong Kingston's *The Woman Warrior* (1976). This popularity continues in other media as well in the 1990s and the early twenty-first century, with mainstream blockbuster films such as *The Sixth Sense* (1999), television shows such as *Medium* (2005) and the first season of *American Horror Story: Murder House* (2011), and the proliferation of romance and detective fiction containing ghosts. The play *The Woman in Black* has the distinction of being the second-longest running non-musical production of all time on the London stage (Craig). Based on a 1983 novel of the same name by Susan Hill, *Woman in Black* was made into a film by Hammer Studios in 2012.

Not surprisingly, ghost stories authored by women have different thematic concerns than those written by men. In *Haunting the House of Fiction*, Lynette Carpenter and Wendy Kolmar argue that ghost stories authored by male writers perceive the world as dualistic, "defined by 'debates' between reason and unreason, science and spirituality, conscious and unconscious, or natural and supernatural" (11), whereas ghost stories written by women "portray natural and supernatural experience along a continuum. Boundaries between the two are not absolute, but fluid, so that the supernatural can be accepted, connected with, reclaimed, and can often possess a quality of familiarity" (12). Female writers of ghost stories participate in a tradition of writing that considers the conditions of women's lives (Lundie 1), particularly themes common to the Gothic novel such as domestic violence, women being dispossessed of their property, the need to know women's history, and bonds between women in this life and even beyond the grave that help ensure their survival (Carpenter and Kolmar 10).

Many of the thematic concerns of the Gothic are also central to YA

## 1. Subversive Spirits

ghost stories authored by women, where girls are nearly always subject to violence in the home. However, the violence in these texts that I am analyzing is represented as overregulation rather than physical abuse. In addition, the haunted protagonists in these stories are particularly vulnerable since they are minors lacking the full legal rights and autonomy of adulthood, and they are frequently either orphans with no one to protect them, or are mothered by women who are themselves too brutalized to stand up for their daughters. Many of these narratives are also concerned with the importance of bonds between women, living and dead.

In this chapter, I examine six YA ghost stories with teen female characters who are haunted in a variety of ways, ranging from indirect communications with wraiths to possession of their consciousness or their bodies by a disembodied spirit. In each, the haunted character appears to the outside world as an unproblematic model of white, middle-class adolescent girlhood. However, the ghost's activities reveal the difficulties of being a young, white female in various times and places. Through the ghost's intervention, the haunted female recovers the repressed or disavowed knowledge she needs — and it saves her life — metaphorically in some instances and literally in others. To put it another way, the haunted girl is in danger of being extinguished not by the specter who haunts her, but by representatives of a patriarchal culture, such as her father or other male relatives. The ghost, as a double of the girl it haunts, becomes a co-owner of her disavowed knowledge; hence, it functions as what Sigmund Freud calls "insurance against extinction of the self" (141–42). Via the ghost, the haunted girl has access to knowledge she must eschew in order to be normatively feminine. However, because the haunted girl receives this knowledge through the mechanism of haunting, she appears to be merely a passive conduit for the emergence of this forbidden knowledge. Forced to disavow knowledge and behaviors that would make them strong and autonomous, these adolescent girls are similar to the ghosts who haunt them in that they are pale substitutes for the selves they could be if untrammeled by the confines of traditional femininity.

While the ghost in each of these texts aids the female protagonist, there are limits to its intervention. The ghost that protects the female protagonist from being victimized by the extremes of patriarchal culture is a subversive rather than a revolutionary or radical figure: it does not encourage open mutiny against a hegemonic culture that authors oppressive models of gender since, because the haunted girl is still a minor at the moment, her obvious defiance of authority would bring about severe repercussions. Instead, due to the ghost's intervention, the haunted female protagonist continues to appear to adhere to her restrictive gender role, but with a difference: her performance of gender is subtly altered so that she "call[s] into question the regulatory practice of identity itself" (Butler *Gender* 32). The conclusions in all of the novels hint at greater changes in the future when the protagonist reaches adulthood and will have more autonomy. But for the moment, the ghost enables the haunted female character to nurture her strength quietly, in ways that do not draw the attention of those with the ability to circumvent her efforts. In this way, the ghost is also a feminine figure, subtly influencing the girl it haunts rather than actively causing change to occur.

Of the three chapters in this work, this chapter about ghosts is the most lengthy, as the ghost story is the largest subgenre of horror fiction, overshadowing even vampire and zombie fiction in the number of works that have been published. Perhaps this is because the ghost story itself straddles so many different genres, from the Gothic to mystery to the possession narrative. I have broken this chapter into two sections, each examining a different mode of ghost story. In the first section, "The Conventional YA Ghost Story," I analyze conventional ghost stories with female protagonists haunted by spirits who want justice for harm committed to them in life. All or part of these novels are set in the historical past when women had comparatively few rights and so were far more dependent on men for protection. As a consequence, it is easy to understand how the greatest menace to female characters is found in the patriarchal home, which is supposed to protect women from the rough outside world. The second section, "The Modern Gothic Ghost Story," examines ghost stories that are a more modern variation on the Gothic. In the modern Gothic ghost story, the ghost is a round character, as fully developed as the girl that he or she haunts. These novels are set in the late twentieth and twenty first centuries, where women have and expect more ability to control their lives than was available to their mothers or grandmothers. The family patriarchs in the modern Gothic ghost story menace the female protagonists by putting them in extreme circumstances in which they are the objects of far greater control than are their contemporaries.

Five of the novels I consider, Phyllis Reynolds Naylor's *Jade Green*,

## 1. Subversive Spirits

Nina Kiriki Hoffman's *Stir of Bones* (2003), Laura Whitcomb's *A Certain Slant of Light* (2005) and its sequel *Under the Light* (2013), and Kathryn Reiss's *Dreadful Sorry* (1996) are ghost stories in the female Gothic tradition, where domesticity imperils the heroine rather than protects her. In *Jade Green*, the orphaned Judith comes to live with her wealthy Uncle Geoffrey whose house is haunted by the ghost of his former ward, Jade Green. Unknown to Uncle Geoffrey, Jade was murdered by his lecherous son Charles when she resisted his attempt to rape her. Judith is so virginal that she cannot fully appreciate that Charles is menacing her when he makes double entendres or violates her personal space by standing too closely to her. Only Jade can protect Judith from being similarly victimized by Charles. Nearly every aspect of Susan's life is controlled by her tyrannical and abusive father in *Stir of Bones*. If Susan fails to conform to her father's wishes, he brutally beats his wife so that his daughter may see her own imperfections reflected in her mother's bruised flesh. Susan can only find respite from the tyrannical gaze of her abusive father after she is befriended by the ghost of a boy who died 64 years ago. Jennifer and her mother are similarly threatened by domesticity in Laura Whitcomb's *A Certain Slant of Light* and the sequel, *Under the Light*. In Jennifer's fundamentalist Christian family, women are coerced into restrictive gender roles that were more typical in the 1950s. In Jennifer's family, women must submit to the authority of their husbands and fathers, and are financially and emotionally dependent on men, who dictate everything from what they wear to what they think. In Reiss' *Dreadful Sorry*, Clementine Horn, the ghost who haunts Molly, died resisting a restrictive gender role that would have completely submerged her identity into domesticity. Clementine, who was a young woman at the beginning of the twentieth century, just wanted to continue her education and travel the world, developing her intellect and living a life that she found meaningful. But the orphaned Clementine's uncle Wallace, her legal guardian, forced her to labor as the family's unpaid nanny, and thwarted her efforts to escape this limited role.

Whitcomb's *A Certain Slant of Light* and *Under the Light*, and Kathryn Reiss's *Dreadful Sorry* are possession narratives as well as ghost stories in that the ghosts either take over the body or tap into the consciousness of the girls they haunt. These works differ from the standard possession narrative in that the spirit helps the girl whose body she inhabits rather than harms her, as in the case in William Peter Blatty's *The Exorcist* where the entity that takes over adolescent Regan O'Neill's body is a demon whose nature is to do harm rather than the disembodied spirit of a dead woman seeking to have her voice heard. In *A Certain Slant of Light*, the spirit of Helen inhabits Jennifer's body, and in *Under the Light*, she enables Jennifer to resist her father's attempts to eradicate all aspects of her self. Molly, the teen protagonist of *Dreadful Sorry*, has her consciousness hijacked by Clementine Horn, the ghost of a girl who lived in a time before women had the right to control their bodies and destinies. Through Clementine's intervention, Molly can finally appreciate all of the benefits she enjoys due to first- and second-wave feminism.

These novels are typical examples of the YA ghost story. Four of the six novels are set either partially or entirely in the historical past, a device which denaturalizes the construction of gender by revealing how women in other time periods were coerced into occupying subordinate gender roles far more restrictive than contemporary ones. *Jade Green* is set in the late nineteenth-century American South, while *Stir of Bones* takes place in 1981, 22 years before the novel's publication in 2003. *Dreadful Sorry* and *Ruined* go from the late twentieth and early twenty-first century of the haunted protagonist to a century earlier, when women still lacked the right to vote. Placing all or part of these narratives the past makes it easier to demonstrate how normative femininity is a subject position that is interpellated through various cultural institutions. Convincingly situating these narratives in historical periods different from those of the reader requires that the author do more than imbue her characters with the trappings of another time: she must also explain how the cultural institutions of the period employed unique disciplinary practices to manipulate women into restrictive subject positions.

Two of the five writers examined here denaturalize the construction of gender by placing their heroines in situations that are extreme in relation to how women of their class and race can expect to be treated given the time period when they are alive. Susan, Hoffman's haunted protagonist in *A Stir of Bones*, is dominated by an abusive father who keeps her isolated from her peers and who insists that she always dress and behave in an unambiguously feminine manner. Susan's father's version of femininity is at odds with conventional femininity in the United States in 1981, the time period in which the novel is set, when changes precipitated by second-wave feminism nurtured a generation of girls accustomed to speaking their minds and having more autonomy. In *A Certain Slant of Light* and *Under the Light*, Jennifer's fundamentalist Christian family requires that women demonstrate their piety by submitting themselves completely to their husbands or fathers in ways that are unthinkable for most twenty-first century American women. Through these extreme situations, both novels emphasize how normative femininity is a constructed subject position rather than something natural and therefore immutable.

The YA ghost story in which a teen girl is the object of haunting differs from the wider genre of ghost story by its emphasis on the painful process through which girls become women. The YA ghost story with a haunted female protagonist is also distinctive from those in which a male is the object of haunting[1] in that the family patriarch (or his analogue) is "the source of danger to women and children" (Carpenter and Kolmer 4). The family patriarch, who represents the wider patriarchal order, employs various micropractices of discipline targeting the protagonists' bodies in order to facilitate an erasure of the self to better form the girl into a compliant young woman who accepts her subordination. The teen girl's protagonist's subjectivity is mired in domesticity and compulsory heterosexuality, and necessitates that she limit mobility, smother her feelings, and strangle her words so that she can ultimately be put "in her place," either as a wife and mother, or in some instances, even as the type of woman whose treatment at the hands of men signals to many in a patriarchal culture that she deserves no respect. This element of the YA ghost story is derived from the genre's roots in the Gothic.

Ghost stories in which teen girls are haunted also diverge from those in which a pre-teen is the object of haunting, where the ghost menaces rather than helps the girl it haunts. For example, in Mary Downing Hahn's *Wait Till Helen Comes*, the haunted children are endangered by the ghost rather than empowered by it. Helen is a lonely ghost who attempts to entice Heather into a premature demise so that the child can become the wraith's eternal playmate. This is also the case in Patricia Clapp's *Jane-Emily*, where the ghost of Emily, a willful and spoiled child who made herself die to punish her parents for not giving her their undivided attention, possesses the pre-teen Jane, who must be rescued by her adolescent cousin.

The overwhelming majority of YA ghost stories have haunted female rather than male protagonists, arguably because women are traditionally perceived as more "open" than men, and so are more susceptible to haunting.[2] The haunted female character of the YA ghost story is typically middle-class and white, perhaps because white middle-class girls are expected to be quieter and more controlled than their working class and non-white counterparts, resulting in their feeling "trapped in their own goodness and perfection" (Brown *Raising* 95) when they manage to successfully embody this ideal of femininity. Even their anger must be disavowed. Lyn Mikel Brown's research about the politics of girls' anger reveals that white middle-class girls find it "transgressive to even speak their justified anger directly and publicly" (*Raising* 94). In this way, white middle-class girls moving into the dominant social construction of femininity are deprived of their voices in ways that are sometimes so subtle that they are not immediately obvious to us. Reclaiming this lost voice and the agency that comes with it are difficult for adolescent girls not only because they live in a sexist culture, but because the institutional forces that have contorted them into their uncomfortable feminine subject positions are invisible. As a result, their subordination is often presented as the product of an irresistible biological imperative rather than an effect of power which can be resisted — and potentially reversed.

## The Conventional YA Ghost Story

In the ghost story, a disembodied spirit haunts a person or place with the goal of receiving justice denied to it in life. In the YA ghost story however, the ghost does not merely reveal to the person she haunts the injustice she suffered in life: the ghost is also the uncanny representation of feelings that the haunted female character must repress in order to fit into her culture's idea of appropriate femininity. The repressed does not disappear. Instead, it seethes beneath the surface, waiting for an opportunity to emerge. In the conventional YA ghost story, the repressed re-emerges in the unfamiliar figure of the ghost, who is a sort of double of the girl she haunts. Freud understands the figure of the ghost as the embodiment of the uncanny, something "that was long familiar to the psyche and was estranged from it only through being repressed" (147–48) and that returns in a disturbing and not wholly familiar form. As the embodiment of all which is disavowed, the ghost can enable the haunted protagonist to reclaim her silenced voice in order to resist her dangerous subordinate subject position. In this way, the ghost is also her ally.

The conventional YA ghost story is exemplified by Kathryn Reiss' *Dreadful Sorry*, Phyllis Reynolds Naylor's *Jade Green*, and Paula Morris's *Ruined*. The ghosts in these novels understand just how dangerous the subject position of normative femininity can be. Both Jade (*Jade Green*) and Clementine (*Dreadful Sorry*) were orphans during their lifetimes who had no one to effectively protect them from the family patriarch or his analogue. And after the death of her white father in *Ruined*, the Creole Lisette lacks anyone to ensure that she is protected in New Orleans in 1853, where laws are changing a decade before the Civil War to disenfranchise free people of color and make their condition more legally similar to slavery.

The haunted teen girls in the conventional ghost story are endangered because they are being schooled in restrictive gender roles in preparation for adult womanhood. However, the dangers of normative femininity are not immediately obvious to these haunted female protagonists (or to the reader) because they see their gender roles as natural and far less restrictive than those of their foremothers. The ghosts in these narratives, who serve as doubles for the girls they haunt, are able to show the objects of their haunting what might happen to them if corrective actions are not taken.

So the spirits in the conventional ghost story do more than seek justice for themselves — they also help the girls they haunt by helping them understand the vulnerabilities inherit in their own subject positions. Or to put it another way, in the conventional YA ghost story, the ghost's quest for justice is broader than merely righting the wrongs she endured while alive. Instead, justice for the ghost involves bonds of sisterhood through which she improves the life of the girl she haunts.

## *Discipline and Silence*

Conventional femininity is not a monolith, but a subject position that varies over time and across cultures. Nevertheless, one of its most salient features is a cultural silencing that facilitates women's subordination. In *Waking Sleeping Beauty*, Roberta Seelinger Trites discusses how feminist children's novels focus on their characters' articulateness (47), a quality that is equated with autonomy. Trites observes how some psychological theorists "consider cultural silencing to be one of the dominant forces that shape female growth" (47). Clementine, Jade, and Lisette were silenced during their lifetimes, and all were ultimately silenced through death—Jade and Lisette are murdered, while Clementine dies attempting to escape the life that Uncle Wallace tries to force her into. The return of each girl as a ghost is a testament to the strength of their resistance to the silencing they suffered in life and through to their final breaths. Clementine's, Jade's and Lisette's silencing was accomplished in part through discipline. In *Discipline and Punish*, Michel Foucault describes discipline as a mechanism of power which shapes the behavior of individuals through regulation of their activities. This regulation is enforced through a complex system of surveillance (O'Farrell). Reiss' and Naylor's ghosts are subject to bodily discipline in life that is meant to cow them into a restrictive model of femininity that makes them more easily controlled. This discipline is administered in *Dreadful Sorry* by Clementine's Uncle Wallace, and in *Jade Green* by both Jade's benefactor Geoffrey and other well meaning people in the community, and secretly by Uncle Geoffrey's lecherous son Charles. Lisette in *Ruined* is subjected to discipline by the law and cultural institutions that give women and non-whites far fewer rights and privileges than those afforded to white men.

In life, Clementine and Jade were especially vulnerable to the excesses of discipline since they were orphans with no family fortune to support them after their parents died. Thus, both Clementine and Jade are put into situations where they are at the mercy of those who abuse them. When she is eleven years old, Clementine Horn is sent to live with her wealthy and sternly patriarchal Uncle Wallace, who takes control of her body as payment for his largesse: Clementine is to compensate him for her room and board by serving as the family's unpaid governess until the last of his children leaves home. Uncle Wallace subjects Clementine to discipline by controlling where she lives and goes. Over the next seven years, Uncle Wallace prepares Clementine for what he has decided will be her adult role, a lower middle-class feminine subject position with strictly regulated parameters. Thus she is permitted the luxury of a high school education, but only so that she may more effectively tutor her cousins. Clementine has little leisure time, and cannot socialize with her teen peers because Uncle Wallace insists that she return directly from school each day to care for his children, who will be her permanent charges once she graduates. In the distant future, when Clementine's cousins no longer require the services of a governess and her "debt" to the family has been repaid, Uncle Wallace plans to select a local boy to be her husband. In this way, Clementine is not that much different from Jennifer in *A Certain Slant of Light* and *Under the Light* in the next section of this chapter, whose family hopes to exert a similar level of control over her adult life.

Clementine attempts to resist this discipline. Instead of spending her life in tiny Hibben, Maine, she wants to attend college and travel the world. When Uncle Wallace vetoes her plans, even after Clementine says she will not ask him for financial assistance, she solicits the help of her teacher and even tries to run away. Clementine's attempts to resist her uncle's discipline reveal to her that his will is enforced through a complex network of surveillance. Because Uncle Wallace is the wealthiest inhabitant of Hibben, which is located on a small island in the Atlantic, he can depend on residents reporting to him when Clementine behaves in ways that he would not approve of. So, for example, when Clementine confides in her favorite teacher that she wants to go to college and see the world, the teacher not only chides the girl for having ambitions that are counter to her uncle's will, she also reports their conversation to Uncle Wallace. Clementine's attempts to run away from home are similarly thwarted by townspeople who tell Uncle Wallace when they realize that she is planning to leave.

While Uncle Wallace's plans for Clementine are in keeping with a conventional idea of femininity for a girl of her race, sex and class in 1916, they are counter to Clementine's ambition to continue her education and see the world, as well as wildly different from conventional femininity in 1996, the year that *Dreadful Sorry* was published. But as an orphan minor living in a time when even adult women had few rights, Clementine's wishes are easily silenced by her uncle, who at one point imprisons her in the family home so that she cannot escape her "duty." In this way, Clementine is a type of Gothic heroine, a female whose house becomes a prison from which only death will free her. Diane Hoeveler posits that lying below the surface of the female Gothic novel

> is the sense that middle-class women can only experience the male identified patriarchal-capitalist home as either a prison or an asylum. A woman is reduced in such a home to the status of an object, decorative or functional depending on her husband's class [19].

Clementine's Aunt Ethyl is an example of domesticity as prison. Her continuous pregnancies demonstrate her subordination to Uncle Wallace and make her doubly a prisoner, in her home and in her flesh: she is too weak to do anything more taxing than sipping tisanes in bed and so passive that she does not even read.

While most disciplinary practices in these novels target the body, others focus on the mind. Disciplinary practices connected to reading, writing, and learning from other media are commonly employed to silence many of these girls' voices. In *Meeting at the Crossroads*, for example, Lyn Mikel Brown and Carol Gilligan "describe the transformation of adolescent girls from being outspoken and confident at the age of eight or nine to being so concerned with being socially acceptable that they have learned to silence themselves by the age of thirteen or fourteen" (47). Writing is a particularly important component of articulateness. Writing, "which has so much potential to help people understand their agency" through reflection and revisioning, is one way that characters learn to use their voices. In fiction, "those who are denied speech, denied language" are also denied community, and subsequently, their full potential as humans (Trites *Waking*, 62, 63). In "The Laugh of the Medusa," Hélène Cixous explains how writing and speech have been usurped and used in the oppression of women: "writing and speech have been one with the phallocentric tradition ... a locus where the repression of women has been perpetuated" by grossly exaggerating "all the signs of sexual opposition (and not sexual difference), where woman has never had her turn to speak" (Cixous, Cohen, and Cohen 879).

In *Dreadful Sorry*, Uncle Wallace knows the subversive potential of reading and writing, and so he attempts to limit Clementine's literacy. When Clementine tries to run away the first time, Uncle Wallace burns the atlas that belonged to her late father, the one book in her possession, and locks her in her room. Clementine used to look through this atlas and dream of all the places she would like to visit. Uncle Wallace's destruction of the atlas demonstrates how threatened he is by Clementine's reading, which has encouraged her to imagine a life beyond the narrow servitude he has in store for her.

Uncle Wallace also views women's education as threatening because it encourages literacy and independent thinking. Uncle Wallace provides unequal educational opportunities for his children: the boys all leave home

## 1. Subversive Spirits

to attend university, while the girls are sent to ladies' finishing academies where they will be disciplined into a subordinate upper-class femininity. While Uncle Wallace permits Clementine to attend high school so that she can be a better governess to his children, he forbids her from attending college because he believes that higher education will turn her into "one of those ridiculous suffragettes" (Reiss 130) who agitate for the empowerment of women.

Jade, the eponymous character of *Jade Green*, is subject to more rigorous, and eventually, more sadistic bodily discipline than are her middle-class sisters. The daughter of one of the town prostitutes, Jade has to beg for food and sleep in the gutter. When Jade's mother dies, the town's religious community takes control of her so that she may be disciplined into a working-class femininity that will enable her to become a productive member of the subordinate classes. To this end, Jade is sent to live with Judith's Uncle Geoffrey's housekeeper, who comments about the girl's undisciplined behavior: "it was only with the greatest difficulty that [Jade] learned to live as civilized people do" (Naylor 37–38), and wear stockings and sleep in a bed. While Jade cannot be induced to attend school, she works well with her hands, and so excels in a relatively unladylike job deboning chickens in a butcher's shop. Her sponsors hope that she can at least be made into a productive member of the working class.

Because the orphaned Jade has no one to protect her, she is subject to a particularly violent variety of discipline targeting the body. Charles, the lecherous, ne'er-do-well son of Uncle Geoffrey, subjects Jade to sexual harassment culminating in her death after she resists his attempts to rape her. Charles hacks off Jade's right hand with the meat cleaver she uses to fend off his attack, leaving her to bleed to death, silencing her forever. Because Jade is a member of the subordinate classes, no one investigates her death, which is improbably explained as a suicide. Later Charles will similarly menace Judith, his orphaned cousin who comes to live with his father. Charles' behavior with Jade and later Judith are part of a wider culture in which sexual violence against women frequently goes unpunished because its threat ratifies the interests of patriarchy. This type of violence is what Foucault terms an illegality, an illegal behavior that is tolerated by a regime in part because it supports its interests (*Discipline* 84–87).

The threat of sexual violence is a micropractice of discipline that polices the borders of gender and class. On a personal level, sexual violence aims to put the victim "in her place;" on a global level it serves to turn her into an example to others who might be tempted to escape their own subordinate positions. Arguably, this is why Jade's death was not viewed as murder by the coroner, but rather, an improbable suicide by one of those "strange unaccountables" (Naylor 39), members of the subordinate classes who according to common wisdom are beset by inexplicable violent whims that resist interrogation. When sexual violence is viewed as a "natural" consequence of masculinity, the victim rather than the perpetrator is to blame. As a result, the threat of this violence serves as another institutional control on women's bodies; it perpetuates the lie that if women regulate their appearances, curtail their presence in public spaces, and even limit their own knowledge of human sexuality, then they will be safe from harassment. Author Phyllis Reynolds Naylor emphasizes how this sort of violence is a type of institutional control in *Jade Green* by never representing the victims as being complicit in their fates.

Lisette in *Ruined* is silenced during her brief lifetime by laws and customs governing race in antebellum New Orleans, restricting where blacks can live, work and congregate, such as laws prohibiting them from meeting or even playing music in public (Morris 199) and ultimately making it possible for whites to kill blacks with impunity. Lisette is not a slave, but a free woman of color. In antebellum New Orleans, it was customary for wealthy white men to have two families, one with a white woman, who was his legal wife, and a second one with a genteel free woman of color, his mistress. Lisette was the daughter of this second type of union. While interracial marriage was forbidden, the relationships between wealthy white men and their black mistresses often had many of the trappings and benefits of marriage: the man would purchase a home for his partner and visit with their children, pay for their education, and sometimes even provide for them in his will. In this way, Lisette lived a life of relative privilege as a black woman in the nineteenth century antebellum South. Nevertheless, her life is less valuable to the white people in power than the lives of other whites. Lisette, like Jade, is silenced when she is murdered and the circumstances of her death are covered up.

Lisette is killed by Mrs. Bowman, the enraged wife of her father, who had just learned within hours of her husband's death that he had a second family and provided for them in his will. Lisette is in the Bowman family

*1. Subversive Spirits*

home when Mrs. Bowman makes this discovery, having been called there a few days earlier by her father, who was dying of yellow fever. Longing to see Lisette one last time, Mr. Bomwan sent for the girl to nurse him, believing that she would not be noticed by his wife, who did not know Lissette, and was occupied nursing their daughter, who was also dying of yellow fever. Lisette's father had no fear of that he might infect his daughter, as African-Americans were generally immune from yellow fever.

When Mrs. Bowman spots Lisette in her home, she sees the girl's resemblance to her late husband and realizes that this is his daughter by Rose Villieux. A furious Mrs. Bowman attacks Lisette, fracturing the girl's skull on the stairs and subsequently killing her during the scuffle before the two are separated by the family attorney and physician, literal representatives of the patriarchal order, who are immediately present to "handle" a narrative that ensures the continued stability of the status quo. They tell Lisette's mother that the girl succumbed to yellow fever, and was quickly buried in a mass grave, something happening all over New Orleans at the time due to the epidemic outbreak of the fever throughout the city. Lisette's body, however, is secretly sealed in the Bowman family tomb along with the body of her father so that it can never be examined in order to contradict this story. While Lisette's mother Rose does not believe this story, Mrs. Bowman is not charged with murder, as she is white and a member of the city's ruling class. In fact, the word of the family physician and attorney are sufficient to prevent Lisette's death from even being investigated. The protections of the patriarchal order then benefit Mrs. Bowman, though her husband's expression of his patriarchal privilege by maintaining two lives with two separate families are what caused her to lash out in the first place.

Yet Lisette and her mother Rose refuse to be silenced permanently; both of their voices are heard beyond the grave. Rose places a terrible curse on the Bowman family, condemning the next seven daughters to die at sixteen, Lisette's age at her death. Rose's curse, however, also inadvertently condemns Lisette to linger in this world as a ghost rather than pass into the next life: she always appears to the doomed Bowman daughters just a few months before they are about to die. While in life, Rose and Lisette were invisible to nearly all of the Bowman family, after their deaths, the terrified Bowmans are all too familiar with mother and daughter and whisper their story as they unsuccessfully attempt to break the curse.

Clementine, Jade and Lisette owe their ethereal existences to extreme forms of discipline that permanently silenced them in life. Yet though the girls they haunt are also silenced as part of their gender training, this process does not seem extreme or terribly restrictive given when each girl lives. In fact, the silencing of girls today is so commonplace that the process is frequently invisible to the reader. The ghost then points to the unseen discipline that deprives the haunted girls of their voices.

## *The Invisible Disciplining and Silencing of the Haunted Girl*

The disciplinary practices that have shaped Molly's body are not obvious in *Dreadful Sorry* in part because Clementine's intervention does not save Molly from being subordinated by the family patriarch. However, Clementine's intervention in Molly's life eventually helps her appreciate the freedoms and class privilege she has taken for granted. Nevertheless, Molly, like other American girls in the twenty-first century, is silenced by cultural forces that have taught young women her age that feminism is not important because either all of the goals of second-wave feminism have now been achieved and women have the same opportunities available to men, or that the goals of second-wave feminism were not relevant to women's actual lives. Thus, Molly and girls like her are often less likely to speak out about injustice since they lack a contextualizing framework of women's history to articulate their own experiences. After all, women's history is still not fully part of the school curriculum or promoted by mass media. In this way, Molly and other girls like her are silenced.[3] However, Molly's silencing is not obvious to readers because it is the sort that happens every day, and so is relatively invisible to contemporary readers of *Dreadful Sorry*.

It is also not readily apparent how Judith has been silenced in *Jade Green* or how her body is the site of disciplinary practices that have contorted her into a subordinate subjectivity, since she seems to willingly embrace her gender role. Rather, Judith's acceptance of the crippling conventional femininity of her time is in part a function of the narrative's setting, late nineteenth-century South Carolina, in which woman's subordinate status is eroticized rather than viewed as disempowering, a phenomenon typical of the historical romance novel. Prevailing discourses of gender in Judith's time, and our own, falsely suggest that appropriately feminine behavior would ensure that women are protected against sexual violence. Jade's violent death, however, exposes that protection as illusory.

Rebecca Brown in *Ruined* is temporarily disciplined and silenced by restrictive gender roles after she is forced to stay for six months with a family friend in New Orleans while her father makes a lengthy business trip abroad. A middle class girl from New York City, Rebecca has a good deal of agency in her life, and was never required to behave in keeping with a strict model of femininity. However, Rebecca's situation in New Orleans changes when she attends Temple Mead Academy, a private girls' school. Here Rebecca learns of the city's strict racial and gender hierarchy that she will participate in as a Temple Mead student. Temple Mead is de facto racially segregated—except for Rebecca's mixed race host's daughter Aurelia, the school is nearly all white, and most students and their families only come into contact with non-whites as their servants. Temple Mead's pupils are expected to behave in an unambiguously feminine manner while at school, training them in a type of womanhood that is compatible with values in the Deep South. Students' uniforms consist of an unfashionably long plaid skirt and blazer instead of the unofficial and unisex "uniform" of New York teens, jeans and sneakers. Moreover, the students of Temple Mead are expected to "comport [themselves] as young ladies at all times" by refraining from hoydenish behaviors including "running along the street" (Morris 29) and sitting on the school steps. Also, Rebecca is expected to abide by Temple Mead's unofficial rules that reinforce racial and social hierarchies, such as only attending the formal dance with a student from St. Simeon's, the all boys school affiliated with Temple Mead (Morris 30).

Rebecca finds these rules annoyingly archaic, and she ignores as many of them as she can get away with. As a consequence, she runs afoul of Helena Bowman and Marianne Sutton, the school's reining mean girls, who control their peers through their ability to have their enemies shunned by their classmates. Helena's and Marianne's ancestors founded the prestigious Mardi Gras Krewe of Septimus, and the girls live in two of the nicest mansions in the most exclusive neighborhood in New Orleans, so they are given special privileges at school and exempted from rules such as coming to class on time, or at all. Helena's and Marianne's peers also give them special privileges by allowing them to become the school's queen bees. Although Rebecca vows to "not be intimidated by two snooty juniors" (Morris 33) or to care overmuch about the spoken or unspoken rules of the school, Helena and Marianne punish her for scorning the rules by making sure that she is ignored by her classmates so often she has to eat lunch alone. Eventually, Helena's family will attempt to permanently silence Rebecca when they try to kill her to lay to rest the 150 year old curse that claims the teen daughters of the Bowman family.

### *Insurance Against Extinction: The Ghost as Double*

So far, I have discussed how the family patriarch or his analog attempts to discipline girls into a docile feminine subjectivity, which might seem to imply that these ghosts and the girls they haunt have been seamlessly cowed into submission. But that is not the case. Instead, when these protagonists realize that they are being groomed for positions in which they will have far less freedom than their brothers, they become angry and resist, although these open acts of defiance eventually prove fatal. The ghost's intervention, however, enables these female protagonists to successfully resist subordination through more subtle acts of rebellion. That these YA authors turn to the extreme and destabilizing figure of the ghost to combat patriarchy suggests how difficult it is for young women to resist traditional femininity as well as the importance of doing so. The ghost reveals that conformity can be a life and death struggle. Resisting patriarchal imperatives to conform to oppressive gender roles is so difficult that supernatural intervention is necessary. The non-realistic elements of the texts encourage the reader to remake reality in order to imagine alternatives.

Ghosts in the conventional ghost story provide lurid examples of the fate of girls who openly defy patriarchal authority when they lack the financial, social and legal resources to be autonomous. When poor, penniless Jade is murdered by Charles, his class privilege protects him from being held accountable for his crime. Lisette is similar to Jade in how class privilege also protects her murderer. Clementine's defiance also results in her death. Desperate to escape Uncle Wallace, Clementine feigns love for a local boy and convinces him to elope with her. But on the stormy night when the two attempt to escape their island community, their boat capsizes and they drown. Jade's, Clementine's, and Lisette's deaths warn readers of the very real dangers in openly defying rigid gender roles, but also set the stage for the girls they haunt to rebel in a way that is less obvious but more subversive.

While the haunted girl is momentarily silenced, she eventually regains her voice along with the ability to protect herself through the assistance of the ghost. The ghost, as "insurance against the extinction of the self" (Freud 142), is the keeper of the repressed to which the haunted character must have access, lest she also become a ghost. The repressed, that which is silenced or otherwise hidden from view, can never be completely banished, but always returns. The ghost in the conventional ghost story represents the repressed, and is a double of the girl that it haunts. The ghost embodies those aspects of the haunted girl that are incompatible with her family's or her culture's ideas of normative femininity. So when the repressed inevitably resurfaces, it emerges in the uncanny form of the ghost. The ghost gives to the girl it haunts knowledge about the patriarchal culture in which she lives.

Ghosts are quite literally insurance against the extinction of the self in *Jade Green* and *Ruined* because they protect the girls they haunt from being murdered. Jade and Lisette do this by showing Judith and Rebecca hidden information about people who have harmed these ghosts in life, and who will also harm the girls they haunt if this knowledge is not passed on to them. Specifically, Judith and Rebecca need to understand that they are menaced by more than rogue individuals, but rather, people who have been able to get away with harming young women because of their relatively privileged position in a patriarchal culture. Clementine in *Dreadful Sorry*, on the other hand, will help Molly elude the potentially crippling force of institutional sexism by revealing its existence and by encouraging Molly in her development.

The ghost is uniquely able to help the girl it haunts defy restrictive gender rules because it is her double who permits her to contemplate her subject position from a different vantage point. This new perspective is necessary for the haunted girl to understand how to subvert the people and institutions that would deny her autonomy. Thus, the haunted girl realizes that gender is not a stable identity, but rather, as Butler would describe it, a more precarious and shifting identity that is performed through "a stylized repetition of acts" (*Gender* 140). While an illusion of the stability of gender is maintained through the constant repetition of stylized acts, these iterations also open the opportunity for transformation in how they can reveal "the arbitrary relation between such acts" through "the possibility of a failure to repeat" (Butler *Gender* 140).

Robyn McCallum sees the figure of the double as useful in revealing how subjectivity is constructed dialogically. Because "an individual's identity is formed in dialogue with others and with social discourses, ideologies and practices," we "can never see ourselves directly." Instead, "we construct a sense of ourselves by appropriating the position of the other, outside the self" (McCallum "Other Selves" 17–18). To put it another way, the ghost as Other is a mirror of sorts. Its similarity to the girl it haunts permits her to see herself in the object rather than the subject position. The haunted girl's new perspective subsequently exposes how the limitations of her present feminine subject position are constructed and therefore are open to disruption, rather than as boundaries that are natural and therefore unchangeable. This knowledge permits the haunted girl to formulate a strategy for resistance, ranging from small incidents of sabotage to larger acts of subversion. Clementine, Jade, and Lisette are doubles of Molly, Judith, and Rebecca, who, like the ghost of Christmas Future in Charles Dickens' "A Christmas Carol," show them what could be, helping them to resist a similar fate and even personally intervening in some cases.

Clementine is more than a double of Molly: she is her alter ego,[4] living a life that Molly might have shared had it not been for first- and second-wave feminism. Via haunting, Clementine offers Molly knowledge of women's history that was not repressed by her, but was simply previously unknown. It is a past that Molly has never experienced, one where women lacked the right to vote, to control their bodies, or to have an independent existence apart from fathers and husbands. The knowledge that feminism has given her more agency will permit Molly to take advantage of the opportunities afforded her by her relatively privileged upbringing. One of Clementine's most treasured possessions during her life was her only doll, Mollydolly. Like most girls, Clementine projected all of her hopes onto her plaything. It is fitting then that Clementine chooses to haunt Molly, a girl with the name of her doll. In this way Molly too is Clementine's alter ego, as she is able to do what Clementine never could.

In Naylor's text, Jade is viewed as a monstrous Other, both by Charles, and later by those who refuse to investigate her strange and bloody death, because her failure to take up her proper gender role threatens the stability of the symbolic order. When Charles murders Jade, he has identified her as abject and subsequently cast her out, thereby buttressing the symbolic order. The example of Jade's bloody abjection serves to reinforce a status quo that manipulates women's behavior through the threat of sexual violence at the hands of an anonymous maniac.

Jade is both an Other and a double of Judith. Though the terms "Other" and "double" are often used interchangeably, I am making a distinction here between the two. While both literary tropes represent disavowed or repressed aspects of the self, the Other's striking characteristic is its *difference* from the original, which makes it monstrous. The double, on the other hand, is characterized through its uncanny *similarity* to the original. In life, Jade's inability to strike a pose of conventional femininity due to her class status makes her an Other, particularly in relation to the gently-bred Judith. As a ghost, Jade's grisly manifestation as a disembodied right hand further defines her as monstrous Other. Throughout the novel, Jade's severed hand appears and literally points to things before it scuttles away. Yet Jade is also a double of Judith: both are orphans and wards of Uncle Geoffrey, and we learn how each has been subjected to Charles' harassment. Certainly Charles sees both girls as similar in his selection of them as targets for his abuse.

Lisette is a double of Rebecca and is marked as an Other, as she is non-white. Lisette is also a double of all of the Bowman daughters because of her mother's curse on the family. The curse, in fact, originated because Lisette is also a Bowman daughter, and Mrs. Bowman resented the girl because she and her mother were doubles of her husband's white family. This novel posits the live girl as a sort of double of the ghost. Rebecca is a double of Lisette due to the Bowmans' belief that they can kill her to fulfill the curse with a seventh Bowman daughter, thereby sparing their daughter Helena. In killing Rebecca, Helena's family would solidify her role as Lisette's double by replicating her death.

Lisette keeps Rebecca from being murdered. Approximately fifty years after Lisette was killed, Claudia's great-grandmother Miss Cecilia, a well-known Voodoo priestess in the city, shared a vision she had about how the curse would conclude: the seventh Bowman daughter would "fall to the ground" (Morris 246) amidst flames and people in masks and colorful costumes, shivering in the cold, imagery suggesting that the events would take place during the Septimus Mardi Gras parade. Because Helena, older than Rebecca by a few months, is the seventh Bowman daughter, the family engineers a meeting by torchlight between the two girls after the parade. The Bowmans drag Rebecca to their family tomb, where they try to kill her as a way to satisfy the conditions of the curse by substituting Rebecca for Helena as the seventh daughter to die. Lisette, however, intervenes to save Rebecca, something she has never done for any of the other Bowman daughters, who became terrified after they saw her since Lisette has always appeared to their predecessors before their deaths to predict their demise. Yet Rebecca is unlike the other Bowman daughters in that she has been friends with Lisette since they first met, in part because Rebecca did not initially realize that Lisette is a ghost and so did not run away in fear.

Lisette saves Rebecca through an act of friendship, taking the living girl's hand, which makes her momentarily invisible so that she can escape by climbing on top of the Bowman family tomb. During her climb, Rebecca accidentally dislodges the life-sized stone angel topping the mausoleum, which crushes Helena and completes Rose's curse by claiming the seventh Bowman daughter. An underlying theme here is that sisterhood allows women to live and have agency in their lives. Had Helena befriended Lisette when she first saw her instead of screaming in terror, perhaps she too might have lived. Or perhaps if Mrs. Bowman would have viewed Lisette as someone who also grieved the recent death of Mr. Bowman rather than as an abject Other to be beaten and killed, then there would never have been a curse placed on the Bowman family.

## *Performative Acquiescence and Passive Transformation*

Yet while the ghost enables the girl she haunts to formulate strategies for resisting domination, the haunted girl is still a minor with relatively little power to control her life, and so she cannot openly rebel against those who attempt to subordinate her lest they increase their efforts to repress her. Thus, when the ghost supplies the girl she haunts with this repressed knowledge, she does it stealthily so that the girl does not appear to be actively resisting her subordinate gender role. Indeed, the ghost is a fitting vehicle for this repressed knowledge because it comes unbidden to those it haunts. After all, the haunted girl is an adolescent who is rarely in a position of sufficient power to completely resist societal control, and outright rebellion would be suicidal given the power imbalance. So, when the haunted girl is in possession of what was once repressed, she still *appears* to remain within the boundaries of normative femininity. The ghost plants the seeds of subversion with the repressed material that she supplies, and the narrative implies that in the future, the haunted girl will be in a position to more openly resist these forces and have more control of her life. The reader, as well, after exposure to the haunted girl's experiences with the ghost, has been presented with alternatives to subordinate feminine gender roles.

When the haunted girl gains access to this repressed knowledge about the past, she is in a sense reborn. While the haunted girl appears to be no different than she was before her supernatural encounter, she has been subtly transformed into someone stronger, more resilient, and therefore better able to resist her oppressors and/or help others resist oppression now that she is in possession of this missing knowledge. The haunted girl's rebirth is suggested through the birth imagery found in all of these novels. *Jade Green* and *Dreadful Sorry* are set near the sea and make use of other water imagery, which signifies parturition. Water imagery and the color green predominate in *Jade Green*. Uncle Geoffrey's house overlooks the Atlantic Ocean, and Judith will be within sight of this body of water when she is reborn as someone stronger. The color green, in this context, is another facet of the novel's birth imagery. Green is traditionally associated with spring and renewal, and it is also the color of the Atlantic. Green was Jade's favorite color— indeed, she was named after a shade of green—and its presence in the house where she died has the power to evoke her spirit. Judith will later be reborn in a sense when Jade comes to her aid in the novel's denouement, saving Judith from Charles so that she can live to eventually embrace a fairly conventional womanhood as a wife and mother.

Birth imagery is also prevalent in *Dreadful Sorry*. Clementine has a symbiotic relationship with Molly, which allows Molly to be reborn, emphasizing the importance of sisterhood to girls' development. Clementine died a watery death, drowning at sea on the stormy night that she attempts to run away with a local boy, and the only way off of the island is by boat. Meanwhile, on the night that Clementine drowns, Aunt Ethyl is dying in childbirth. While Clementine lived with Uncle Wallace's family, she was not only responsible for caring for her cousins, but was also her aunt's midwife during her numerous pregnancies, which have exhausted her body. Aunt Ethyl's final pregnancy is an inversion of what birth imagery usually symbolizes in that it is not a literal or figurative rebirth for anyone, but rather, a testament to her slow death of spirit and body due to her marriage to Uncle Wallace, whose insistence on feminine subordination extends to requiring that his wife continuously bear children. On the night that Aunt Ethyl dies in childbirth, her body is so weak from being pregnant so many times that she would not have lived, even if Clementine had stayed home to attend her, and her child is stillborn as well.

Birth imagery is also embedded in Molly's story of the near-death experience she has before she can undergo a similar rebirth. Molly's phobia of water is so severe that she cannot pass her private school's mandated swimming requirement, putting her in danger of not graduating. During a party, one of the guests decides to help Molly overcome what he sees as a baseless fear of water by throwing her into the swimming pool. Molly nearly drowns, and the experience causes her to go into her first fugue state during which she sees not the blue and white tiles of the pool, but dark water, seaweed, and splintered bits of the wrecked boat and Clementine's hatbox floating above. Molly's near-death experience precipitates a series of fugue states over the course of the summer during which she experiences fragments of Clementine's thwarted existence. While Molly has no knowledge of Clementine's life at the time of her near-drowning, it seems as if Clementine has sought out Molly to uncover the mystery of her disappearance over eighty years ago. After nearly drowning, Molly elects to spend the summer with her father and his new wife Paulette, who have recently moved to Hibben, Maine and purchased Uncle Wallace's house. Here Molly is surrounded by water while she goes into fugue states in which Clementine appropriates her consciousness to relate her story, which had been suppressed during her brief life. Against this backdrop of birth imagery is Paulette's own life-threatening pregnancy. But whereas Aunt Ethyl's repeated pregnancies signify an end of life, Paulette's pregnancy, freely chosen, is a birth that will solidify her connection with her new husband and step-daughter. So by the end of the summer, Clementine will live again through Molly, who can tell her story, while Molly will eventually be able to live her life more fully due to her better understanding of women's history.

In *Ruined*, descriptions of both water and fire imply rebirth. Morris

## 1. Subversive Spirits

accurately characterizes New Orleans as a moist, humid city, and it is nearly always raining during Rebecca's stay. New Orleans' post–Katrina landscape in Tremé and the Lower 9th Ward are visibly marked by the receding flood waters, while the restoration projects taking place there suggest the city's rebirth. While the water imagery foreshadows revival, Rebecca is reborn amidst fire imagery that connects death to the cycle of regeneration. The theme of the Septimus parade is the phoenix rising from the ashes. The Bowman family arranges for Rebecca to ride in the parade as one of the maids in order to engineer the torchlight meeting between her and Helena that Miss Cecilia predicted would be part of the conclusion of the curse. As one of the maids of Septimus, Rebecca rides on one of the floats depicting a tableaux of the theme, and she is costumed as fire, inadvertently emphasizing her own potential for rebirth. After the Bowmans' plans to kill Rebecca are thwarted, one of the descendents of those involved in Lisette's murder burns down the Bowman family home where Lissette was killed so that the families affected by the curse can then start over.

When the haunted girl is reborn, the transformation is not readily apparent to all around her since she seems to still adhere to her restrictive gender role. But the haunted girl has been altered by the knowledge that the ghost has supplied to her. She is no longer someone whose fate in a patriarchal society seems inevitable due to her sex. Rather, the haunted girl is now someone who understands the constructed nature of gender and of subjectivity, and who will be able to use this knowledge in order to eventually resist subordination more effectively, and to help others resist as well.

Rebecca is not obviously transformed at the conclusion of *Ruined*. Because Rebecca comes from New York and has a father who supports and encourages her empowerment, she already has a great deal of agency in her life even before she is haunted by Lisette. Although Rebecca openly questions the oppressive social structure of upper class New Orleans, her resistance to this culture is not a full-scale revolt against contemporary patriarchal institutions. Rather, *Ruined* represents New Orleans' hierarchal social structure with its rigid gender norms as a throwback to earlier and less enlightened times which are out of sync with modern social norms in the United States. Thus Rebecca's resistance to the norms of upper class New Orleans does not constitute a full-scale revolt against contemporary patriarchal institutions, which are never even considered in the novel. However, Rebecca has a broader view of the world after her experience with Lisette, so she can better appreciate the history of New Orleans, and she is now sufficiently sensitive to the spirit world to become a medium to other restless ghosts seeking justice and peace. Rebecca uses these abilities in Morris's sequel to *Ruined, Unbroke*n. However, I have not included *Unbroken* in my analysis since it is more of a murder mystery than it is a ghost story per se.

The transformation of the haunted girl is also not terribly obvious in *Jade Green*, which exemplifies what Hoeveler terms gothic feminism, a passive-aggressive strategy employed by the heroine of the female Gothic novel that permits her to survive while not being unsexed. In the female Gothic novel,

> women who ostensibly appear to be conforming to their acceptable roles within the patriarchy ... actually subvert the father's power at every possible occasion and then retreat to studied postures of conformity whenever they risk exposure to public censure [Hoeveler 6].

Hoeveler has come to describe this posture as gothic feminism,

> a version of "victim feminism," an ideology of female power through pretended and staged weakness. Such an ideology positions women as innocent victims who deserve to be rewarded with the ancestral estate because they were unjustly persecuted by the corrupt patriarch.... The gothic feminist always manages to dispose of her enemies without dirtying her dainty little hands [6–7].

Judith is an excellent example of a gothic feminist. Her seemingly unbelievable ignorance of male sexuality marks her as appropriately feminine while putting her in danger of being raped and killed by Charles. This potential for victimization further marks Judith as appropriately feminine.

Jade as monstrous Other possesses the knowledge of human sexuality that Judith *cannot* acquire because doing so would make her no longer conventionally feminine. The only acceptable way for Judith to have access to this knowledge is via Jade's haunting. Judith's dependence on Jade to communicate this material constitutes the passive aggressive gothic feminist strategy described by Hoeveler. Jade, not Judith, understands what Charles is planning, so in an act of sisterhood, Jade comes to Judith's rescue since Jade has already experienced Charles' violence. In the novel's denouement, Jade's hand that was cruelly hacked from her body materializes and strangles Charles before disappearing forever. Left behind is a tableau implicating Judith's would-be rapist and murderer while preserving Judith's innocence.

## 1. Subversive Spirits

Charles lies dead with his trousers undone, clutching the knife with which he planned to murder Judith. Because he was killed by a ghost, the bruises on his throat disappear, and so his death cannot be possibly linked to Judith, a gothic feminist who survives to inherit the family estate. Jade's intervention has saved Judith's life and allowed her to remain prime marriage material in a culture that prizes female virginity. Judith also remains "innocent" after her final encounter with Charles since it was not necessary for her to "dirty her little hands" with any unseemly knowledge of male sexuality or sexual politics to preserve her life.

As a result of Jade's ghostly intervention, Judith can subtly subvert the existing order. Creed observes that horror brings about "a confrontation with the abject (the corpse, bodily wastes, the monstrous-feminine)," only to eventually eject and "redraw the boundaries between the human and non-human" ("Horror" 46). *Jade Green* concludes with Jade's hand, the symbol of her as abject, disappearing forever into the churning sea. In this way, the abject has been purged, and the symbolic order has been stabilized. However, the boundaries between human and nonhuman are not re-established, but re-*drawn*. While Judith might appear to be unchanged by her encounter with the abject, she has been transformed and subsequently empowered. She now has a better understanding of sexual politics, at least in its more dangerous forms, and will be in a superior position to protect herself in future. The novel's conclusion implies that Judith will eventually inherit her uncle's sizeable estate. Wealthy herein, Judith will have more autonomy and control over her life in spite of living in a time period where women had less agency and fewer legal rights than they do today.

Clementine's transformation of Molly is arguably the most radical. While other spirits in YA ghost stories are the keepers of personal knowledge that the girls they haunt have been compelled to repress, Clementine is unique in that she is the repository of knowledge repressed by an entire culture. Clementine returns information to Molly that has been suppressed by the media and the educational system in the interests of re-instituting the subordinate subject positions that women occupied before second wave and even first wave feminism.

Though Molly is the daughter of parents who helped shape cultural changes brought about by second wave feminism, she lacks any appreciation of how these changes have benefited her. Neither of Molly's parents embodies traditional gender roles. Her mother is a successful attorney with her own male secretary, and she earns enough money to send her daughter to an expensive private school. Freed of the need to be normatively masculine, Molly's father displays emotion and is nurturing instead of sternly patriarchal. Yet Molly does not appreciate the advantages she has due to class privilege or the advancement of women's rights brought about by second-wave feminism. Molly's ignorance of the fundamental changes to gender roles that her parents' generation fought for is part of a post-feminist mindset which erroneously believes that all of the goals of second-wave feminism are irrelevant to the lives of contemporary young women. This mindset puts Molly (and other girls like her) in danger of losing some of these rights.

It is not surprising that Molly fails to appreciate the gains made by feminism since women's history is not very thoroughly taught in school, nor is it part of the popular consciousness. Instead, the project of feminism is frequently represented by the media as dead after either equality between the sexes had been achieved or after the wider population viewed the goals of feminism as unworthy. As a result, girls are often reluctant to identify themselves as feminists, who are still characterized as rabid man haters who do not wear make-up or shave their legs. Nevertheless, young women who do not identify as feminists support feminist ideals of equality between the sexes and freedom of choice (Baumgardner and Richards).

Molly's initial reaction to Clementine's story could be characterized as post-feminist in the most common meaning of the term, suggesting that the goals of second wave feminism are no longer relevant. After experiencing Clementine's story, initially Molly is unchanged: she comments that Clementine was "the most selfish person [she's] ever met" (327) since her decision to run away cost her deluded beau his life, and she also left her Aunt Ethyl to die in childbirth rather than serve as her midwife once again. Molly's first reaction is not surprising since even after reliving Clementine's life, she lacks a contextualizing historical frame of reference. However, by the novel's conclusion, Molly's consciousness has been raised so that she can better understand the importance of sisterhood in helping women live their lives to their fullest potentials. Molly's stepmother puts her on the path towards third-wave feminism by helping her understand that Clementine was not monstrously selfish. Instead, Clementine wanted "what all the girls I know today want for themselves — and expect they'll get ... a good education ... work that paid a fair wage ... [and] an independent life" (328). With this realization, Molly comprehends how she has benefited from both first- and second-wave feminism, and it is indicated that she is on her way to becoming part of the third wave of feminists who will use the gains made by their foremothers to work towards feminist goals.

## The Modern Gothic Ghost Story

The modern Gothic ghost story is more metatextual; it is aware of the conventions of the Gothic and the ghost story. The modern Gothic ghost story has many of the same elements of the conventional ghost story, including a protagonist who is endangered by domesticity, and whose body is subject to overregulation by the family patriarch. Moreover, like the protagonist of the conventional ghost story, the protagonist of the modern Gothic ghost story is saved by the ghost, whose intervention provides her with information that enables her to resist subordination and ultimately live a life in which she has more agency. However, the modern Gothic ghost story differs from the conventional ghost story in that its characters subvert the conventions of the Gothic in order to have more control over their lives. The haunted female protagonists in the modern Gothic ghost story are acutely aware of their oppression and so work to resist it. This awareness is due in part because the family patriarch requires that these characters adhere to gender roles that are far more restrictive that those of other girls their age in the time and place where they live.

The ghost in the modern Gothic ghost story is also a round character rather than a spectral wraith whose story in life can only be told by appropriating the consciousness of the girl it haunts, as is the case in *Jade Green* and *Dreadful Sorry*. Rather, the ghost in *A Stir of Bones* tells his story directly to the girl he befriends, while in *A Certain Slant of Light* and *Under the Light*, the ghost narrates the story of her life to the reader. These ghosts require more than just justice — rather, like the girls they haunt, they need help accessing their repressed knowledge so they can create a coherent narrative of what happened to them in the last moments of their lives and rest in peace. The girls haunted in these novels help the ghosts escape their limited perspective in order to construct a sense of themselves dialogically, to know themselves through the perspective of others as well as themselves, which ultimately allows them to escape their restrictive spectral forms.

## *Regulating the Body and the Mind through Discipline*

In the conventional ghost story, the haunted girl's coercion into a subordinate feminine role is not obvious. Yet in the modern Gothic ghost story, the haunted girl is so over-regulated that her resistance is an important element of the plot. But in spite of their resistance, the haunted girls' oppressors temporarily rob them of their voices in order to facilitate their subordination. As a result, the haunted girls are similar to the ghosts who haunt them in how they frequently *feel* alienated from their bodies. Patriarchy predisposes teen girls to feel disembodied as their bodies mature. Brenda Boudreau explains that as an adolescent girl's body takes on visibly sexed characteristics, it "becomes an obstacle to autonomy and self-agency as [she] tries to reconcile her body to the demands of a socially proscribed gendered identity, leading paradoxically, to feelings of disembodiment" (43). In *A Stir of Bones* and *A Certain Slant of Light/Under the Light*, Susan and Jennifer have their bodies over-regulated by their fathers, building upon feelings already set in place by wider patriarchal culture, exacerbating their feelings of disembodiment.

In *A Certain Slant of Light*, Jennifer's body has been so thoroughly regulated that she cannot exist as an autonomous subject. In fact, Jennifer's "self" has been repressed so violently that she is only a minor character in the novel. What we are shown of Jennifer over the novel's six-day time frame is filtered through the consciousness of Helen, the ghost who briefly inhabits Jennifer's vacant body. Helen, the actual protagonist of *A Certain Slant of Light*, lived some time before the American Civil War, and had more freedoms in life as a woman than those allowed to Jennifer, a contemporary girl who should be the beneficiary of gains for women made by first- and second-wave feminism. In Jennifer's skin, Helen exposes how Jennifer's spirit has been eradicated by her parents, who stamped out all of their daughter's resistance to their attempts to completely subordinate her. Given no place to be, Jennifer's spirit has evacuated her flesh, leaving behind an empty and obedient vessel with a pleasing shape, her family none the wiser. This soulless Jennifer is a sort of Stepford child, who only speaks when spoken to,

## 1. Subversive Spirits

and then only mouths acceptably pious sentiments. Jennifer's resistant behavior resumes, however, when Helen takes possession of her body. The over-regulation of Jennifer's body continues in *Under the Light*, the sequel to *A Certain Slant of Light*, wherein Jennifer has returned to her body and begun to fight for some agency in her life.

In *A Stir of Bones*, Susan's over-regulated body similarly "becomes an obstacle to autonomy and self-agency" (Boudreau 43). While Jennifer literally flees her body, Susan mentally disassociates herself from her flesh. She never feels pain, and can watch burns, cuts, and scrapes "blister and bleed with clinical detachment, as if they were happening to someone on television" (Hoffman 2). Susan's father has so thoroughly disciplined her body that she no longer remembers having much control over it.

Another important component of the modern Gothic ghost story is the figure of the family patriarch, the representative of the wider patriarchal order. As in the conventional ghost story, the family patriarch in the modern Gothic ghost story disciplines his daughter into a restrictive gender role that is mired in domesticity and compulsory heterosexuality. The family patriarch is the enforcer of feminine subordination in *A Stir of Bones*, *A Certain Slant of Light*, and *Under the Light*. Jennifer's and Susan's fathers employ various micropractices of discipline that focus on their teenaged daughters' bodies in order to coerce them into subordinate roles preparing them for a womanhood in which they will be devoid of agency. Both fathers control their daughters' bodies by limiting their mobility and deciding what they can wear and to whom they can talk. These fathers are aided by their wives in disciplining their daughters. Michelle Massé observes that women in the female Gothic "do not merely reflect but help to shape [the] system" (5) that oppresses them through internalizing its values. Because Jennifer's and Susan's mothers have bought into the belief that feminine subordination is natural and desirable, they serve as models for their daughters' behavior and as accomplices to their husbands' discipline.

In *A Certain Slant of Light*, Jennifer's father Dan Thompson applies various disciplinary techniques to his daughter's body in order to turn her into a docile Christian subject. Dan's obsession with how Jennifer's body is displayed derives from the family's Christian fundamentalism, which requires that women submit to men in all matters. One way that female members of the Thompsons' church demonstrate their faith is by dressing in attire that codes them as unambiguously feminine, and therefore, different from and subordinate to men. As *pater familias*, it is Dan's job to ensure that Jennifer embodies their church's conception of Christian womanhood. For this reason, he inspects his daughter's wardrobe daily to insure that her body is acceptably concealed: there can be no jiggling or exposure of bra straps, and her hem line must be no shorter than an inch above her knees.

Dan controls Jennifer's body further by chronicling its rhythms and limiting its mobility. Even Jennifer's menstrual cycles are not private; he has directed Jennifer's mother Cathy to track them on a calendar, presumably to ensure that her reproductive capabilities are in working order in preparation for marriage and motherhood. Dan also limits his daughter's access to her peers. Although Jennifer is fifteen years old, she is not allowed to date and she is not allowed to ride the bus to school, but must be delivered and picked up by her mother so that she has little opportunity to socialize. When Jennifer is eventually permitted to socialize with boys, her outings will not resemble the sort of free mélange of associations that characterize teen heterosexual relationships in the United States. Instead, Jennifer will only be allowed to date boys who are members of the family's church, providing that both sets of parents approve of the relationship.

Dan's tight control over his daughter's body exemplifies attitudes towards women in his ultra-conservative religious community. As Christian fundamentalists, they view the Bible as the literal word of God rather than a historical document. Using passages from the Old Testament that represent women as inherently inferior to men, Dan and his fellow fundamentalists hold that feminine subordination is a natural consequence of being female rather than a cultural construct. However, because the Thompsons live in the modern United States, where such extreme feminine subordination is no longer typical, more stringent measures must be taken to form Jennifer into someone who accepts that all authority resides in the hands of men. Dan's discipline of Jennifer's body, then, is calculated to re-form her into a woman like her mother, who blindly accepts her subordinate position within the family unit and their church.

In *Under the Light*, which is told alternately from Jennifer's and Helen's perspectives, we learn that disembodiment is a momentarily liberating experience for Jennifer. "Was anything possible now?" (12), Jennifer muses after leaving her body for what will be a six-day absence. And anything is possible

## 1. Subversive Spirits

for her for a while, as she can to venture to other countries, even to the surface of the moon, in the blink of an eye. However, after a few days Jennifer discovers the limitations of disembodiment in how she lacks the ability to completely put her will into action.

In *Stir of Bones*, Susan's subordinate status within her family is similarly reinforced through discipline targeting her body. Throughout the novel, "Father" is the only name by which Susan's male parent is referred, emphasizing his role as family patriarch. Like Dan, Father also controls his daughter's appearance and limits her mobility and access to peers. Father makes the rules about her dress and grooming: he personally selects Susan's unambiguously feminine wardrobe and chooses her hairstyle. Appropriately, Susan thinks of Father as a "property owner" and of herself as a piece of land he manages (Hoffman 69–70). Hoffman represents this view as objectionable by immediately showing readers that Susan is pleased when Father's "property" is defaced in small ways. For instance, Susan is elated to find a bruise on her thigh from gym class because the mark is a way of temporarily disrupting Father's ability to enjoy the perfection of his "property."

The property-property owner simile that Susan uses to illustrate her relationship to Father is also an apt description for his relationship with her mother, whose body he disciplines through violence. Whenever Susan does something to displease Father, Mother serves as a surrogate for punishment, and Susan is forced to see her own "flaws" illustrated in Mother's bruised flesh. Mother views these beatings as a legitimate disciplinary practice, demonstrating how she helps shape the system that oppresses her. Mother describes herself to Susan as someone who deserves her husband's abuse because she is "stupid about things," and Father is a "good man at heart" (Hoffman 133). Such statements reveal how Mother has been conditioned by Father to believe that *she* is responsible for his violence. To Mother's way of thinking, her abusive marriage has its compensating joys. Mother tells Susan that she has all she ever wanted as a girl: the family has "so many beautiful things, and a housekeeper to keep them pretty" (Hoffman 133). In this way, Mother is Father's accomplice in indoctrinating Susan into what he sees as her appropriate gender role—a model of delicate femininity, a woman with impeccable grooming who is *always* deferential to masculine authority. This model of femininity would precondition Susan to viewing abusive relationships as normal rather than pathological.

Father also disciplines his daughter's body by limiting its movement. He sends her to private school not to give her a solid educational foundation, but to isolate her from common public school children and to monitor her comings and goings. Each day, Susan must directly return home from school. She is not permitted to associate too freely with her more privileged peers outside of school since they could also induce her to resist Father's authority. Like Jennifer, Susan has no expectation of privacy: her possessions are searched, and even her dirty laundry is periodically inspected by Father for evidence that she has left the house without permission.

Yet as we soon see, Susan does not completely accept Father's regulation of her body. Instead, we see her formulating strategies for resistance at the beginning of the novel when she plans a research project for school so that the necessary gathering of information will require her to leave the house, unsupervised, for several hours a day. This resistance enables Susan to make friends, who give her a support system, and to meet Nathan, the ghost who will help her thwart Father's ability to control her or harm Mother.

However, Father's and Dan's discipline goes further than the body. They also subject their daughters to discipline targeting the mind. The subversive potential of literacy is a prominent theme in *A Stir of Bones*. Because Father recognizes that reading, writing, and even access to other media have the potential to incite rebellion, he monitors Susan's reading material, and requires that she show him all of her school work, as much to give him the opportunity to scrutinize her thoughts as to check on her academic progress. Father similarly understands the subversive potential of popular media since it creates a virtual community that permits people to realize their full potential as humans. To ensure that Susan's mind is untainted by influences that might make it less malleable to his will, he limits her access to popular culture: she can only watch educational programs on public broadcasting — no MTV, cartoons, or even prime time dramas or comedies which might promote a model of femininity that is far less repressive than Father's conception of girlhood.

As a successful trial attorney, Father has a unique appreciation for the power of language to manipulate others. Susan describes this ability as "word magic," implying that he has some incomprehensible ability to transform reality through language. Father's "word magic" serves to further silence Susan. If Susan were to report Father's abuse of Mother to the authorities,

## 1. Subversive Spirits

she has every reason to suspect that her complaint would not be taken seriously since Father has previously demonstrated that he can convince emergency room personnel that his wife is merely clumsy on those nights when his violence necessitates she receive medical treatment. Father's "word magic" has similarly silenced a string of family housekeepers who have witnessed the effects of his violence. When they attempt to speak out, Father discredits their words and threatens to deploy his "word magic" against them to invite harassment from the police. Father's use of language to bully is typical of abusers, who often rely on male privilege and in some instances, class privilege, to negate the speech of others, particularly women, whose words are frequently viewed as unreliable due to gender stereotypes.

In *A Certain Slant of Light* Dan understands the subversive potential of reading and writing, as is demonstrated by his attempts to limit his daughter's literacy. Dan and his wife routinely search Jennifer's book bag and the contents of her room for unacceptable literature. Even *Jane Eyre* is considered too controversial for their daughter to read with its plot about a young woman's relationship with her married employer. Jennifer's personal reflections in her diary are similarly regulated. When her parents discover that she has expressed unacceptable thoughts in this medium, the pages are torn out, and she is forced to use the rest of the book to copy biblical passages about obedience. The last date of Jennifer's expurgated diary entries coincides with the day her camera, another tool of self-expression, is taken away as punishment for her continuous questioning of the family's faith (*Certain* 217). It is not surprising that Dan would censor his daughter's diary since in this medium, even Jennifer's very private use of writing encourages her to see herself as an autonomous subject. In *Under the Light*, Dan characterizes his daughter's private thoughts written in her journal as wicked (5). When Jennifer leaves her body, the first place her spirit travels to is an art museum and the library. In the museum, she is able to see for the first time free displays of the human body in paintings and photographs, something that her mother "would have considered borderline pornography" (*Under* 13). Jennifer is at first elated when her spirit travels to the library, believing that she "could read anything [she] wanted now, uncensored" (*Under* 14). However, Jennifer quickly realizes the fallacy of her thinking after discovering that without a body, she is unable to pull a book off of the shelf to read or to even turn pages. True agency requires control of both the mind and the body.

In *Under the Light*, readers see just how subversive literacy is when Helen communicates with Jennifer through a hymnal and the Bible while the girl is in church. Although Helen has now vacated Jennifer's body so that the girl can live in her own flesh, Helen still needs to maintain communication with Jennifer to help the girl take full control of her own life. Helen initiates this communication while Jennifer is in church, guiding the girl's attention to relevant passages in the Bible, a book that her parents have used as justification for her subordination. While Jennifer's parents often cite parts of the Bible that enjoin women and children to obey their "masters," Helen directs the girl's attention to Biblical passages that encourage sisterhood. As a hymn entitled "This Is My Father's World" plays in the church, Helen draws Jennifer's attention to a passage in the Book of Ruth, where, in an expression of sisterhood, Ruth famously promises to follow her mother-in-law until the death of both (*Under* 109).

## *Awareness of Oppression as a Way of Resisting It*

The haunted female protagonists of *A Stir of Bones*, *A Certain Slant of Light*, and *Under the Light* are different from their counterparts in *Dreadful Sorry* and *Jade Green* in that they are painfully aware of their own oppression in a patriarchal culture and do not accept their subordination as part of the status quo. Rather, Jennifer and Susan subtly resist their fathers by contemplating how they have been made into disciplined subjects. Susan can explore this relationship only after she has a private space for self-expression, a place away from Father's jealous gaze. She does this by sneaking out of the house with her friends and exploring an abandoned house, where everyone can have "a room of one's own" to do what is not possible at home. Susan's room is a space where she contemplates the parameters of herself as a disciplined subject, which ultimately enables her to formulate a more effective method of resistance. Nathan provides Susan with this space to experiment with methods of resistance, permitting Susan and her friends to have rooms in the abandoned house he haunts. Nathan owned this dwelling in life, and now that he is a ghost, no one can open the house's doors to enter without his permission.

Jennifer explores her subjectivity through photography. Hidden in Jennifer's room are self-portrait photographs documenting her oppression. If, as Pamela Bettis and Natalie Adams observe, "bodies prove that we are real" (12) then these photographs are signs of Jennifer's resistance, where she claims her body through self-representation. Jennifer's photographs, discovered by Helen while she inhabits Jennifer's flesh, are disturbing in that they show the girl's body with its soul inside, since they were taken before Jennifer's spirit left her flesh. Trites explains that YA novels employing photography "create many opportunities for characters to explore the relationship between subject and object, between acting and being acted upon" (*Disturbing* 123). Clearly Jennifer is exploring this relationship. In one photograph, Jennifer is nude and in fetal position, representing how her relationship with her parents makes her feel infantilized. In another photograph, captioned "the ghost waits," Jennifer has a sheet over her head and a suitcase at her feet, illustrating how she has been made into a ghost of sorts by parents who demand she stifle not only all anger, but even all independent thought. Jennifer's self-portrait photographs represent her simultaneously in both the object position and the subject position: as the photographer, Jennifer visually represents what her parents have done to her.

However, these photographs do more than reproduce Jennifer's experience of being subordinated: they allow her to meditate on her subordination to formulate strategies for resistance. The suitcase in the second photograph, for example, foreshadows the possibility of escape via the ghost. The third photograph, a shot of Jennifer's face, taken in the dressing table mirror where she looks to be "absolutely at peace" (*Certain* 178), is the most defiant of the collection, indicating that Dan and Cathy have not yet completely eradicated their daughter's stubborn individuality. In this picture, Jennifer is more than a subject who is acted upon. Here she is in the object position both as photographer and as a photographic subject who looks back at the viewer.

Yet Dan and Cathy momentarily succeed in disciplining Jennifer into a model of feminine subordination. When they take away even the most private places for self-expression from Jennifer, her spirit flees her body and she becomes the daughter they have always wanted, one who obeys instructions without question and speaks only when spoken to. During *A Certain Slant of Light*'s six day time frame, Jennifer is an absence rather than a presence. We never see events through her perspective. Instead, we learn Jennifer's story through Helen, the disembodied spirit who takes possession of

Jennifer's uninhabited body for less than a week. Helen in this capacity is a sort of archeologist who pieces together the particulars of Jennifer's life through interacting with her family and examining artifacts she left behind after vacating her flesh. And as we discover, Helen's archeology helps make Jennifer's life livable.

## Reclaiming the Body to Be Reborn

When Jennifer reclaims her body in *Under the Light*, Cathy and Dan continue to try and discipline her. However, as the couple is now divorcing, each makes separate attempts to control their daughter. Dan, believing that Cathy let Jennifer "get out of control" (149) attempts to force his daughter to come live with him and his new partner Judy Morgan, so that he can more effectively subordinate her. Cathy, desperate to prevent her now-estranged spouse from taking her daughter away, works to reign in what she views as Jennifer's defiance, which includes her questioning of her parents' actions and communicating with people that they do not approve of. One of the more extreme measures that Cathy resorts to is allowing the women of the church to perform an exorcism on Jennifer, which is ironic as Jennifer's body was possessed earlier.

Susan and Jennifer try to resist their fathers, but find it difficult to do so alone. Both Susan's and Jennifer's fathers have isolated them so that they can break their daughters' spirits without interference. Susan's and Jennifer's mothers do not intervene in their husbands' treatment of their children because they too have been thoroughly subordinated by these men. Susan's mother is beaten by her husband, who has convinced her that she deserves the abuse because she is too stupid to care for herself or her daughter. While Dan does not beat Cathy, he is emotionally abusive, and he and the members of their church have convinced her that if she fails to be subordinated to her husband's will, then she is both a bad wife and a bad Christian. As a consequence, Cathy is fearful of interfering with Dan's instructions about parenting Jennifer even when she feels that his actions are harmful to their child.

Nevertheless, Susan and Jennifer reach out to peers in order to help them resist their fathers' control. Susan sneaks away from the watchful gaze of Father, ostensibly to visit the library to do research for a school project,

## 1. Subversive Spirits

where she meets Edmund, Deirdre, and Julio, the son of Susan's family's housekeeper. This friendship gives her some strength to resist Father. However, their influence alone does not allow Susan to resist Father in a meaningful way that will prevent him from crushing her spirit and beating Mother. In *Under the Light*, Jennifer seeks out Billy, the boy in *A Certain Slant of Light* whose body James inhabited when he courted Helen while she was in Jennifer's body. While Helen and James inhabit vacant bodies of Jennifer and Billy, Jennifer's and Billy's spirits meet and become friends. When Jennifer returns to her body, she looks for Billy, whose spirit has also returned to his flesh. Billy, however, is consumed with his own problems — before his spirit fled his body, he stood by while one of his friends at the time raped a girl. Now he is charged with being an accessory to rape and must work to stay out of jail as well as distance himself from people that he realizes were poor companions. As a result, Billy rejects Jennifer's overtures because he is convinced that the world would be a better place without him in it, and that he would only harm her if he she is near him. Discouraged by Billy's rejection of her, Jennifer at first decides "to be completely cooperative," with all her parents require of her, including going to church, being homeschooled by Judy Morgan, and using "a camera only to take pictures at birthday parties and Christmas" (199). She muses that she might even "learn to be happy" so long as she "didn't care what happened to [her] next" (199).

Susan and Jennifer can only effectively resist their fathers with the help of the ghosts who haunt them. These ghosts empower Susan and Jennifer both by acting as their doubles and as well as by being fully supportive of them. The ghost of Nathan in *Stir of Bones* empowers Susan by serving as her double. Nathan, the only male ghost haunting a female protagonist in the novels that I have surveyed, represents all the masculine qualities that Susan is compelled to repress in the interest of embodying Father's narrow concept of femininity. Nathan is a double of Susan in that she also experiences herself as a kind of ghost, one living under Father's watchful eye. As McCallum notes, the figure of the double infers opportunities for resistance, for "the double represents another possible position that the character might occupy, an internalized aspect of otherness" (*Ideologies* 77). Hence, it is appropriate that Susan is haunted by a male rather than a female ghost since what has been most violently repressed by Father are those qualities of herself that are traditionally associated with masculinity, such as being independent and outspoken, as well as the ability to use her body in ways that would cause her to get dirty and disrupt the illusion of femininity that Father requires her to maintain. When Nathan reacquaints Susan with these repressed aspects of herself, she sees further possibilities for resistance.

In *A Certain Slant of Light* and *Under the Light*, Helen serves as a double of Jennifer. It is difficult at times to differentiate Jennifer from Helen since they cannot talk directly to one another the way that Susan and Nathan are able to do. Jennifer has returned to her body in *Under the Light*, but at first she is only dimly aware of Helen's presence, and at one point, she even believes that she is having a psychotic episode rather than being haunted. The action in *A Certain Slant of Light* takes place during the six days that Helen possesses Jennifer's body, and at this time, she effectively *is* Jennifer, since she cannot completely do as she wishes while inhabiting this body that is controlled by Jennifer's parents. But Helen does not merely use Jennifer's body to mouth her words. Rather, Helen and Jennifer have similar ideas. Both are distrustful of those who claim to know the fate of someone's soul after death. Before Jennifer vacated her body, what her parents find most disturbing about her is that she questions the tenets of their fundamentalist faith, a privilege not even accorded to male members of their church. When Helen occupies Jennifer's flesh, she too questions the family's faith, challenging members of the congregation about their hierarchal belief that clerical intervention is necessary for individual salvation. Relying on her own authority as a spirit, Helen in Jennifer's body excoriates her family's co-religionists as presumptuous people who "have no idea what it's like to die or go to heaven or not go to heaven" (Whitcomb, *Certain* 248) and therefore cannot tell others who will be saved or damned.

Helen is also Jennifer's double in that she reacquaints Jennifer with her sexuality. In that respect, the text defies the moralizing stance on sexuality that Trites observes is a staple of much YA fiction. One of the major concerns exhibited by works in the genre regards the need to teach "teens to repress their liberated sexualities" (Trites, *Disturbing* 92) through continuously reminding readers of the dangerous consequences of sexual activity — dangers ranging from a broken heart to contracting AIDS. Helen's relationship with Jennifer is contrary to this stance. Helen initially possessed Jennifer's body so she could consummate her relationship with James, another disembodied spirit who has taken up residence in a vacated body. As Helen uses Jennifer's body to express her love for James, she is also enabling Jennifer to have a relationship with a boy her own age, which is conventional behavior for heterosexual teen girls in the United States in the twenty-first century.

Helen's influence continues to allow Jennifer to be reacquainted with her sexuality in *Under the Light*, where she no longer inhabits Jennifer's body but still communicates with her via haunting. After Jennifer reclaims her body, she looks for Billy, who has also reclaimed his own flesh. Now completely in control of their bodies, Jennifer and Billy explore their mutual attraction and consider what they might have in common in spite of their seeming to be so different from one another. Yet Helen continues to assist Jennifer via haunting. With Helen's encouragement, Jennifer recalls the repressed memory of what her father did to drive her from her body for six days — forcing her to read to her parents parts of her diary in which she describes a dream where a boy at her school put his hand under her shirt. When Jennifer hesitated to read aloud this very personal passage, Dan threatened to have her mother read it to her. Afterwards, Dan took away anything that Jennifer could use to express herself: he destroyed the offending pages of Jennifer's diary and forced her to transcribe Bible verses about obedience in the book's remaining pages, and took away her camera, her CD player, and all of the clothing that she loved.

Helen's relationship with Jennifer in both novels mimics the convoluted relationship between spirit and medium, or between the individual and God, as envisioned by Spiritualists. Spiritualism, which began in the 1840s, was an anti-hierarchal faith whose adherents believed that individuals could have direct access to divine truth through spirit communication. Unlike other faiths of the period, many Spiritualist leaders were women. Also, all Spiritualists were feminists in that they believed in equality between the sexes (Braude).

Ann Braude's history of the American Spiritualist Movement explains how women who served as mediums for spirits of the departed were simultaneously conventionally feminine and empowered. While "mediumship was closely identified with femininity" (Braude 23),

> mediums did not model a simple abrogation of accepted feminine norms. Instead, mediumship gave women a public leadership role that allowed them to remain compliant with the complex values of the period that have come to be known as

the cult of true womanhood [which] asserted that woman's nature was characterized by purity, piety, passivity, and domesticity [Braude 82].

While the spirits might cause their hosts to make statements incompatible with conventional femininity, mediumship did not unsex women. Indeed, in the nineteenth century, merely the act of speaking publicly was believed to be antithetical to women's nature. Mediumship, however, "did not require a decision to rebel against a domestic role" (Braude 83) because Spiritualists believed that mediums did not consciously choose their roles; rather, they were chosen by the departed to be their conduits. In this way mediumship mimicked pregnancy in that the medium was a passive vessel for the spirit.

The female medium then was not unsexed through her congress with the dead since her relationship with ghosts was an extension of normative femininity of the period. Rather, mediumship permitted women to subtly subvert prevailing notions of gender while appearing to uphold these conventions. While in the posture of normative femininity,

> with the encouragement of spirits, [female mediums] did things that they themselves believed women could not do ... [and the spirit] presence helped women overcome internal doubts as well as external sanctions [Braude 83].

The spirit, then, functioned as a sort of double for the medium. The medium, while possessed by a spirit, could publicly challenge a sexist culture that saw her as physically and intellectually unsuited for autonomy, while her behavior could be attributed to the superior intellect of the spirit rather than the feelings of the medium herself. As mediums, women could simultaneously critique their subordinate status while appearing to maintain the subject position of normative femininity. In this way, Spiritualism helped women reclaim their voices in order to subtly subvert existing power structures, while not openly appearing to threaten them.

The haunted female character in YA ghost stories is frequently a medium, someone temporarily possessed by a spirit who speaks *through* her. As Helen's medium, Jennifer can reclaim her silenced voice. This does not imply that as Jennifer's double Helen puts words in her host's mouth; rather, Helen permits Jennifer to express herself more emphatically.

In the conventional ghost story, the haunted girl is reborn through the ghost. In the modern Gothic ghost story, however, both ghost and haunted girl are reborn due to their connection with each other. This rebirth manifests itself in the new master narrative that ghost and haunted girl construct about themselves. This narratives allows both to reclaim agency in their lives — the ghost can pass into the next life, while the haunted girl can counter narratives that those more powerful than her have crafted as part of their attempts to control her. Birth imagery accompanies this transformation, and often the haunted girl is reborn in a feminine space — the haunted house, for example, in *Stir of Bones*, or the reclaimed house of the patriarchal family in *A Certain Slant of Light* and *Under the Light*.

Susan is reborn in multiple ways in *A Stir of Bones*. First, Susan is reborn through her relationship with Nathan, who empowers her by awakening the repressed knowledge of her own strength. After their first meeting, Nathan gives Susan a finger bone from his skeleton, a piece from a body part that represents the will: it does not so much give Susan power as it reveals a strength that she was previously unaware she possessed. Nathan's gift demonstrates what Trites says of feminist power, that it "is more about being aware of one's agency than it is about controlling other people" (*Waking* 8). Once Susan becomes aware of her own strength, she can begin the process of reclaiming her silenced voice. This process commences almost immediately. When Susan's friend punches her arm, Nathan's bone in her hand grows hot, traveling up her arm and warming her vocal cords until she can tell her friend "Don't. Hit. Me" (Hoffman 63). Susan's ability to vocalize this objection surprises her since "at home there was nothing she could do about people hitting people," but "out here, where it was supposed to be safe, she didn't want anyone to hit her" (Hoffman 63).

Susan is further reborn through her newfound ability to see *how* Father is able to manipulate others. Nathan's presence in Susan's life occasions her contemplation of what she has always known but until now could not articulate: Mother participates in her own victimization. As a consequence, Susan realizes that Father cannot completely control her. Instead, Susan's "brain and all the landscapes and architecture in it belonged to her" (Hoffman 70). It is a space uncolonized by Father, and therefore the site of future resistance.

*Stir of Bones* is also full of water and nautical imagery suggesting rebirth. The novel is set in Washington State, near the Pacific Ocean, from which Susan has taken one of her most treasured objects, a smooth stone that she found when a visiting aunt took her to the beach. Five years later, the day stands out as memorable to Susan: her trip allowed her to momentarily defy Father, who has limited her contact with relatives and has never permitted her to go to the beach because he considers the sand to be too messy (Hoffman 12). Through this stone, which Susan keeps in her pocket, the sea persists as a significant theme: the stone has been worn smooth by the ocean, yet also contains a faint fossil of a shell, a spiral shape suggesting regeneration and eternity. As Susan comes to understand the constructedness of her subject position, the stone takes on new significance as something reminding her of her own resilience. The stone prompts Susan to consider that "things could survive a lot of grinding" (Hoffman 13). Susan ponders that maybe she "had some sand in her too" (Hoffman 13) since deceiving Father in order escape the house has emboldened her to attempt other things she has never done before, such as making friends with kids her own age.

Susan's most significant and obvious rebirth experience occurs on Halloween night, when Nathan enables her to be quite literally reborn as a pre-discursive subject, someone whose body has not yet been inscribed by culture.[5] On this night of the year, spirits have supernatural abilities beyond what they normally have, and Nathan uses his to alter Susan. There, in Susan's house on Nautilus Road under the moon in the salt-soaked air, Nathan transforms her into what he describes as a reflection of her inner self. The name of Susan's street also suggest rebirth: the nautilus is a spiral-shaped sea creature. Susan's changed body is armored, a manifestation of what Nathan describes as her inner skin that keeps her alive and also alone (Hoffman 143), with arms and legs that feel stronger than they do in her other body (Hoffman 140). But most importantly, the reborn Susan is a sort of pre-discursive subject that is beyond gender: her transformed body is "a sexless thing" (Hoffman 142) with short hair. Susan's invulnerability in this body is *because* she has no sex on which a subordinate subjectivity can be erected. Unlike the gendered Susan, this Susan is not contained by any boundaries, including those of the physical universe. Ghostlike, Susan can pass through walls or walk on the surfaces of rivers.

However, because it is impossible to escape the ubiquity of culture, Susan's existence as this pre-discursive subject is unstable and cannot be maintained indefinitely. Thus, at the end of the night, Susan cannot keep her new body and leave the old one behind forever, since leaving her old body uninhabited could quite possibly cause both to dissolve (Hoffman

## 1. Subversive Spirits

156). Instead, at the end of the evening Susan must return to her old body and find a more permanent way to be reborn in order to escape Father's oppression.

Susan can only be more permanently and effectively reborn as a *discursive* subject. This rebirth occurs within the feminine space of House, the abandoned dwelling where she and her friends first meet Nathan and where all have a room of their own where they can develop their talents. House is in marked contrast to the heterogeneous disciplinary space that she calls home. In Father's home, Susan uses her "house sense," an ability that helps her detect where anyone is inside the house so she can evade Father's gaze. Inside of House, however, Susan is most fully reborn. When Father discovers that Susan has been sneaking out, he puts an end to her outings. Despairing of ever being beyond Father's control, Susan contemplates suicide in order to eternally put her body out of his reach, and escapes to visit House one last time. But Susan's ghostly and living friends are there waiting, and they refuse to let her end her life. Instead, to make her life more bearable, they transfer some of their collective power to her via a magical ceremony. Susan, who can use this power once in any way she wishes, will draw upon it to undermine Father's ability to manipulate through using his wife's bruised flesh to illustrate his daughter's supposed imperfections. In this way, with the help of the ghost and her friends, Susan constructs new narrative of herself as someone who deserves to live and who is strong enough to resist Father's violence and to protect others from it.

Jennifer is similarly reborn in *A Certain Slant of Light* and *Under the Light*, which are also full of water imagery. When Helen first enters Jennifer's vacant body in *A Certain Slant of Light*, she is transformed yet again from the Thompsons' literally spiritless daughter to someone more insistent on expressing herself. This transformation occurs due to her relationship with Helen, which renews her strength so that she can eventually be reborn as someone who can comfortably inhabit her own flesh and reclaim her silenced voice now that she no longer has to repress so many of her desires that are not in keeping with her family's idea of Christian femininity. When Helen realizes that her inhabiting of Jennifer's body is untenable for both, she entices the girl's spirit to return to her flesh by putting the body through a near-death experience. Helen gets in the bath and takes all of Jennifer's sleeping pills, bringing the girl close to drowning in an environment suggesting amniotic fluid. With the body near death, Helen's spirit exits and Jennifer's returns in the newly feminine space of the Thompson home, made so by Dan's departure earlier that day, after he abandoned the family for his more compliant mistress. This newly reclaimed feminine space nurtures sisterhood, which is so important for women's development. Jennifer and her mother momentarily nurture their spirituality and repair their relationship, which was fractured by Dan's continued insinuation of himself in between the two. However, Dan continues to interfere with Jennifer and Cathy's relationship in *Under the Light*, so Jennifer must undergo a second rebirth experience, where she becomes someone who can more forcefully resist her father's efforts to completely control her and her mother. This second rebirth occurs when Cathy turns her daughter over to the other women from church, as she believes that Jennifer is possessed by demons since the girl has been talking about feeling that she is a completely different person and has had some recent loss of memory, which, unknown to Cathy, was due to Helen inhabiting the girl's body. The women of the church perform an exorcism on Jennifer, holding her down while interrogating her about her supposed relationship with the devil and flicking salt water into her eyes to cast out demonic influences. Helen helps Jennifer through this experience by showing the girl Helen's own repressed memory of the last moments of her life where she drowned in the cellar after taking her toddler daughter there to shelter during a storm. Jennifer's relationship with Helen allows her to re-live the ghost's terrifying last moments before drowning, a memory that further suggests amniotic fluid and rebirth.

After Helen shares her most painful memory with Jennifer, she encourages Jennifer to remember her own most painful memory, the one that drove her from her body when her father humiliated her by forcing her to read aloud a passage from her diary where she recounts a sexual dream. Helen, however, encourages Jennifer to stop repressing this memory, and to instead remember it, and then take control by "creating a new version of her nightmare" where she tears down the old narrative in which she is powerless against her father's invasive discipline and replaces it with a newer story where she has agency (213). Thus, when Jennifer recounts the story of her humiliation again, she calls out her parents for their treatment of her and each other rather than being ashamed of the experience. Changing this memory is empowering for Jennifer because by being openly angry with her

## 1. Subversive Spirits

parents, she asserts her right to have feelings. She then recalls a time when her mother did defy her father for her. As a little girl, Jennifer was dressed up and taken to a funeral at church, where she was predictably bored and uncomfortable. When Cathy allows Jennifer to lie in her lap, Dan commands that his daughter sit up and pay attention. Instead of forcing Jennifer to obey her father, Cathy objects that the child is nearly asleep, and then whispers in her daughter's ear that she's "a good girl" and that "God loves [her]," and she can do whatever she wants because she's "one of his angels." Dan clears his throat "against secrets being shared between his wife and daughter," (215) disrupting their relationship, but Cathy continues to whisper comforting words to Jennifer. This memory shows Jennifer the potential for sisterhood between mother and daughter.

After Jennifer reconstructs the narrative of how her father humiliated her, she is reborn as someone much stronger who can draw on resources that she forgot that she had, such as the power of her own voice. While Jennifer is experiencing Helen's memory and reliving her own painful repressed recollection, she is also being held down by the women of her parents' church who are performing an exorcism on her, an antithesis of the nurturing sisterhood she has experienced with Helen. Jennifer emerges from the memory to command the women to "let go" (218) of her, which they immediately do now that she "carried a new authority in her voice" (218). Jennifer's newfound defiance fosters sisterhood between her and her mother, emboldening Cathy to be similarly reborn as someone who will no longer blindly submit to authority, particularly when it attempts to drive her away from her child. After Jennifer demands that the women from the church unhand her, both mother and daughter pepper them with a barrage of questions about their role in concealing Dan's affair with another church member and their own hypocrisy in claiming that Jennifer is possessed because she says that she has seen a ghost and has had sex out of wedlock when some of them have done the same. This stronger Jennifer thwarts her father's attempt to force her to go live with him and his new partner.

At the end of *Stir of Bones*, Susan too is transformed. As a result, she can subvert Father's ability to control her, but he cannot detect how his influence has been diminished. Susan, for her part, still seems to be the same compliant daughter who can be cowed into submission. But Susan is different, stronger: she now has friends who can give her moral support and contradict Father's warped version of a normal family. These friends are a resource, people who are "ready to howl as necessary, or send her power" (Hoffman 209). Susan uses the magical gift given to her by Nathan and her living friends to confound Father's attempts to manipulate her through violence against Mother. After Mother has received a particularly savage beating, Susan heals her bone-deep bruises with the gift she has received from her friends. When Father cannot see evidence of his handiwork on Mother's body, he is utterly confounded. Another sort of magic occurs when Father is "confused and uncertain" (Hoffman 208) since he appears to have lost the ability to control his daughter's body through beating his wife.

Because *A Stir of Bones, A Certain Slant of Light,* and *Under the Light* are modern Gothic ghost stories, the ghost also needs the girl it haunts to help it get closure in its own life. Being a ghost is an uncomfortable condition. Nathan cannot leave his now-abandoned family home and pass into the next life until he remembers how he died. Eventually, Nathan and the reader learn that he hung himself in the family home when he was the only family member remaining after World War I and the influenza pandemic afterwards claimed everyone else. Helen too must remember the painful last moments of her life, which she has repressed all this time because she believes that she accidentally caused her toddler daughter's death. Before meeting James and inhabiting Jennifer's body, Helen wandered among the living unseen and unheard, attaching herself to a series of hosts who never knew of her presence. So in the modern Gothic ghost story, to be a ghost is to be denied the fellowship of both the living and the dead who has passed into the next life, since the ghost is too burdened with its own guilt to quit this world.

Susan and Jennifer have symbiotic relationships with Nathan and Helen respectively through which all are reborn. Helen dies a watery death, only to be born anew as a formless spirit because she is unable to completely relive the memory of her death by drowning, something she must do before she can be reunited with her loved ones in the Light. For the next century and a half, Helen avoids the pain of being a bodiless spirit by attaching herself to a series of living hosts who are never aware of her spectral presence. When Helen's most recent host marries and begins to speak of having a child, the impending pregnancy prompts her to search for a new host. Instead, she finds James, another ghost who has taken possession of the body of Billy after his spirit fled during a near-fatal drug overdose. James encourages Helen to take over Jennifer's uninhabited body so that she too can be reborn in this way, clothed in the flesh of someone else.

During Helen and James' six day courtship, Helen realizes that indefinitely inhabiting someone else's flesh is untenable. Helen and James' very adult love for one another cannot be expressed through bodies so tightly regulated by others. The couple cannot just run away clothed in this purloined flesh: since Jennifer is only fifteen years old, her parents have the legal authority to keep her from seeing other people. And when James quits his borrowed body to fully cross into the spirit world, Jennifer's body soon becomes a prison for Helen: she has no one in whom she can confide because she cannot tell anyone among the living who she actually is. As a result, Helen resolves to leave Jennifer's body so that she can be completely and finally reborn as one of the Light. After Helen exits Jennifer's body, she must face her hell of her own making by fully recalling the night that she died, trapped in a flooded cellar with her toddler daughter. The water in this small space also suggests a womb-like environment. After Helen allows herself to relive this event, she fully passes over to the other side to learn that she saved her child from the flood before she died. This knowledge permits Helen to be reborn as one of the Light who can be reunited with James and her now-departed family in the realm of spirits.

Nathan in *Stir of Bones* also needs Susan. Before she came along, Nathan was imprisoned in the house where he died for the past 63 years. But "there's something special about" (Hoffman 93) Susan: Nathan's house, which is like a living being, responds to her, opening doors for her that remain shut to others, and Nathan is able to leave the house if he wishes. Nathan's friendship with Susan and her friends has allowed him to experience emotional growth just as Helen has grown through her relationship with Jennifer. So on Halloween, the one night of the year when spirits can fully wander the earth and even decide whether or not to move on, Nathan decides to stay another year "to gain power and knowledge" (Hoffman 153).

# Conclusion

In *The Psychic Life of Power*, Butler muses that rather than laboring to discover *what* we are, we should *refuse* what we are, which is the result of how we have been individualized and totalized by the various institutional discourses that enact our subjectivities. Butler enjoins her readers "to promote new forms of subjectivity through the refusal of this kind of individuality which has been imposed on us for several centuries" (101) through varying the repetition of "what we are." In *Gender Trouble*, Butler says that because "all signification takes place within the orbit of the compulsion to repeat," agency "is to be located within the possibility of a variation on that repetition" (145). Monsters are examples of the sort of variation hypothesized by Butler. If iterations of the monstrous feminine can be understood as a purification of the abject that breaks down boundaries and calls their naturalness into question rather than as something that reinforces these boundaries, then horror is rife with subversive potential, thwarting the ability of various institutional discourses about sex and gender to individualize and totalize.

The haunted girls in the novels examined in this chapter are in the process of "refusing what they are," though that refusal is not always obvious to other characters in the books. With the assistance of the ghost, the haunted girl has refused to repeat some of the stylized acts that perpetuate normative femininity. Due to the ghost's intervention, the haunted girl has reclaimed her voice and can subsequently resist domination. Their resistance can take many forms, ranging from a quiet but effective subversion of patriarchy to becoming a more active participant in the world.

Rebecca in *Ruined* refuses what she is when she returns to New York with her father after breaking the Bowman family curse. Although she is a member of this prestigious family, she has no desire to participate in the rigid class and gender structure that claiming this position would require. When Rebecca returns to New Orleans in Morris's second novel in the series, she is still refusing what she is in a sense. She does not come back in order to pick up where she left off with the Bowman family, but rather, she returns at the request of a ghost to help release him from wandering the earth as a spirit by enabling him to accomplish a task he failed to do in life.

In *Jade Green*, with Jade's help, Judith refuses Charles' attempt to define her as abject and therefore worthy of harassment. When Judith fights back against Charles, she has "refused what she is" by varying some of those stylized acts of gender which have made her vulnerable to victimization. Judith has subverted one of the more pernicious forms of patriarchy in which women are controlled through the threat of violence. Judith will never again

## 1. Subversive Spirits

be so naive that she is easy prey for someone like her lecherous cousin, and her eventual wealth will insulate her from other situations in which she is put in peril due to financial exigency. However, while Judith has refused Charles' attempt to define her as abject through his actions, she has not refused the limits on her as a white, middle class heterosexual woman. The novel concludes with an indication that Judith's life will eventually culminate in the marriage plot in which she becomes a wife and mother in a patriarchal marriage in which she is subordinate to her husband's will, so she has not refused (or even thought much about) the role that she is expected by her culture to occupy.

Molly in *Dreadful Sorry* "refuses what she is" by discarding a notion of female maturity that is predicated on rejecting the mother, who is often portrayed as someone "whose stifling presence must be escaped in order for the daughter to develop fully" (Trites, *Waking* 103). *Dreadful Sorry* opens with Molly blindly rejecting all her mother has to offer, such as her wealth and intellect to ensure that her daughter receives an excellent education and her own example of a positive role model of a strong woman. Yet because the possibility for agency lies in the variation of the repetition of stylized acts that perpetuate gender, Molly's growth will not be founded upon her rejection of her mother. Instead, Molly's growth derives from sisterhood that includes maintaining her ties with her mother as well nurturing her relationship with her new step-mother and using women's history to understand her own connection to other women through time. The novel concludes with Molly embracing a feminist paradigm of female growth, one that allows "the daughter to mature without necessarily breaking from her mother," permitting "both mothers and daughters to be strong" (Trites, *Waking* 103). Within the frame of this paradigm, Molly can vary the repetition of those stylized acts to "alter what she is," to paraphrase Butler, rather than to outright "refuse what she is." After her experience with Clementine, Molly returns to her mother, resolved to conquer her fear of water so that she can pass the school's swimming requirement and graduate in order to embark on a future in which she has far more control over her own life than Clementine ever had.

It is more obvious how haunting has transformed Jennifer in *A Certain Slant of Light* and *Under the Light* and Susan in *A Stir of Bones* in ways that open up possibilities for subverting the agendas of their more immediate oppressors. Susan's relationship with Nathan has radically altered her perceptions of power and subjectivity, giving her numerous opportunities to fail to repeat some of the stylized acts of gender that Father requires of her. As a result, Susan is in a stronger position to refuse what Father (and patriarchal culture) define her as being. Because Susan must live in the same house with her oppressor until she turns eighteen, for now, she can only reclaim and nurture through stealth those parts of herself that Father has attempted to eradicate. For the moment, Susan has reclaimed enough of her own strength to make the remaining years in Father's home bearable for her.

Jennifer and her mother Cathy most obviously refuse what they are according to Dan's concept of Christian womanhood. At the end of *A Certain Slant of Light*, Cathy too now openly questions the tenets of their religion which made it possible for Dan to manipulate them in the first place. Cathy tells Jennifer that she no longer knows "what to think about God" (268) and wonders if Dan lied when he used God as an excuse to control every facet of her existence. The novel indicates that Jennifer too will continue to refuse what she is, and explore with her mother what each can be. Here too female maturation is not precipitated on an outright rejection of the mother, but instead is built upon an expansion of the mother/daughter relationship through which both can be strong. In fiction, a woman's capacity to grow is so frequently represented as being contingent on her repudiation of her mother that it appears to be a necessary condition of female development. The expansion of the mother/daughter relationship in *A Certain Slant of Light* then is another one of those variations in which the possibility for agency lies. By the end of *Under the Light*, Jennifer and Cathy have further refused Dan's narrow concept of Christian womanhood, and strengthened their connection to one another.

As these novels show, the figure of the ghost provides an important tool in feminist YA literature. The ghost as a double of the self permits the author to denaturalize feminine subordination by laying bare its genealogy and causing the reader to wonder "if gender is constructed, could it be constructed differently" (Butler *Gender* 7)? This exposure opens up possibilities for readers to imagine their own strategies for resistance.

CHAPTER 2

*Blood and Bitches: Sexual Politics and the Female Lycanthrope in Young Adult Fiction*

THOUSANDS OF YEARS OLD, the figure of the werewolf is unique among supernatural entities: as a creature that is simultaneously human and animal, its monstrous Otherness is a part of its body rather than an external component. In this regard, the young female werewolf differs from the haunted girls considered in Chapter 1: while those protagonists have stifled all that their culture considers to be anathema to their sex, the female werewolf is incapable of suppressing the feelings and physical traits that are considered incompatible with conventional femininity.

YA werewolf fiction exposes the pressure that teen girls face to be conventionally feminine, a subject position that necessitates they eschew their desires for sex, and sometimes even food, while simultaneously stifling the resulting justifiable anger. While the male werewolf typically exhibits behaviors that are well within the parameters of normative masculinity, the female werewolf represents heightened monstrosity because her lupine body puts her outside of conventional femininity, confirming patriarchy's worst fears about women's relationship to nature.

The werewolf is more animal than human, and is associated with blood and the moon. Women are represented in high and low culture "as closer to nature and therefore lacking a spiritual dimension," an idea that "so pervades the imagery and language of civilization that the concept takes on an air of reality" (Griffin 26). In this way, the figure of the female werewolf is a continuation of negative associations of women with nature: in fact, she embodies patriarchal fears about the uncontrollability of nature and uncontrollable women.

Other facets of the female werewolf's monstrosity are her anger and her desire for sex and meat. While these characteristics are compatible with normative masculinity, they are antithetical to normative femininity. When the female werewolf is angered, she will answer back to her antagonist, sometimes with violence. Her sexual needs are so great that she is capable of taking on the role of aggressor. Even her desire for meat is incompatible with conventional femininity, as meat eating is more closely associated with masculinity, as Carol Adams points out in *The Sexual Politics of Meat* (26).

The contemporary representation of the werewolf is far removed from the figure first imagined two thousand years ago, which dates back to Ovid and Virgil. In the Middle Ages, the werewolf was represented in Marie de France's "Bisclavert" as a sympathetic monster who was more sinned against than sinning. The werewolf did not become popularized until the nineteenth century, where it appeared in both fiction as well as in accounts "developed by antiquarians, folklorists, mythologists, historians and other social commentators" (du Coudray 14). The Victorian incarnation of the werewolf established it as "the beast within," a trope derived from a concept of the human mind as a conscious-unconscious duality, whereby the unconscious "was regularly associated with the bestial, instinctive life of the natural, material world" (du Coudray 66). In these theories, the unconscious mind always threatened to erupt, transforming the hapless human into a raging, uncivilized beast that lacks control over its baser desires. This trope of the werewolf is similar to the one we are familiar with today. However, the essential elements of the modern werewolf tale did not crystallize until the early twentieth century. The werewolf in its contemporary form derives from one literary and two filmic sources: Guy Endore's novel *The Werewolf of Paris* (1933), and the Universal Studios films *Werewolf of London* (1935) and *The Wolf Man* (1941). These sources continue to represent the werewolf as the repressed, bestial part of every civilized man that is always threatening to erupt while also evolving the popular mythology of lycanthropy.

One of these changes includes positive representations of lycanthropy as a condition that enables humans to shake off some of the repressive effects of civilization that have made humans estranged from beautiful and useful aspects of themselves. In the 1960s, some feminist writers used the werewolf as an affirmative "symbol of female identity." (Dziemianowicz 680). While the female werewolf in these later works is still positioned within the nature/culture dichotomy, nature and woman's alleged closer association with it are positively revalued, thereby challenging women's negative positioning as man's Other (du Coudray 130). Contemporary affirmative treatments of the female werewolf include the character of Elena Michaels in Kelley Armstrong's Women of the Otherworld Series and Shakira's song "She Wolf." All represent lycanthropy as a condition allowing women to express desires that women are encouraged to repress as they are viewed as anathema to hegemonic femininity.

The contemporary trope of the werewolf as a feminist repositioning of woman as man's Other is also uniquely able to elucidate how teen girls struggle for autonomy in a patriarchal culture. The trope of the werewolf mirrors contemporary discourses of adolescence that characterize teens as hormonally-crazed savages who must learn to master their baser impulses before they can mature into productive adults. The werewolf's sudden growth of body hair and aggressive behavior, which is similar to the changes primarily associated with male puberty, particularly connect the creature with adolescence. Recapitulation theories of human evolution single out adolescence as a crucial time when individuals either leap "to a developed, superior Western selfhood or [remain] in an arrested savage state" (Lesko 34). In this way, the teen werewolf is an atavistic monster incapable of mastering its "primitive" emotions in order to become an adult. Tony Rivers, the hapless protagonist of the 1957 film *I Was a Teenage Werewolf*, fits this description. Tony's immaturity is demonstrated by his inability to control his anger, which constantly erupts into fights with his peers. Dr. Brandon, the therapist whose experimental treatments are supposed to help Tony manage his anger, instead cause his patient to regress to a primitive state of human evolution, exacerbating the youth's adolescent immaturity and transforming him into a dangerous werewolf who must be destroyed.

But if the werewolf is a creature whose monstrosity derives from its propinquity to transgress the boundaries that allegedly separate human from animal, civilized from savage, and child from adult, then the female werewolf is doubly transgressive. While in her lupine pelt, the female werewolf is at odds with our concept of what it is to be both a civilized human *and* stereotypically feminine. The male werewolf is a monster because his desires for violence, sex and food are so intense that they fall well outside the concept of civilized humanity. Nevertheless, the male werewolf's transformation does not unsex him, for his proclivities are all extreme iterations of hegemonic masculinity, a subject position whose single most evident marker is violence (Kimmel 132). Therefore, both Tony Rivers and Larry Talbot, the werewolf protagonist of the film *The Wolf Man* (1941), are dangerously uncivilized, yet unambiguously masculine.

The female werewolf, on the other hand, is monstrous because her lupine body puts her outside of conventional femininity, confirming patriarchy's worst fears about women's supposedly closer relationship with nature. In the nineteenth century, female lycanthropy was represented as a demonized femininity, in response to how first-wave feminism provoked anxieties about "sexuality, gender differences and reproduction" (du Coudray 46). The female werewolf was considered the inverse of the chaste Angel of the House: either a femme fatale who seduced her victims or a mother bent on destroying children rather than nurturing them. Additionally, the female werewolf recalls a "pervasive cultural association of femininity with nature, embodiment and biology" (du Coudray 112). These ideas inform most accounts of female werewolves.

Yet the female werewolf can do more than merely reproduce in monstrous form the sexist nature/culture dichotomy. Like the ghost, the werewolf is a powerful trope because it reveals the constructedness of gender. The werewolf is not so much an animal as it is *an animal in drag in a human skin*, a position that calls into question the parts of ourselves that we designate as animal Others. In *Gender Trouble*, Judith Butler muses on the ability of drag to expose the sex/gender link as constructed rather than natural (2). The werewolf's shapeshifting ability similarly breaks both the sex/gender link and the human/civilization link. Because women are perceived as being closer to nature than are men (Griffin 26), to be normatively feminine is also to repeatedly perform stylized acts that keep at bay a woman's supposed animal nature. In this way, while some female werewolves merely confirm patriarchy's worst fears about the supposed essential animal qualities of women, other female werewolves expose how categories of gender are highly constructed subject positions rather than immutable conditions dictated by biology. Moreover, as a monster, the female werewolf can, in Elizabeth Clark's words, "show us other ways of being" (10) because she is what literature scholar Daniel Punday would describe as a "hopeful monster," a "desirable alternative to the present" (12) rather than something that is merely abhorrent.

The teen female werewolf is monstrous because at a time in her life when she is supposed to start demonstrating her maturity by mastering her "baser" impulses, her body cannot be contained within the boundaries of conventional femininity. The haunted protagonists discussed in Chapter 1 suffer because they succeed too well at maintaining poses of stereotypical femininity. But the teen female werewolf's budding lupine body will not permit her to be groomed into culturally sanctioned boundaries of femininity: it is strong and athletic, and sprouts hair in places where women are supposed to be smooth, and her "unfeminine" appetites for sex and meat as well as her capacity for anger make her incapable of acting like a good girl for long.

Perhaps this is why one defining feature of the female werewolf is her capacity for extreme anger, an emotion incompatible with stereotypical femininity. Lyn Mikel Brown explains how anger is antithetical to a conventional femininity that is predicated on self-abasement: "anger, *because* it is tied to self-respect, must be excised if a girl is to move seamlessly into today's culture [and it is to] remain unchanged by her presence" (*Raising* 12). While the haunted girl has disavowed her anger to the degree that she, like the ghost, becomes a sort of wraith or a pale substitute of herself, the female werewolf cannot stifle this emotion. Rather, the female werewolf experiences her anger as a normal and desirable attribute because it makes her strong and powerful. Moreover, the female werewolf is capable of acting on her anger.

A hybridization of human and animal, the female werewolf emphasizes the dangers of denying repressed emotions and desires to the point that the body is painfully contorted. Similarly, the trope of the female werewolf can transform a reader's consciousness and permit her to "refuse what we are" (*Psychic*, 101) to borrow Butler's idea, by reconstructing these boundaries. The creature's ability to pass back and forth between the boundaries that supposedly separate animal from human, and male from female, undermines these categories by revealing their permeability. The teen female lycanthrope, whose overt sexual desire and anger are essential facets of her being, can swallow these feelings only at her peril, thereby providing an object lesson to girls about the dangers of repressing feelings and denying the body in order to be normatively feminine. In this way, the teen female werewolf is a hopeful monster who can show us other ways of being.

In this chapter, I consider two YA novels, a short story, and four films with teen female werewolf protagonists. The inclusion of film is central to my discussion since the figure of the werewolf as we know it owes as much to its cinematic as to its literary predecessors. The short story "Boobs" by Suzy McKee Charnas; the films *Blood Moon* (2001) and The Ginger Snaps Trilogy (*Ginger Snaps* [2000], *Ginger Snaps 2: Unleashed* [2004], *Ginger Snaps Back: The Beginning* [2004]); the novels *Blood and Chocolate* (1997), by Annette Curtis Klause and *The Blooding* (1996), by Patricia Windsor depict the utility of the figure of the female werewolf for exploring the situation of teen girls.[1] Like the ghosts discussed in Chapter 1, the werewolf offers resistance to feminine subordination. However, the figure of the werewolf represents a more physical and graphic manifestation of the Other than does the figure of the ghost. The texts I examine have achieved sufficient popularity to be well-known. The Ginger Snaps Trilogy is included in my study of YA werewolf narratives in part because *Ginger Snaps*, the first film in the trilogy, was well-received by critics and was the recipient of several awards.[2] *Blood Moon* (also known as *Wolf Girl* in Canada, where it was produced) has received little critical attention, but is a cult horror classic.[3] "Boobs" was a 1990 Hugo Award winner for Best Short Story and is widely anthologized, while *Blood and Chocolate* and *The Blooding* are owned by at least 800 libraries worldwide.

As of this writing, I have identified no YA narratives of lycanthropy with female protagonists of color, so all of the werewolves I examine here are white. However, unlike the haunted girls I analyzed in Chapter 1, many of these werewolf protagonists are working class. These representations of the werewolf as a member of the working class is not surprising as many nineteenth-century narratives of lycanthropy characterized the werewolf "as a threat emanating from the underclasses" (du Coudray 45). For the protagonists of *Ginger Snaps* and "Boobs," lycanthropy is an expression of their rejection of their family's middle-class values.

The films I discuss fit the definition of YA fiction as a type of coming-of-age narrative with an adolescent protagonist whose development is connected to what she learns about power and subjectivity. Moreover, as I indicated in the introduction, YA fiction is not limited to literary texts. Indeed, the Young Adult Library Services Association argues for a broader definition of the genre that includes visual texts such as "picture books, comics, and graphic novels" (Cart "Value") in addition to literary works. Film certainly falls under this expansive rubric. Finally, my inclusion of film in this study is necessary given that the contemporary representation of the werewolf is derived from both literary and filmic sources. To understand the YA werewolf, then, we need to examine both novels and films.

I have broken this chapter in to two sections: "The Lycanthrope as Femme Fatale," in which I examine representations of the teen female werewolf that embody patriarchal fears about teen girls, and "The Werewolf as Model of Liberated Feminine Subjectivity," which considers representations of the creature as a "hopeful monster" offering the possibility for female freedom and power. The Lycanthrope as Femme Fatale analyzes filmic representations of the teen female werewolf. *Blood Moon* and The Ginger Snaps Trilogy are fairly typical examples of the horror film in that they offer more conservative representations of monstrosity. *Ginger Snaps* follows "the basic formula for the horror film in which normality is threatened by the Monster" (Wood 117). The main character of the movie, Ginger Fitzgerald, evokes Carrie White, the eponymous heroine of Stephen King's 1974 novel. Like Carrie, Ginger is an outsider who experiences late menarche: she is nearly sixteen years old when she finally gets "the curse." Moments after her first menstrual flow unexpectedly courses down her legs, Ginger is attacked by a werewolf who is attracted by the smell of her blood. As a result, over the next lunar cycle, Ginger transforms from a human girl with no interest in boys or dating into a violent and sexually insatiable beast for whom desire and anger are inextricably linked. As a consequence, Ginger must be "put to sleep" for the protection of humans. *Ginger Snaps 2: Unleashed* picks up where *Ginger Snaps* left off, with Ginger's sister Bridgette now struggling to control her own lycanthropy, which is connected to her sexual desires, so that she does not similarly harm others. *Ginger Snaps: The Beginning* pinpoints a moment in the late eighteenth century when the failure to euthanize Ginger's infected ancestor loosed the curse of lycanthropy on North America.

*Blood Moon* (2001) challenges viewers' concept of the werewolf. Set in an anachronistic traveling freak show, *Blood Moon* bombards viewers with side show "oddities" — but these "freaks" are not the monsters of the film. Rather, the "normal" people who pay their money to gawk at the side show's attractions are the actual monsters, an idea derived from Tod Browning's controversial cult film *Freaks* (1932). *Blood Moon* expands this idea to consider how women are made to feel monstrous if their bodies do not conform to an increasingly narrow standard of feminine beauty. Tara the Wolf Girl, the show's main attraction, suffers from hypertrichosis, an extreme form of hirsutism that covers her body in long silky hair and gives her a lupine appearance. Yet Tara becomes a monstrous Other only after she sheds her fur. After Tara partakes of an experimental depilatory drug, she transforms from a dog-faced vegetarian pacifist into a smooth-skinned beauty who dispenses violence to those who tormented her when she was a "freak." This representation of woman as a potentially violent animal is not new, but a strain of Romanticism, which Griffin describes as "eros and nature" melded into "one simultaneously fatal and evil force" (13) that is personified as woman. *Blood Moon*'s treatment of issues of appearance and belonging is particularly relevant for female adolescents.

The second part of this chapter, The Werewolf as Model of Liberated Feminine Subjectivity, examines three literary representations of the werewolf, Suzy McKee Charnas' story "Boobs" (1989), Patricia Windsor's 1996 novel *The Blooding*, and Annette Curtis Klause's 1997 novel *Blood and Chocolate*.[4] Because all are works of fantasy as much as they are horror fiction,[5] they envision the werewolf as a creature representing female freedom and power. Nature and wolves specifically are presented in a more sympathetic manner in these works of dark fantasy than they are in the horror genre (du Coudray 59). "Boobs," *The Blooding,* and *Blood and Chocolate* characterize the female connection to the natural world as a strength and question the idea that woman's presumed closer relationship with nature makes her into an irremediable, abject Other. "Boobs" is a relatively straightforward representation of the werewolf as the embodiment of female freedom and power that is denied to women in a patriarchal culture. *Blood and Chocolate* and *The Blooding*, on the other hand, also draw on the genres of Gothic and paranormal romance as well as horror, and their teen protagonists, older than Charnas's by several years, have had more time to be persuaded by cultural messages that women's subordination to men is natural and romantic. Thus, Windsor's and Klause's romantic heroines labor to unpack beliefs about feminine subordination that they have previously viewed as desirable signs of their relative maturity, while Charnas's younger protagonist has not yet fully bought into these crippling sexist ideals.

While the protagonists of *The Blooding*, *Blood and Chocolate*, and "Boobs" all originally desire to be "normal girls," their lupine bodies cannot be conventionally feminized, nor can they control their "unfeminine" desires for meat or sex, or fully repress their anger. But most importantly, these lycanthrope protagonists exhibit hybridity: they are not animals trapped in human bodies, but rather, powerful combinations of human and animal who can pass back and forth between their two forms at will. Ultimately, this hybridity reveals that gender is constructed rather than innate, and so calls into question the naturalness of the gendered order. In this way, these lycanthropic protagonists are Punday's "hopeful monsters" who, in the words of Butler, "refuse what they are" and so hint at a different way of being (Clark 10). Ginger and Bridgette (The Ginger Snaps Trilogy) and Tara (*Blood Moon*), on the other hand, lack this hybridity, and so each girl eventually becomes trapped in one form.

For Kelsey Bornstein, the eighth-grade protagonist of "Boobs," the female body is a liability that invites sexual harassment from boys, whose actions are excused as a sign of their immature masculinity rather than punished as undesirable behaviors. Kelsey receives negative attention from her classmates because her breasts have developed over the summer, while the majority of her female peers still have childish figures. On her first day of junior high school, Kelsey has her nose broken by Billy Linden, one of the school bullies who calls her "Boobs" and makes a grab at her breasts. When Kelsey shoves Billy away, he retaliates by punching her in the face. However, Billy is not disciplined for his actions, which are excused as "natural" adolescent male behavior. Kelsey can only exult in her human female body after she learns that she is able to change into a werewolf once a month. Because Billy will not stop harassing her, Kelsey dispatches him when she is in her werewolf form. Afterwards, Kelsey is relieved that she can now "walk through the halls [of her school] without having anybody yelling 'Hey, Boobs!'" (Charnas 491) since Billy was the ringleader who orchestrated her persecution by her peers. As a result, Kelsey can pursue her education without fear of harassment, partake in nurturing female friendships, and enjoy her human female body.

In *The Blooding*, sixteen-year-old Maris spends the summer working as an au pair in a remote English village. During her employment, she becomes attracted to Derrick, her handsome and brooding employer who might have murdered his wife. Nevertheless, Maris ignores both her gut feelings and the advice of older women, refusing to believe that Derrick is dangerous and should be avoided. Instead, Maris lets Derrick turn her into a werewolf, which he does to make her more dependent on him and therefore easier to control, as she will rely on him to mentor her in how to hunt in her new form. Maris's faith that Derrick has good intentions towards her in spite of evidence to the contrary follows the plot trajectory of the typical Gothic romance, where the heroine similarly romanticizes dangerous and controlling behavior in men. However, *The Blooding's* conclusion deviates from the typical romance plot in how Maris's own inner strength, combined with her newfound lycanthropy, enables her to avoid becoming a controlled and exploited gothic victim.

In *Blood and Chocolate*, Vivian is born a werewolf, and has always lived with other members of her species in an extended family pack. Initially, the adolescent Vivian is disdainful of lycanthropy: she sees werewolf culture as more openly sexist than human culture, and lycanthropy as a condition that weakens werewolves, who must repress much of their anger and sexual impulses to pass among humans. Yet ultimately, Vivian learns to accept her lycanthropy, which includes coming to terms with her attraction for the pack's new leader. In learning to accept her sexuality and her anger, Vivian avoids the damaging repression of anger and other emotions detailed by Brown in *Raising Their Voices*.

While not all the protagonists in these narratives experience happy endings, each text highlights the pressures that human girls feel to feign weakness, repress their anger and deny their sexual feelings in the interest of being accepted as conventionally feminine. As a result, these protagonists invite readers to consider alternatives to conventional femininity in how they expose this subject position as something constructed which can be changed rather than something natural and therefore immutable.

## The Lycanthrope as Femme Fatale

*Blood Moon* and The Ginger Snaps Trilogy follow the standard formula of the horror film in which "normality is threatened by the Monster" (Wood

117), although both are open to subversive readings, as Elizabeth Clark points out, in that horror is often a genre "that asks radical questions and provides conservative answers" (119). In *Blood Moon* and The Ginger Snaps trilogy, the female werewolf is an iteration of patriarchal fears about the "nature" of woman as a dangerous, sexually insatiable beast governed by her hormones, a characterization that justifies her subordination. For this reason, in the hostile patriarchal world she inhabits, the female werewolf must be destroyed if order is to be maintained. This summarizes Ginger Fitzgerald's situation in *Ginger Snaps*, as well as the position of her sister Bridgette in *Ginger Snaps 2: Unleashed*. In *Ginger Snaps: The Beginning*, the prequel to *Ginger Snaps*, we learn that the failure to destroy Ginger's ancestor three hundred years ago allowed the blood-born agent that transmits lycanthropy to continue to infect people so that Ginger would herself become infected in the twenty-first century. Tara in *Blood Moon* is similarly threatening, though in a less straightforward way than the Fitzgerald sisters of The Ginger Snaps trilogy. Tara knows too well that she is viewed by others as a dangerous animal due to her hypertrichosis. As a consequence, Tara embarks on a series of experimental treatments that make her conventionally feminine in appearance. However, the treatments alter Tara's mind as well so that she is no longer the gentle vegetarian who refuses to eat "anything with a face." Now Tara is a feral animal in an alluring form who is more dangerous than she ever was when covered in fur. Tara's transformation from "beast" into a beauty reveals that the demands of a patriarchal culture which compels women to repress their feelings and groom their bodies into an acceptable veneer are unnatural and undesirable. One of the most important lessons of horror is that repression is dangerous: the repressed always returns, in monstrous form, to wreak havoc on members of the culture who have necessitated its banishment. The figure of the monster, the horrifying representative of the abject, is also a portent. "The word 'monster' derives from the Latin *monere*, meaning 'to show'" (Fonseca and Pulliam *Hooked on Horror, Volume III* 155). This return of the repressed then is more than retribution on the part of the monster; it is a warning about the dangers of disavowing certain knowledge or parts of the self. These female werewolves show that normative femininity is not the natural consequence of having a female body, but instead, a fragile construction that can be maintained only at a terrible cost to young women.

## *The Beauty Myth*

The female werewolf's appearance is the most obvious manifestation of how she is at odds with conventional femininity. In spite of the gains made by first- and second-wave feminism, girls are still encultured to spend an inordinate amount of time grooming themselves to attract the attention of potential male partners.[6] Their bodies must be carefully controlled: regularly depilated, deodorized and dieted into a smooth, slender form that is graceful rather than strong. The female werewolf breaks all these taboos. In her lupine form, she has hair where women are supposed to be smooth. Moreover, she is often stronger than any human male in the narrative. This strength flies in the face of a patriarchal culture where women's participation in sports, particularly competitive sports and those that are not conducive to developing a lithe and petite female body, is still discouraged, in spite of changes ushered in by Title IX to encourage female athleticism. Competiveness and athleticism are still traits reserved for normative masculinity.[7] Clark postulates that the horror of the female werewolf "lies in a female body becoming grotesque through the taking on of masculine/male traits" (3).

Beauty standards are part of a wider sexual politics that maintain feminine subordination. Susan Brownmiller observes that biological femaleness is not sufficient to differentiate women from men, and so it is necessary for women to perform their gender through a stylized repetition of acts that constitute femininity. Femininity "constantly reassures its audience by a willing demonstration of difference, even when one does not exist in nature" (Brownmiller 15). Women are enjoined to construct their femininity by grooming their bodies to fit this aesthetic, and they are increasingly valued according to their ability to fit into these nebulous standards. Naomi Wolf explains that in a post-second-wave-feminism world where men feel threatened by women's increased economic independence, beauty standards have replaced the feminine mystique as a way of controlling women (10–11). Wolf dubs these ubiquitous standards the Beauty Myth, a term that emphasizes the impossibility of maintaining these standards. Women who deviate from this feminine aesthetic are viewed as unfeminine, and as a result can be rejected by potential male mates, the eventual power brokers in a patriarchal society, and even shunned by their peers. In fact, a woman who does not conform to the cultural standards of beauty might find her employment opportunities limited, a consequence that significantly diminishes her ability to be autonomous (Wolf 20–57).

Not surprisingly, the Beauty Myth affects adolescent girls' feelings of self worth. Joan Jacobs Brumberg argues that this myth encourages adolescent girls to "make the body into an all-consuming project in ways young women of the past did not" (xvii). Both Wolf and Brumberg conclude that the societal expectations that push women to aspire to be beauties deprive them of agency. If women are kept occupied by a "body project" that necessitates eternal vigilance against hairiness, odor, weight gain and aging, then they are less likely to notice, let alone challenge, cultural forces that perpetuate their subordination.

Young women pursue the Beauty Myth, in part, because it is represented by mass culture as something that will empower them by making them irresistible to men and the envy of other women. Trites characterizes YA fiction as concerned with subjectivity and power: in the YA novel, teens "learn to negotiate the levels of power that exist in the myriad social institutions within which they must function ... including social constructions of sexuality [and] gender" (*Disturbing* 3). Given the centrality of the theme of power in YA texts, it is not surprising that the Beauty Myth is an important element of this genre of fiction when the central characters are female. The Beauty Myth promises power to the girl who has dieted, exercised and manicured her body into a magical combination of perfection. Yet the Beauty Myth cannot deliver this power, in part, since the ideal can only be achieved by the genetically fortunate few. Furthermore, the aging process ensures that this ideal cannot be maintained indefinitely by anyone. Since beauty is a primary characteristic of conventional femininity, girls wishing to grow up into strong, autonomous adult women must learn to see through the fiction of the Beauty Myth.

The opening scene of *Ginger Snaps* establishes that Ginger and her sister Bridgette already have rejected the Beauty Myth. Before Ginger becomes a werewolf, the teen sisters set themselves apart from their peers with their dark-hued thrift shop finery and teased Goth hair, a sartorial defiance that is part of their larger rejection of hegemonic femininity and of the white middle-class values of their community. But everything changes for Ginger once she is bitten by a werewolf. Ginger suddenly buys into the Beauty Myth, changing her appearance to conform to a more conventional standard of teen female beauty that encourages girls to show their "maturity" by dressing in sexualized ways. The day after Ginger is attacked, she comes to school sporting a stylish hair-do and form fitting clothing, drawing appreciative glances from the boys and disapproving glares from other girls. Little do they, or Ginger, know that she is quite literally turning into a femme fatale who can use her appearance to lure her prey to her.

Ginger's new embracing of the Beauty Myth also makes her monstrous in that she becomes a hormonally-driven, sexually-insatiable animal. Susan Griffin notes that pornography is filled with associations between women and animals (24), a connection that permits men to deny what they perceive as their own bestial impulses by projecting these feelings onto the body of a woman. According to this logic, a woman's body, by inspiring desire in a man, recalls him to his own mortality and subsequent vulnerability, an association which is terrifying for him because "nature can make him want. Nature can cause him to cry in loneliness, to feel a terrible hunger, or a thirst. Nature can even cause him to die" (Griffin 28). The sinister association of women with the natural world, however, is not limited to pornographic fantasy, but is also reproduced in high and popular culture, including horror fiction. In *Ginger Snaps*, Ginger's transformation is governed by the phases of the moon, an association that connects lycanthropy to menstruation and nature. As Ginger becomes more sexually desirable, she also becomes more animal and difficult to control, and therefore dangerous.

In *Ginger Snaps 2: Unleashed*, Ginger's sister Bridgette also spends an inordinate amount of time grooming her body into normative femininity, though she does this to keep from attracting attention to her budding lycanthropy, a condition which makes her monstrous in appearance because it puts her body outside of the borders of both her gender and her species. Because Bridgette has been dealing with her lycanthropy longer than her sister Ginger ever did, her body is more greatly transformed. Thus, Bridgette must periodically shave her back and stomach and even cut off the tips of her ears, which are elongating into lupine points, so that she will continue to look both human and feminine. But Bridgette's attempts to maintain an outwardly feminine appearance only delay her inevitable transformation into a hairy beast.

Tara in *Blood Moon* becomes a monster *because* of her desire to conform to the Beauty Myth. Tara so craves the approbation that accompanies being a conventionally feminine beauty that she willingly destroys all about her that makes her a compassionate and autonomous young woman. At the beginning of the film, Tara is stereotypically feminine in all but appearance. She is modest, shy, and so gentle that she is an ethical vegetarian who will not eat "anything with a face." These qualities are at the heart of what Lynn Phillips terms the "Pleasing Woman Discourse," part of a set of "prevailing ideas or cultural messages" (16) about normative femininity and masculinity. Contemporary discourses about gender communicate that a "good" woman cherishes "the feminine 'attributes' of modesty, attractiveness, and sacrifice for others, particularly men" (Phillips 39). Though Tara is self-sacrificing and modest, her extreme hirsutism eternally bars her from being both normatively feminine and normatively human. The aesthetics of beauty impose "a childlike state of hairlessness" (Brownmiller 140) on women, and body hair located anywhere but on a woman's head is associated with an "animal-like aspect" that is characteristic of "werewolves, witches, barbarians and madmen" who all appear "uncontrolled and fierce" (Brownmiller 144). In this way, the silky hair covering Tara's body signifies that she is not female and not human, negating any other behaviors or bodily characteristics that demonstrate the opposite. As a result, Tara's hirsutism makes her an eternal Other. During one of Tara's rare journeys outside of the freak show, she is recognized by two local boys who have seen her Wolf Girl performance. One tells Tara that she "looks really freaky" and that he "puked the first time" he saw her, a confession which only reinforces Tara's status as abject Other.

Tara understands better than most girls the perils of not fitting into her culture's standards of beauty. In fact, she is lucky to be alive. As an infant, Tara was abandoned by her desperate mother to Harley Dune, the freak show's proprietor. Born in the aftermath of Ceausescu's Romania, the infant Tara was nearly killed by superstitious villagers who believed that her hirsutism indicated that she was the spawn of Satan. Harley's freak show has at least given Tara a place to exist in a more enlightened culture, if only to occupy the subject position of professional Other. Furthermore, Tara is luckier than other "freaks." One of the side show's attractions includes "the dime museum," a collection of preserved deformed infants known to fellow performers as "the baby show." Harley explains that "most freaks are killed as soon as they are born."

Tara and her fellow freaks make their livings as professional Others who reassure their audiences of their own comparative normalcy. If being normatively feminine, normatively masculine, or even normatively human are tenuous categories that must be continually constructed through a stylized repetition of acts, then these categories also need reinforcing through the presence of the Other, that personification of the abject. Building on Lacan's concept of the mirror stage, Creed describes identity as "a structure that depends on identification with another. Identity is an imaginary construct, formed in a state of alienation, grounded in misrecognition" ("Horror" 57). Because "the self is constructed on an illusion" (Creed "Horror" 57), it is always inherently unstable. Harley Dune's freak show, like the horror film, "puts the viewing subject's sense of a unified self into crisis, specifically in those moments when the image on the screen [or the performers, as is the case in the freak show] become too threatening or horrific to watch, when the abject threatens to draw the viewing subject" (Creed "Horror" 57) to that place "where meaning collapses," as Julia Kristeva would say. But meaning eventually reconstitutes itself when the spectator stops looking, in part to "reconstruct the boundary between self and screen," or performer in the freak show, in this instance, "and rebuild the self that had been "threatened with disintegration" ("Horror" Creed 58).

Tara, however, no longer wants to be a professional Other. Instead, she longs to be a "normal" teen girl whose appearance draws admiring glances which would give her another sort of power. So when Dr. Klein's son Ryan offers Tara the chance to test his mother's experimental drug to cure hypertrichosis, she does not hesitate to try it, regardless of the possible dangerous side effects. Without Dr. Klein's knowledge, Ryan injects Tara with the drug, which works as promised. After three treatments, Tara is a "normal" girl with smooth skin instead of silky fur.

Yet Dr. Klein's drug makes Tara much more than "normal" or unremarkable. Instead, she is the embodiment of the Beauty Myth's promise of power. Tara becomes a ravishing beauty whose looks give her a preternatural ability to hypnotize others. As Tara leaves the freak show for good, she encounters Crystal, the ringleader of a group of local teens who have been heckling her at her Wolf Girl performances. Dr. Klein's depilatory drug has so transformed Tara that Crystal does not recognize her as the Wolf Girl. Furthermore, Crystal is so enchanted by Tara's beauty that she does not question why this seeming stranger is alone and naked in the woods in the middle of the night. Instead, Tara is similar to Samuel Taylor Coleridge's Geraldine or Joseph Sheridan Le Fanu's Carmilla, succubae who cast glamours on all who encounter them. Tara's beauty permits her to similarly cast a glamour on Crystal, who shyly reveals her most closely guarded secret of how she too is not conventionally feminine: she is sexually attracted to girls. Crystal makes a pass at Tara, but when she leans in to kiss her, Tara has become so completely animal that she bites off and swallows Crystal's tongue. This act deprives Crystal of agency by robbing her of the power of speech. Because cultural silencing "is one of the dominant forces that shape female growth" (Trites *Waking* 47), when Tara bites off Crystal's tongue, she has made her former antagonist more stereotypically feminine. Yet Dr. Klein's depilatory treatment has also deprived Tara of the power of speech, which makes her both more conventionally feminine and also more animal.

## *Sisterhood and Rivalries Among Women*

Not only does the Beauty Myth divest women of agency by keeping them occupied pursuing impossible standards of physical perfection, it also deprives them of a collective strength in how it undermines sisterhood. Wolf observes that the Beauty Myth prevents sisterhood by encouraging women to "see each other as beauties first" (56) who are in adversarial relationships with one another in order to attract the attention of men. The Beauty Myth undermines solidarity and urges "women to believe that it's every woman for herself" (Wolf 56). Sisterhood is extremely threatening to patriarchy because a unified group of women is more powerful than any individual woman. United through sisterhood, women, who are the majority of the population, could undo the effects of patriarchy in multiple ways and compel changes to the status quo that would give them truly equal opportunities.

The Beauty Myth is one factor isolating Ginger and Tara from other women in how it encourages girlfighting, Brown's term for the bitchy, backbiting relational aggression that frequently characterizes girls' relationships with one another. Brown explains how "girls take out their anxieties and fears about matching up to or resisting ideals of feminine beauty and behavior on each other" (*Girlfighting* 32) by excluding from the group members of their sex who do not meet certain cultural definitions of girlness or femininity, such as those found in the Beauty Myth. The result is a "climate of division and distrust among girls [that] eventually undermines women's psychological strengths and their political potential" (Brown *Girlfighting* 33). In this way, girlfighting maintains the status quo — girls grow into women who see one another as rivals for the attention of men, the power brokers in a patriarchal society, rather than become women who question the value of this attention in the first place. Lycanthropy in these films only exacerbates the effects of girlfighting in that it for a time makes the teen female werewolf better conform to conventional notions of feminine beauty as well as better able to answer back to her antagonists.

Tara has benefited from a powerful intergenerational sisterhood with her fellow freak show performers. Yet as Tara becomes more of a beauty, she rejects the sisterhood of those who were part of her support system. In this way, Tara is both more conventionally feminine and more monstrous. Before Tara becomes a beauty, Athena the Fat Lady and Christoph/Christine the hermaphrodite serve as her mentors. Both women have a unique understanding of the Beauty Myth because their bodies lie far outside the parameters of stereotypical femininity. Christoph/Christine whose body is neither clearly male nor female encourages Tara to value herself and other people for qualities other than their ability to be "normal." Athena tells Tara that the outside world, with its normal people, is highly overrated. Indeed, Athena's act is all about inverting the Beauty Myth. During Athena's performances, she wears sexy lingerie and is glamorously made up. Athena delights in how her 665-pound body frightens spectators because it quite literally overflows the boundaries of conventional femininity. Athena's weight additionally signifies to audiences her capacity to cross boundaries in a way that threatens the social order — 665 is one number short of 666, the Biblical mark of the beast and a harbinger of the End Times. After viewing Athena, the boyishly thin Crystal feels so insecure about her own ability to be stereotypically feminine that she puts her finger down her throat to purge the small amount of cotton candy she has eaten lest this morsel cause her to swell to the performer's size.

As Dr. Klein's depilatory treatment begins to transform Tara, she rejects this intergenerational sisterhood, distancing herself from both women, as well as from the other members of the freak show. In this way, Tara is policing the borders of femininity "by excluding and rejecting and ostracizing 'other' girls who don't match up" (Brown *Girlfighting* 59). At the end of the film, when Tara has been transformed into a flawless beauty, it is indicated that she will also be a sort of lone wolf, passing through a landscape where there is no one else like her. In the concluding scene, the Beauty Myth's promise of power is revealed as hollow. In her new and "improved" form, Tara is isolated from all other members of her species, and she is mute, representing how she has been divested of agency as the price for feminine beauty.

The Ginger Snaps trilogy also examines girlfighting and its ability to undermine sisterhood among women. Because The Ginger Snaps Trilogy follows the rules of horror, sisterhood is represented negatively as something that can, at the very least, stunt women's growth by undermining heterosexual relationships, and at worst, create monsters who are able to disrupt civilization. In *Ginger Snaps*, even before Ginger was bitten by the werewolf, she and her sister Bridgette were victims of girlfighting. The sisters' running feud with other female peers is established in a scene during gym class. Ginger and Bridgette make nasty comments about Trina St. Claire, one of the school's more popular girls, supposedly outside of her hearing. But Trina overhears the sisters' remarks, and the violence of her retaliation demonstrates the long-standing nature of their grudge. During a game of field hockey, Trina knocks Bridgette to the ground in a way that appears accidental from the gym teacher's distant perspective. Brown describes the hidden nature of girlfighting, which permits this relational aggression to fly under the radar of adults who could intervene in what they might see as bullying behavior: "Part of being an acceptable girl in a culture so deeply infused with white middle-class values" is to appear to be "nice." Thus, "girls who buy into prevailing views of femininity are likely to hide the 'bad' or 'shameful' parts of their relationships" (*Girlfighting* 6). This type of "accidentally on purpose" violence is one way that girls hide from adults their aggression towards one another.

When Ginger begins her period and is bitten by the werewolf hours later, the power dynamic shifts between her and the girls who excluded her: while Ginger is still the target of girlfighting, she can now defend herself. Nevertheless, from her new position, Ginger still perpetuates these persistent divisions between women rather than attempting to overcome them. The werewolf's bite has put Ginger through a sort of accelerated puberty, so she changes overnight from someone who scorns beauty culture to a beauty whose appearance gets her attention from boys. This change makes her into Trina's rival. Soon after Ginger's transformation, she begins dating Jason McCardy, one of the more popular boys in school. While Ginger is now more like a "normal" girl, other girls are even less likely to feel any solidarity with her since winning Jason's attention makes her more formidable competition for a boy whose popularity positions him as one of the school's power brokers. Furthermore, Ginger's changed status alters her relationship with her sister Bridgette. While the sisters are still close, fights erupt because of Ginger's new interest in boys, and Ginger's momentarily privileging of her relationship with Jason over her relationship with Bridgette. Nevertheless, Ginger's close relationship with Bridgette is presented as something that stifles the younger sister's growth rather than something that is a source of comfort and strength. Ginger's love for her sister was overly possessive even before she became a werewolf, and at times Bridgette seems to have no identity of her own. In a scene where Ginger is sent away from the table for speaking disrespectfully to her mother, for example, Bridgette gets up to leave too, prompting her mother to instruct her to sit down as she is not the one being punished, but her sister.

But if girlfighting deprives women of sisterhood, then that is a desirable outcome from the perspective of patriarchy since women's solidarity with one another makes them better able to resist patriarchal control. Lycanthropy in these films keeps women isolated from one another in that the female werewolf cannot maintain deep connections with anyone once the condition has fully transformed her into the raging animal that men have always suspected that she is at heart. In The Ginger Snaps Trilogy and *Blood Moon*, the transition from human to beast is not periodic, whereby the sufferer turns into a werewolf every full moon. Ginger's, Bridgette's and Tara's transformations occur only once, gradually, and are not reversible. In *Ginger Snaps*, towards the conclusion of the twenty-eight day cycle during which Ginger changes into her permanent werewolf form, she becomes increasingly jealous of Bridgette. Ginger eventually expresses this jealousy violently when she rips apart an elderly school janitor who, according to Ginger, was only kind to Bridgette because he was a pedophile trying to look at her breasts. Bridgette exhibits similarly violent sisterly feelings for Ghost in *Ginger Snaps 2: Unleashed*. When Bridgette believes that a young man has raped Ghost, she allows him to be torn apart by the fully changed male werewolf who has been following her throughout to mate with her after she has fully transitioned into her new body.

Bridgette's sisterly feelings for Ghost make her vulnerable to manipulation by the younger girl, who has a terrible fate in store for her. While Bridgette might find comfort in the support of her sex, Ghost is extremely skilled at girlfighting, and feels no obligation to protect other women. Bridgette learns too late that Ghost is not a poor near-orphan whose grandmother accidentally set herself on fire while smoking in bed. Instead, Ghost set her grandmother ablaze to be free of the control of a woman who has done nothing abusive to her as far as we know. In the film's conclusion, while Bridgette is momentarily helpless while fully changing into her wolf form, Ghost imprisons Bridgette so that she can be unleashed on the girl's enemies.

*Ginger Snaps: The Beginning*, a prequel to *Ginger Snaps*, further considers the connection between feminine monstrosity and sisterhood. According to the film, lycanthropy came from a windigo, which appeared soon after whites interacted with Native Americans in the late eighteenth century. The Native American characters predict the coming of two sisters who must fight to the death if the curse that turns humans into werewolves is to be lifted. The two predicted sisters are Bridgette and Ginger, ancestors of the same sisters in *Ginger Snaps* who have the same first and last names of their descendents. The film's opening also emphasizes the sisterly bond between Ginger and Bridgette: the two make the same pact to remain together forever that they made in *Ginger Snaps*. After Ginger is bitten by an infected child and will soon transform into a werewolf as a result, Hunter, a young Native American man, counsels Bridgette to kill her sister to prevent the disease from spreading: "She dies by your hand or you die by hers. You have no choice" to prevent the spread of her lycanthropy. Ginger is positioned by the narrative as the vector of disease that can introduce chaos into the world and so must be destroyed, not the white male child who bit her, and who was eventually euthanized, or the werewolf who infected the child. Moreover, Hunter's words of advice carry particular weight, as the film stereotypically represents Native Americans as having a mystical bond with nature, which makes him the expert about phenomena that whites cannot explain through science. In this way, Hunter's declaration presents girlfighting as something natural if unpleasant that is necessary to maintain order rather than as an artificial situation that women are put in by patriarchy.

So once again, girlfighting is the answer to maintaining the social order, which is always threatened by the monster in the horror film. But Bridgette kills Hunter instead of Ginger because he was threatening her sister so the lycanthropy spreads. A voiceover narrated by Ginger in the film's final scene explains that this bloody act of sisterhood marked "the day the curse grew stronger" because now the sisters are "together forever," "united in blood." So if girlfighting perpetuates feminine monstrosity, as we see in *Ginger Snaps* and *Ginger Snaps 2: Unleashed*, then sisterhood begins it.

## *Lycanthropy and Sexual Maturity*

Lycanthropy is also connected with an idea of unbridled sexual desire, which patriarchy has so often associated with something that has the potential to transform a civilized human into a raging beast who is at the mercy of his or her hormones. The female werewolf is particularly terrifying in this context, as she is the antithesis of a "good woman" who is more in control of her sexual desire than are men. Instead, the female werewolf is the embodiment of what men find bestial in themselves and have projected on to the bodies of women (Griffin 24).

Ginger's lupine characteristics are closely tied to her becoming a sexually mature young woman. At the beginning of *Ginger Snaps*, both Ginger and Bridgette scorn what they characterize as the "total hormonal toilet" of high school culture: neither girl dates or demonstrates any romantic interest in boys or girls. The film implies that the sisters' disdain for their peers is due to more than their intellectual superiority (Bridgette, the younger sister, is in classes with Ginger because her high test scores permitted her to skip a grade). Instead, this disdain is a product of their relative sexual immaturity: neither nearly sixteen-year-old Ginger nor the fifteen year old Bridgette has entered menarche, and the sisters' physical immaturity contributes to their outsider status among their peers. But when Ginger starts her period and is bitten by a werewolf almost immediately afterwards, she becomes simultaneously a sexually mature woman *and* a monster. Thus, the natural world of the wolf and the category of woman are connected. After these two events, Ginger becomes sexually mature. However, while her normatively feminine peers manage to keep their sexual desires under control, these feelings erupt violently in Ginger, who has been transformed into a teen femme fatale.

When Ginger is about to ovulate, she is so eager to lose her virginity that she sexually assaults her boyfriend Jason. In the back seat of his car, Ginger's desire to have sex is so fierce that she starts ripping off Jason's shirt. Jason encourages Ginger to slow down, reminding her "who's the guy here," which only enrages her. Ginger then sexually assaults Jason while he screams.

Although Ginger is dangerous to others while she is ovulating, she poses an even greater threat on the night of the full moon, when she is about to menstruate for the second time in her life. On this night, when Ginger will fully transform into a werewolf, she is also at her most sexually active: she attempts to sequentially seduce several men. Afterwards, Ginger will become fully werewolf, a metamorphosis that has been taking place over the past twenty-eight days since she was first bitten. The relationship between the werewolf and menstruation is nothing new. Walter Evans sees the werewolf, regardless of its sex, as being related to the menstrual cycle because its "bloody attacks ... occur regularly every month" (357). As a female werewolf, Ginger is doubly linked to the phases of the moon. Lunar cycles are generally associated with femininity as women's menstrual cycles loosely follow the moon's phases.

The werewolf's bite has made Ginger monstrous by altering her body so that it resembles what Kristeva terms the abject body, whose manifestation is "the feminine maternal body" (Kristeva 102). The feminine maternal body is the prototype of the abject body because of its lack of corporeal integrity, demonstrated through the secreting of blood, among other things, signifying its link to the natural world (Creed "Dark Desires" 122). The combination of lycanthropy and menarche changes Ginger's body from a girlish one to a maternal one, her behaviors are now regulated by her menstrual cycle, which is in turn controlled by a lunar cycle. She goes from having no desire to date to becoming a slave to the biological imperative to mate. Ginger's werewolf form is horrifically maternal — her chest now has six teats, emphasizing her reproductive capabilities.

Finally, Ginger's lupine body also links her to nature. Before Ginger fully metamorphoses into a werewolf, she is a seductive combination of woman and animal. In this hybrid body, Ginger represents what Griffin theorizes is all that men find bestial in themselves, and in pornography, have projected on to the bodies of women (24). Furthermore, in this context, Ginger's ability to incite desire in all men who come her way is as monstrous as her need to tear things apart. Unlike the woman of pornographic fantasy, Ginger cannot be controlled. Pornography that associates women with animals is created by a pornographer who "imagines himself in control. Where there is a horse, there is a rider. Where there is a lion, there is a lion tamer" (Griffin 28). But in horror, the monster is not so easily subdued, and so Ginger is not controlled by any of the male characters.

Tara's connection to the natural world is more complicated. Tara's name (which means "earth" in Latin) hints at her association with nature. Before her transformation, Tara appears to be more closely affiliated with the animal kingdom than with humanity as the hair covering most of her body gives her a bestial appearance. Yet in this form, Tara is more civilized than the "normal" humans in the film. Ferocity, a characteristic often attributed to animals, is not present in the vegetarian Tara. Rather, Tara is so gentle that when Crystal and her friends taunt her by pelting her with dog feces during her Wolf Girl performance, she can only cry and howl in frustration. Tara only becomes ferocious after exchanging her "animal" body for a "human" one. The film's closing shots affirm Tara's connection with the natural world in her new depilated flesh. As Tara recedes into a wooded landscape, we can see that she has lost the power of speech, no longer wears clothing and now walks on all fours. Her body posture indicates that she is comfortable in this environment and that some "natural" instinct has taken over to guide her in her new life. While those who may encounter Tara might view her as benign, even desirable, the viewer, who has witnessed her savaging of Crystal and other of her tormentors in previous scenes, knows that she is now a dangerous monster.

## *Lycanthropy as Drag*

Ginger's and Tara's metamorphoses are types of drag in which they perform as normatively feminine and human. The combination of the werewolf's bite and hormonal changes brought about by menarche transform Ginger's body, making it more masculine and animal. As a consequence, Ginger must labor to successfully pass as female and human.[8] Tara has been giving a drag performance all of her life. As one of Harley Dune's oddities, Tara performs as animal, augmenting her body hair with prosthetic fangs and nails to give her a more bestial appearance. But when Dr. Klein's depilatory treatment eradicates Tara's hirsutism, she stops performing as an animal only to become a beast performing as a beautiful young woman.

In *Gender Trouble*, Butler sees drag as a performance that can destabilize the category of gender by mocking "the notion of a true gender identity" (137). However, not all drag is destabilizing. Butler notes that "parody by itself is not subversive" (*Gender* 139). While some parodic repetitions are "effectively disruptive, truly troubling," others "become domesticated and recirculated as instruments of cultural hegemony" (*Gender* 139). The latter is the case with Ginger and Tara in their monstrous forms.

Ginger's lupine body is a monstrous perversion of the notion of a stable gender identity. As Ginger becomes more of a femme fatale, she is also more normatively masculine in some aspects of her appearance. She sprouts hair on her chest, and her coccyx elongates into a budding tail, which is alarmingly erect, like a tiny penis. As the tail grows, Ginger must tape it to her leg in order to continue passing for human and female, strapping it down in a way that is similar to how drag queens tape down their penises to more convincingly create the illusion of femininity.

Arguably, this is one reason that Ginger's budding lupine body is so threatening to others. Like the body of the drag queen, Ginger's body also cannot be neatly categorized as male or female, human or animal. As a result, her body calls into question the stability of these categories, since Ginger is a creature that crosses borders. Bridgette's lycanthropic form similarly crosses borders between male and female, human and animal. Creed explains that "the concept of a border is central to the construction of the monstrous in the horror film." Anything crossing this border, or attempting to cross it, is menacing because it brings about "an encounter between the symbolic order and that which threatens its stability" ("Horror" 40–41).

Ultimately, the werewolf's animal nature eradicates its human nature, leaving it incapable of returning to its human form. This is the case for Ginger, who is transformed fully from human to beast in twenty-eight days, and for Bridgette, whose full change is momentarily forestalled by her regular injections of wolf's bane. As werewolves, Ginger and Bridgette are animals that do not resemble any sort of creature found in the natural world. Rather, these werewolves are coarse-haired, hideous grey beasts who walk on all fours and are intent on destroying all humans who cross their paths. In *Ginger Snaps*, Ginger must be "put to sleep" for the protection of humans, while the failure to euthanize her in *Ginger Snaps: The Beginning* is what enables lycanthropy to continue to infect people into the twenty-first century. Bridgette is likewise threatening at the conclusion of *Ginger Snaps 2: Unleashed*, because she can be unleashed at will by Ghost. In this way, Ginger and Bridgette are no different from their more famous male werewolf counterparts such as Larry Talbot (*The Wolf Man*) or Tony Rivers (*I Was a Teenage Werewolf*), who must both be killed to protect humans from their menace. As a consequence, Ginger and Bridgette are not "hopeful monsters." Instead, their drag is merely an instrument of cultural hegemony because of how their performances reinforce sexist concepts of women's supposed essential nature.

Tara too can be understood as a creature in drag, first as the Wolf Girl in Harley Dune's freak show when she is a human performing as a beast, and later as an animal in drag passing as a beautiful young woman. Tara's drag is also an instrument of cultural hegemony. Her performance as the Wolf Girl reinforces the imaginary boundaries between human and animal, male and female. As a cultural institution, the freak show embodies a sort of Otherness that confirms the audience's superior sense of normalcy. So patrons viewing the Wolf Girl, Athena the Fat Lady, the Bearded Lady, or the hermaphrodite Christoph/Christine are reassured that they are well within the cultural boundaries that firmly establish them as human, of normal body weight, and unambiguously sexed, rather than challenged to rethink their ideas about these categories, which are based primarily upon physical appearance.

Tara's performance as a beauty at the end of the film has the potential to be one of those "truly troubling" repetitions that Butler describes, but only if the audience can recognize that Tara is in drag, and understand what is so unsettling about her performance. After Dr. Klein's treatments, Tara has gone from performing as an animal to being a full-fledged werewolf, a creature who is simultaneously animal and human. However, Tara's lycanthropy reverses the subject position of the typical werewolf: Tara is a beast trapped within a beautiful human body rather than a human encased in an animal's flesh. As a result, Tara is conventionally feminine: she now embodies

## 2. Blood and Bitches

what the pornographic mind has always believed to be true of women — that lurking behind the alluring form is an animal that can, and must, be mastered by man. But unlike the woman of pornographic fantasy, Tara cannot be mastered. She is a feral creature who in the film's last scene cannot even recognize her own reflection in a pond. Rather, Tara has regressed to a state prior to the mirror stage and the formation of ego.[9] So while it may seem that the film is complicit in perpetuating negative stereotypes about woman's essential nature, it also deconstructs this stereotype in that the viewer has witnessed Tara's deliberate transformation into a beauty without regard for the "side effects."

Although Ginger, Bridgette and Tara struggle with the painful pressures girls face to be conventionally feminine, each loses the battle to escape this constricting subject position. In her influential essay "Visual Pleasure and Narrative Cinema," Laura Mulvey explains that in film, women are "bearer[s] of meaning, not maker[s] of meaning" insofar as they are objectified by the male gaze (29). The male gaze not only recreates women as Other, as objects of desire who provide scopophilic pleasure, but also as harbingers of the castration fear due to their lack of a penis, a deficiency that "constantly endangers the unity of the diegesis and bursts through the world of illusion as an intrusive, static, one-dimensional fetish" (Mulvey 39). This is certainly the case for Ginger, Bridgette and Tara: their monstrosity is intimately connected to how they are assessed by the male gaze.

Vivian (*Blood and Chocolate*), Maris (*The Blooding*), and Kelsey ("Boobs"), on the other hand, can offer the reader possibilities for a liberated female subjectivity, partially because their narratives are not conveyed through a visual medium and so the reader cannot participate in the male gaze in the way she might through film. Outside of the visual realm then, it is easier for Maris, Vivian and Kelsey to escape being codified by the viewer as "static, one-dimensional" fetishes of the werewolf as imprinted into the cultural consciousness by the films *The Wolf Man* and *Werewolf of London* and their various iterations. Instead, Charnas, Klause and Windsor are better able to explore the werewolf as hybrid of beast and human rather than ferocious animal Other. This hybridity is a quality that permits Vivian and Maris to pass back and forth between the categories of animal and human, male and female, a quality that ultimately makes it difficult to confine them to the object position as bearers of meaning.

## The Werewolf as Model of Liberated Female Subjectivity

While Tara and Ginger offer a fairly conventional representation of woman as monstrous Other, Kelsey in "Boobs," Maris in *The Blooding*, and Vivian *Blood and Chocolate* are hopeful monsters in that they hint at possibilities for a liberated feminine subjectivity, which helps readers envision an alternative to patriarchy. Trites states that one of the most important functions of children's literature is "to depict children who enact the agency that children in real life may not have" (*Waking* 29). This in turn enables the reader to imagine her own possibilities for agency. Trites' observations about children's literature can be applied to YA fiction as well. "Boobs" highlights the anger that girls experience after they "see the cultural framework, and girls' and women's subordinate place in it, for the first time" (Brown *Raising* 16), while *The Blooding* and *Blood and Chocolate* emphasize the pressure that teen girls feel to embody a normative femininity that necessitates they disavow their desires for sex — and sometimes even food — while stifling the justifiable anger they experience as a result.

The fantastic elements of these narratives allows readers to imagine alternatives to feminine subordination. Bruno Bettleheim explains how fairy tales foster the reader's ability to work out solutions to complex problems. The fairy tale's unrealistic nature "is an important device, because it makes obvious that the fairy tale's concern is not useful information about the external world, but the inner processes taking place in the individual" (25). Bettleheim's observations about fairy tales also apply to other types of non-realistic fiction such as horror, fantasy, the Gothic and paranormal romance.

### *The YA Lycanthropy Narrative as* Female *Bildungsroman*

Like all YA fiction, the story of the teen female lycanthropy fits into the genre of *Bildungsroman*, or narrative of development, in which the protagonist makes the transition from childhood where she has relatively little autonomy into her adult role. The typical female *Bildungsroman* frequently represents women coming to terms with an adult role in life where they will have less agency than their brothers due to their sex. "Boobs," *The Blooding* and *Blood and Chocolate*, however, conclude with their protagonists on the cusps of an adult womanhood in which they will have more autonomy in their lives than their normatively feminine sisters in that they have the ability to resist being put into restrictive gender roles.

"Boobs" is a fairly typical work of YA fiction in that it is a *Bildungsroman*, albeit a brief one, where the teen protagonist goes from being someone acted upon by outside forces to someone better able to negotiate power relationships. Before Kelsey realizes that she is a werewolf, she is on the path to the type of adult womanhood which will take her from being a relatively empowered and tomboyish girl to a woman whose budding female body is an obstacle to full autonomy. After Kelsey has begun to grow breasts and started to menstruate, she is pressured by her family and her culture to behave in a more feminine manner, which includes not speaking up and swallowing her anger. However, once Kelsey discovers her supernatural abilities, she is on the path to becoming an autonomous young woman whose voice is not silenced. Kelsey with her lycanthropic abilities is what Daniel Punday would call a "hopeful monster," a "new type of human that is a desirable alternative to the present" (811) rather than something abhorrent. Brenda Boudreau's study of adolescent girls reveals that as a girl's body takes on visibly sexed characteristics, it "becomes an obstacle to autonomy and self-agency as [she] tries to reconcile her body to the demands of a socially proscribed gendered identity, leading paradoxically, to feelings of disembodiment" (43).

At the beginning of "Boobs," Kelsey enters eighth grade with a body that matured over the summer. However, instead of this adult body giving her more strength and coordination and the ability to move about more freely, it deprives her of agency, partly because an adult female body is a signifier of women's subordination. Female bodies draw proprietary stares from passers-by and are the target of unwelcome comments from strangers. Women are taught that they are responsible for the harassment they receive from men if they fail to adequately cover up their bodies or if they move about too freely among men. Because Kelsey's developing breasts are larger than those of her female classmates, she is targeted for harassment from her male peers. When Billy Linden, one of the school bullies, calls Kelsey "Boobs," she gets into a scuffle with him and he breaks her nose. Kelsey, however, is blamed for provoking Billy when those with the power to help her do not. They choose instead to excuse his actions as normal teen male behavior rather than as battery that merits punishment. Kelsey's father similarly excuses Billy's behavior to his daughter, telling her that "all boys are jerks at that age" (478), while her stepmother Hilda warns her that she's bound to get hurt if she fights with boys because they "are getting stronger than [Kelsey] will ever be" (474).

Kelsey's agency is further curtailed when she enters menarche. Kelsey experiences her first period as "messy and disgusting" (474) rather than the miracle of womanhood that Hilda said that it would be. The sanitary napkin that Kelsey must wear between her legs during her time of the month constrains her mobility, while she isolates herself from her peers because she fears that they can smell her menstrual odor. Because Hilda wants her stepdaughter to feel empowered in her developing adult body, she insists that Kelsey mark the event of her first period with a special ceremony. However, since contemporary Western culture lacks any coherent rituals to commemorate menarche, Kelsey improvises. In the presence of her best friend Gerry-Anne, she puts away forever her stuffed dog Pinkie that she has slept with since she was three. The deeper motives behind the ceremony, however, reveal that Kelsey is not empowered by this ceremony. Kelsey decided to put away Pinkie so that Gerry-Anne will not think that she is too babyish to be friends with during junior high school (Charnas 475). So the underlying message of this improvised ceremony is that becoming a woman involves an increased willingness to conform to societal norms that strip young adults of much that is comforting.

Kelsey quickly sees that her adult body is something that precludes agency rather than gives her more autonomy. The girl Kelsey was "skinny and fast, and everybody wanted [her] on their team" (Charnas 475), and because she was "strong for a girl," she "used to always wrestle and fight with the boys" (Charnas 473–74). Now, in her woman's body, Kelsey is a target for sexual harassment, and Billy is able to break her nose in part because she is not strong enough to fight young men. Because Kelsey experiences her maturing body as a magnet for ridicule and violence, she conceals it with baggy clothing when she goes to school. Kelsey also becomes aware of her female peers whose bodies have likewise precluded agency. Edie Siler, a girl a few years ahead of Kelsey in school, "starved herself to death" in tenth grade "to keep her body down, keep it normal looking, thin, and strong" (Charnas 476) while Sara, an older eighth grader, has been regularly molested by her father (Charnas 486), allegedly because she too has a maturing female body. Worse still, Kelsey's maturing body means that adults now expect her to participate in child care as a way of schooling her in compulsory heterosexuality. When Hilda becomes pregnant during Kelsey's first half of eighth grade, her parents attempt to convince her that having a younger sibling will be a "fun" way for her to practice for motherhood. But Kelsey knows that the experience will instead further limit her autonomy, and soon she will be like her classmate Mary O'Hare who has the disgusting job of changing her youngest sister's diapers (Charnas 485). In this way, Kelsey is on the path to becoming a typical adult woman whose maturity is demonstrated by accepting that her body justifies her subordination.

Only Kelsey's lycanthropy can give her hope of becoming an autonomous adult woman. Transforming into her wolf body gives Kelsey agency on the most basic level: she describes this change "as something she was doing instead of just another dumb body-mess happening to [her] because some brainless hormones said so" (Charnas 479). In her werewolf form, Kelsey does not have to be afraid of anyone because her "wolf-body was strong" (Charnas 480). Also, Kelsey sees her wolf body as "gorgeous" (Charnas 481), in contrast to how she experiences her human body as something that smells bad and must be concealed with baggy clothing. Kelsey's wolf body also gives her abilities not available to her in her human form. In her wolf form, Kelsey can smell a range of scents unavailable to the human nose, and she can run so fast that she "can almost fly" (Charnas 481). As a werewolf, Kelsey "can see in the dark and run like the wind and leap parked cars in a single bound" (Charnas 473). In this way, Kelsey's wolf body allows her to experience the mobility she had in her pre-adolescent body when she "didn't have boobs bouncing and yanking in front" (Charnas 481–82).

Lycanthropy ultimately gives Kelsey agency as a young woman, in both her wolf and human forms. Because Kelsey can only change into her wolf form during the full moon when she would normally be menstruating, at first she believes that she is doomed to suffer for the remaining twenty-one days before her menstrual cycle when she can change again. After Kelsey's first change when she temporarily lacks access to her lycanthropic form, Billy works to ruin her reputation by telling everyone at school that she made out with him during a drunken party, thus setting her up to be ostracized as the school slut, an abject Other. The slut is found in every high school, cast in this role by her more popular peers in order to mark the outer limits of femininity and serve as an example of what happens to girls who cross these borders.[10] Billy's popularity makes him one of the powerbrokers in the school: he has the ability to decide, for example, what girls will be designated as the school slut, and which ones are popular, so other girls are willing to shun and torment Kelsey in order to curry favor with him, or at least prevent themselves from becoming one of his targets. Thus, Gerry-Anne momentarily stops speaking to Kelsey, while Billy recruits other girls to harass her. Another girl who is now hanging out with Billy and his friends, steals Kelsey's bra while she changes for gym class, giving the garment to Billy, who displays it outside of the principal's office as evidence of the size of Kelsey's breasts.

As a result of these experiences, the second time that Kelsey is able to change into her wolf form, she is already someone better able to take charge of her life. Kelsey's transformation during her second menstrual cycle is the inverse of how women are generally characterized as being during their periods. Kelsey is not an irrational, hormonally-crazed bitch who is having her period, but someone much more able to take charge of her own life. Kelsey knows that Billy will not "grow up," but instead continue to make her life unbearable during high school, so she kills and eats him while she is in her wolf form. With Billy dead, Kelsey can pursue her education and feel comfortable at school now that she will no longer be called "Boobs" when she walks down the hallway. Moreover, Kelsey now spreads rumors about Billy rather than being victimized by his gossip about her. In the days after Billy's death, Kelsey takes pleasure in coming up behind groups of shocked students who are passing around the grisly details about the condition of his body when it was found, adding "a really gross remark or two" (Charnas 491).

Kelsey's ability to transform gives her power that she lacked when she was confined to her human female body. Unlike werewolves in other narratives, Kelsey does not have to kill when she transforms. "Some wolf nights [she] doesn't even feel like hunting" and conjectures that her earlier ravenousness was due to her having stored up "her appetite for a long time" (Charnas 491). Thus, when Kelsey does hunt, she only preys on people who are "looking for trouble" by "sneaking around in the middle of the night"

(Charnas 492). As a result, Kelsey "has done a lot more for the burglary problem" around her neighborhood than "a hundred dumb 'watchdogs'" (Charnas 492). Kelsey's social life has improved as well. Gerry-Anne is talking to her again, so she has the comforting bonds of female friendship, and she is also going on her first double date with her friend, a sign that perhaps Kelsey is being introduced to heterosexual relationships in a safe and comfortable way.

Both *Blood and Chocolate* and *The Blooding* are works of YA fiction that are also paranormal romances, a hybrid genre that gives Klause and Windsor multiple strategies for exposing gender as constructed rather than natural and therefore immutable. Paranormal romance is defined as a narrative with supernatural elements where the love relationship between main characters is the focus of the plot (Ramsdell 4, 221). The Ginger Snaps Trilogy and *Blood Moon* are not paranormal romances; though some of the protagonists have a love interest, the relationship is secondary to the story. In *Blood and Chocolate* and *The Blooding*, however, Vivian's and Maris's romantic relationships are crucial to the development of their emerging senses of self as adult women. Furthermore, these romantic relationships are altered by the figure of the werewolf. In the conventional romance narrative, the heroine must successfully reinterpret the hero's surliness as evidence of his affection rather than behavior that should drive her away. This semantic sleight of hand is not difficult for the heroine to perform (or for the typical romance reader to accept) since contemporary discourses of masculinity have already predisposed her to view his gruff, dismissive behavior as compatible with his gender. The presence of a werewolf figure, however, transforms the typical relationship between the heroine and hero of the romance. Because the female werewolf is the embodiment of all that women are compelled to repress in the interest of being stereotypically feminine, the lycanthropic heroines of these paranormal romances can deconstruct conventional masculinity. As a consequence, they can avoid becoming entangled with someone who would deprive them of autonomy.

Harriet Margolis argues that romance fiction can be read as a type of female *Bildungsroman* in that "it considers questions of female identity, with a particular interest in the female protagonist's subjectivity" (124). Unfortunately, in the romance genre, these questions are usually answered in a way that represents the female protagonist as subordinated and effectively silenced. In the conclusion of most romance novels, the heroine's development is achieved after she finds her true love, with whom she will retreat into the domestic sphere and live a fairly conventionally feminine existence (Margolis 125). Paranormal romance, on the other hand, depicts alternatives for women to the typical marriage plot. Lee Tobin-McClain describes paranormal romance as a genre whose fantastic elements allow "for the exploration of unspeakable elements of contemporary gender identity and relationships" (300) such as women's anger and empowerment and feelings of desire. Lycanthropy enables Vivian and Maris to accept their anger and sexual desires, and to accept themselves as powerful rather than experience such characteristics as abject qualities to be disavowed. As a consequence, each girl can develop beyond the narrow confines of the typical romance novel protagonist. *The Blooding* and *Blood and Chocolate* end with Maris's and Vivian's development into strong and relatively autonomous women who will never quietly and completely retreat into the domestic sphere.

Moreover, the paranormal elements of *The Blooding* and *Blood and Chocolate* enable Maris and Vivian to deconstruct the romance genre's discourses of normative femininity that set women up for victimization. Both girls initially attempt to emulate the conventional romance heroine's behavior, a behavior that is represented as typifying what it means to be a "good" and "normal" woman in our culture.[11] However, eventually each girl realizes that this behavior is self-destructive, both because it is antithetical to her nature as a werewolf and it makes her subject to control by a man who can harm her, as is the case with Maris, or does harm her in Vivian's situation. As a result, both girls come to understand how conventional femininity is a confining subject position rather than a "natural" facet of adult womanhood.

Maris's ideas about adult heterosexual relationships have been shaped by Gothic romance fiction. The reader learns that Maris "liked films where the man seemed remote and almost cruel, but softened in the end" (Windsor 62), a reaction that fits into Tania Modleski's theory of how romance fiction perpetuates "ideological confusion about male sexuality and male violence" by assuring women that a bullying man's meanness "is nothing more than the overflow of [his] love or the measure of [his] resistance to [women's] extraordinary charms" (42). In other words, Maris's exposure to Gothic romance fiction has predisposed her to eroticize men's abusive treatment of women.

## 2. Blood and Bitches

As a consequence, at the beginning of the novel, Maris actively participates in her own victimization. Michelle Massé views the Gothic heroine as someone who helps shape the system that oppresses her through internalizing its values (5). We see this tendency in how Maris is all too willing to gloss over Derrick's dismissive treatment of his wife Barb. Initially Maris views Barb as a woman who is genuinely ill, rather than the chronic malingerer that Derrick believes her to be. But Maris's opinion of Barb changes momentarily when she becomes attracted to Derrick. Afterwards, Maris attributes the couple's fights to what she interprets as Barb's hysterical reaction to her environment rather than Derrick's failure to take over any of the childcare responsibilities or Barb's relative isolation in the family's country home.

Modleski observes how Gothic romance fiction connects a woman's femininity to her ability to ignore the warning signs of abuse. When the Gothic heroine is confronted with evidence that her beloved is a dangerous man, she labors to convince herself that her suspicions are baseless and that "she will have failed as a woman if she does not implicitly believe in him" (Modleski 59). Because *The Blooding* is told from Maris's point of view, we are privy to her internal struggles, so we see her inner battle to redefine Derrick as a brooding gothic hero, in spite of contrary indications. Like Jade's death in the ghost story *Jade Green* that I analyzed in Chapter One, Barbara's death is also labeled a suicide, and her reputed means of dispatching herself are similarly improbable — Barbara supposedly bled to death after biting open her wrists while Jade supposedly took her life by hacking off her right hand with a meat cleaver. After Barb's death, Maris works to convince herself that her suspicions about Derrick's involvement in her demise are unfounded. Maris persists in believing in Derrick's innocence, even after she learns that he is a werewolf who could easily have inflicted these wounds on his wife. Maris will only truly understand how abusive and dangerous Derrick is after she becomes the object of his affection. However, this realization will take some time given that she has been preconditioned by Gothic romance fiction to mistake some of the warning signs of abuse for affection.

The basic framework of *Blood and Chocolate* follows the trajectory of the Harlequin romance: a young, inexperienced woman becomes involved with an older man who is "mocking, cynical, contemptuous, often hostile" (Modleski 36), and his behavior confuses her since the man is obviously interested in her romantically. Like Maris, Vivian is young and inexperienced in the ways of adult relationships (though it is implied that she has been sexually active). Gabriel (the man who will become her partner at the end of the novel) is older than Vivian by about a decade, strong, and more experienced than she. Although Vivian is initially attracted to Gabriel, she dismisses her feelings because of what she sees as his mocking, cynical, and contemptuous behavior, especially towards her. In fact, at the beginning of the novel, Vivian wants nothing to do with the young men of her kind because their swaggering, vulgar, sex-crazed performance of masculinity leads them to attempt to dominate her. Vivian's pursuit of Aiden, a sensitive human boy whose long hair and love of poetry makes him the polar opposite of her fellow werewolves, underscores how she has rejected the sort of masculinity displayed by the young men of her pack. Aiden's interest in the occult and his poem about the beauty of a werewolf in her pelt leads Vivian to hope that he would love the beast within her rather than be repulsed by this facet of herself.

Instead, Vivian's brief relationship with Aiden causes her to become ensnared within the parameters of stereotypical femininity. Because Aiden is a "meat boy," as some members of her pack refer to humans to indicate that they are potential prey rather than the equal of werewolves, Vivian must perform a sort of double drag in his presence whereby she can pass both as human and conventionally feminine. As a werewolf living in a world where her kind is greatly outnumbered by humans, Vivian must always give a convincing performance as a human when she is among them. When Vivian is with Aiden, she must also convincingly perform as normatively feminine so as not to frighten him, even though he is supposedly an enlightened man who does not subscribe to conventional gender roles.

While being conventionally feminine benefits Maris and Vivian in the short run, eventually it sets them up for victimization. Maris's conventional femininity, which is manifested in her willingness to take on an increasing share of the Forrest household's domestic labor after Barb's death, leads Derrick to confess that he "needs her," something that Maris reads at the time as proof that she's a "mature woman" rather than the ignorant child that her mother and other older women believe her to be. Soon after Barb's death, Derrick begs Maris to stay in England and help him with his children, particularly since his mother-in-law, who believes that he drove her daughter to suicide, has threatened to sue for custody. The language of Derrick's request appeals to Maris's need to feel valued and is calculated to manipulate her into making a dangerous and ill-informed choice. Derrick warns Maris that "helping [him] means giving up everything. There's no way back, no way out, no way to undo it. Once it happens, it last forever" (Windsor 190). While Derrick is giving Maris a warning of sorts, he fails to give her all the information she'd need to make an informed choice. However, Maris has already been preconditioned to view the lack of information in this statement as a declaration of love since what Derrick speaks of here can also refer to the idea of marriage as perpetuated in romance fiction. Only after Maris promises to help Derrick does he reveal his lycanthropy to her, and she agrees to be similarly changed as a way of "helping" him.

After Derrick transforms Maris into a werewolf, she soon realizes that he has put her in a situation where she is extremely vulnerable. He has made her into a werewolf not in order to imbue her with supernatural abilities that would make her strong and autonomous, but to make her even more dependent on him. Not only is Maris a stranger in another country, but she is now a monster in a hostile human society. Beset by the unfamiliar new urges that are precipitated by lycanthropy, Maris must rely on Derrick to show her how to survive as a werewolf, as there is no other source of information from which she can learn how to change forms and hunt without being detected by humans. However, Derrick shares knowledge with Maris sparingly, making it difficult for her to leave the house and hunt on her own. After Derrick takes Maris out on an initial hunt, he instructs her to remain at the house to care for his children until he decides when she can hunt again. Meanwhile, Maris's new urges make her a prisoner of her body when she is debilitated by her need to consume raw animal flesh.

Vivian too reaps short-term rewards for grooming her body into a conventional femininity — she momentarily becomes Aiden's love interest. However, when Vivian finally decides to stop performing as conventionally feminine and human, the results are disastrous. On the night they are to consummate their relationship, Vivian reveals her wolf form to Aiden, hoping that he will see "something beautiful, and wild, beyond imagining" (Klause 166). Instead, Vivian out of "drag" is so beyond Aiden's concept of reality that he can only be terrified. When Vivian completes her change in front of Aiden, he begins to cry, then chases her from the room (Klause 168–69).

Aiden's reaction to Vivian's lycanthropic body in effect punishes her for expressing her sexuality. Heterosexual human females find male werewolves attractive, as their lycanthropy is an extension of normative masculinity, particularly as established by the conventions of paranormal romance. This explains some of Maris's attraction to Derrick in *The Blooding*. However, human males find female werewolves repugnant, as they are the antithesis of conventional femininity. Days later, when Vivian corners Aiden to discuss their last encounter, he can only express loathing for her now that he knows her horrible secret: "Every time I think of kissing you I see that other face" and think "what has that mouth done?" (Klause 194). Later Aiden is so horrified by Vivian that he shoots her in order to put her out of the misery he believes she must be suffering because she is a werewolf. Aiden's actions, however, are motivated out of his desire to maintain traditional gender roles rather than protect Vivian.

As I have already noted in the introduction, the supernatural elements of horror denaturalize the repressed, thereby making accessible the terrors of daily life (Pinedo 39), as well as deconstruct and redraw the boundaries that perpetuate subjectivity (Creed "Horror" 46). In this way, "Boobs" uses supernatural elements to critique sexist representations of adolescent femininity in maturing girls who are just beginning to fully realize that they live in a sexist rape culture where their male peers' violent misogyny is represented as a "natural though sometimes unpleasant" facet of their masculinity. *Blood and Chocolate* and *The Blooding* use supernatural elements to critique the sexist representations of erotic love that undergird the romance. Though Windsor and Klause frame their heroines' lives through the conventions of romance, both authors also manipulate these conventions of the genre in order to challenge its sexist assumptions. They do this in part through the use of paranormal elements more commonly found in horror.

Neither Maris nor Vivian can maintain a posture of normative femininity for an extended period of time, particularly as this subject position is represented in the romance genre, since doing so deprives each girl of her own strengths to a degree that puts her in peril. Rather, Vivian and Maris cross boundaries, so they belong to the category of the monstrous even without their lycanthropy. Maris's and Vivian's inability to control their anger, which is a justifiable response to external stimuli, prevent them from being normatively feminine.

## 2. Blood and Bitches

### Lycanthropy as the Antithesis of Conventional Femininity

Lycanthropy is the physical manifestation of all three girls' inabilities to remain within the parameters of normative femininity. All are further characterized as "unfeminine" due to their desires to hunt and eat meat. In *The Sexual Politics of Meat*, Carol Adams describes meat as "a masculine food and meat eating [as] a male activity" (26). In non-technological societies, "meat was a valuable economic commodity" (Adams 34) and men became the hunters who controlled this commodity and consequently achieved power. The female werewolf's ability to kill and eat her prey then demonstrates her bestial nature as well as incipient masculinity; she does not need to rely on a man to supply sustenance, as it were. In fact, her appetites can only be satisfied if she hunts her own prey rather than has it brought to her.

In *The Blooding* we see a power struggle over meat similar to the one that Adams describes as characterizing the distribution of this resource in non-technological societies. After Derrick has turned Maris into a werewolf, he does not want her to change into her lupine form and hunt without him. But the newly-turned Maris is beset by intense cravings for meat, and needs to hunt to supply her own food since her new hunger cannot be satisfied by consuming the store-bought chicken in the Forrests' freezer. Maris's solo outings outrage Derrick, allegedly because he believes that she is too young and inexperienced to be discreet (and therefore runs the risk of exposing his own lycanthropy to a community that is already on edge because a "wolf" has been killing their dogs and livestock). But Derrick's anger is actually about control, as his relationship with Barb reveals.

Ironically, Barb was not a suitable partner for Derrick because she was *too* conventionally feminine and so could never fully transform into a werewolf. When Barb submitted to Derrick's bite, she did so merely to augment his affections for her: she had no innate longing to express the animal side of her personality. Eventually Barb's mental and physical state deteriorates because her body rejects her emerging lycanthropy. The novel implies that Barb's inability to fully change into her wolf form and hunt is related to her Chronic Fatigue Syndrome (CFS), which leaves her too enervated to do much of anything. According to the Centers for Disease Control and Prevention, CFS "occurs up to four times more frequently in women than in men"

("Chronic Fatigue Syndrome: Who's at Risk?"). To put it another way, Barb's CFS makes her the poster child for conventional femininity in how she is extremely passive as a result of her condition, rather than active to the point of being aggressive, which is equated with normative masculinity.

Kelsey, Vivian, and Maris, on the other hand, love the hunt, which further places them at odds with conventional femininity. In general, girls "show higher levels of positive behaviors and attitudes towards animals" (Herzog 7) than do boys, including their attachment to pets, involvement in animal protectionism and aversion to hunting. Kelsey describes herself as experiencing "joy" (Charnas 482) while hunting neighborhood dogs, as well as eating her prey. She compares consuming dogs to "eating honey or the best chocolate malted you ever had" (Charnas 483), while eating Billy is "better than Thanksgiving dinner" (Charnas 490). The human Aiden in *Blood and Chocolate* bemoans that his father tried to make him go hunting with him as a way of making him more normatively masculine, while Vivian thinks that she would give anything to be able to go and kill something with her now deceased father (Klause 79). After Maris is changed, she finds herself longing for "raw flesh and warm blood" (Windsor 235) and feeling a more intense desire to hunt than to eat (Windsor 236). However, when Maris confesses this desire to Derrick, she is so outside the confines of normative femininity that even he seems to be repulsed by her (Windsor 236), showing how femininity is a shifting construct rather than a fixed category.

Another way that the female werewolf resists conventional femininity is her insistence on her own sexual pleasure. At the end of "Boobs," Kelsey is going on her first date and is now sufficiently comfortable in her human female form that she can promise herself that she will no longer "be self-conscious" (Charnas 492) about her breasts. Vivian longs to teach the human Aiden to be "less polite" when they have the chance to be intimate, and the fur on the back of her neck bristles when she smells the musk of her fellow werewolf Gabriel (Klause 52, 135). In fact, in *Blood and Chocolate,* overt sexual desire is a part of normative femininity for female lycanthropes. Maris too desires sex, which for her is connected to and supplanted by hunting. Her new longing to hunt is described in sexualized language. One night Maris is awakened by her own whining sounds, and the wetness she discovers around her mouth is a result of her own now razor-sharp teeth, which have cut her in her sleep and made her bleed. She can only conceive of this feeling as "I want. I need" (Windsor 221), and so cannot stop herself from finding satisfaction by going out to hunt alone.

## *The Value of Women's Anger*

While Maris's and Vivian's aggressive sexual desires are incompatible with conventional femininity, theirs and Kelsey's expressions of anger completely disqualify them from fitting into this category. Brown characterizes anger as "the essential political emotion" in that "it is tied to self-respect, a sense of entitlement, and lucid thinking about wrong-doing" (*Raising* 10). Furthermore, "reasoned anger is critical not only to the healthy psychological development of individual women, but also to their capacity to recognize injustice and organize for change" (Brown *Raising* 11). For this reason, patriarchy needs to suppress women's anger since it is also the catalyst for agency. While Ginger's, Bridgette's and Tara's anger is merely proof that they are dangerously out of control monsters, for Vivian, Maris, and Kelsey, anger is something that puts them on the path to becoming autonomous adult subjects.

Kelsey's anger in "Boobs" stems from her sense of self-respect, and so when Billy calls her "Boobs" and gropes her, she shoves him. However, her expression of anger only gets her beaten up, and she is later blamed by school authorities and her parents for Billy's assault. So the message conveyed to Kelsey is that a woman's anger, even over an injustice as great as sexual assault, is not "legitimate."

At the beginning of *The Blooding* and *Blood and Chocolate*, Maris and Vivian have negative views of women's anger. Maris's family situation has predisposed her to view women's anger as a personality defect rather than a logical reaction to injustice. Her mother is a bitter, seething woman who asserts control in their relationship through continually undermining her daughter. Maris blames her mother's anger for driving off her father. On the day her father left, Maris observes that her mother had "wiped the smile off [his face], and replaced it with anger and pain" (Windsor 66). As a result, Maris grows up predisposed to see *all* women's anger as an irrational response that destroys families and deprives any subsequent children of a nurturing environment.

Maris hopes that her job in England will let her participate vicariously in the sort of domestic life that she has never known, since she views the Forrests as a normal family, which for her means that both mother and father are present, and there is more than one child. However, Maris soon learns that the Forrests' relationship is far from idyllic. Instead, it is characterized by the couple's frequent fights that are provoked by Derrick's poor treatment of his wife. As a result, Maris has yet another opportunity to contemplate women's anger.

Because Maris sees Barb's angry responses out of context, she does not perceive them as emerging from a sense of self-respect. Barb's outbursts never resolve anything between the couple. Instead, after Barb shouts at Derrick about what he has done to upset her (such as undermining her authority in front of the children), he storms out of the house, and she is reduced to tears. As a result, Maris views Barb's anger as irrational and believes that Barb participates in her own victimization. "Why did Barb put up with the fights," Maris wonders. "Why didn't she go home, back to the United States? Why live with arguments?" (Windsor 61). Later, when Maris returns in the wee hours after an evening outing with friends, Barb has a meltdown so severe that the doctor must be summoned to administer a sedative. What Maris does not know at the time is that Barb fears that Maris's late-night absence from the house indicates that she has suffered the fate of their previous nanny, Janice. After Barb's death, Maris learns from her deceased employer's diary that Derrick tried to seduce Janice in the same way that he has seduced her. When things did not work out, Janice suspiciously disappeared in the middle of the night. But at the time of Barb's meltdown, Maris's lack of context for her employer's reaction causes her to judge it, and Barb's anger in general, as further evidence of her mental illness rather than as an understandable response to her husband's mistreatment of her and others. Moreover, Barb's lack of voice in life is further demonstrated by how Maris must obtain this information surreptitiously and piecemeal.

Maris also fears her own anger, and labors to suppress it whenever it erupts. For example, Maris becomes irate after learning that her mother has actively prevented her father from visiting. Yet instead of confronting her mother with what she has discovered, Maris swallows her rage and says nothing, since "to accuse her mother and present concrete evidence meant that everything would be changed forever" (Windsor 68), a situation that would be infinitely worse than her familiar, though unpleasant circumstances.

## 2. Blood and Bitches

Vivian too has a negative view of women's anger. Although Vivian belongs to a werewolf culture that initially views women's anger as healthy, and offers women several opportunities to express this emotion through violence, Vivian perceives anger as an emotion that is at best undignified and at worst extremely dangerous. For example, Vivian is mortified to learn that her mother Esmé has been fighting with Astrid, another female werewolf, over the affections of a man, though Vivian too has harbored the same violent feelings of jealousy. When Kelly, a rival for Aiden's affection, gives Vivian a dirty look, she momentarily contemplates brawling with the girl. But anger is also potentially dangerous, regardless of the sex of the person expressing it. For werewolves, anger is something that can wipe away the human part and permit the "animal to reign supreme" (Klause 171), which endangers the entire pack. A year previously, Vivian's father was killed and the pack forced to relocate because one of their members could not control his anger. As a result, he murdered a human girl, an action that revealed the pack's presence to the people of the community. Frightened humans burned the compound, and Vivian's father, the pack's leader at the time, died trying to save the others. Later Vivian's anger over Aiden's rejection of her prompts her to get drunk, break into Kelly's house, and trash her room. Vivian awakens the next morning with the taste of blood in her mouth and little recollection of the previous night, fearing that she has done more than damage property. When the mutilated body of a biker is found behind a local bar on the night of her blackout, Vivian fears that rage has caused her to behave as an animal lacking the capacity to reason. Later, however, Vivian will discover that the animal has not reigned supreme in her, but rather, that Astrid is responsible for the killing.

All three protagonists reconsider their feelings about the efficacy of anger after mastering and coming to accept their lycanthropic bodies. After Kelsey learns about her ability to change and masters her wolf form, she can mete out violence to those who have angered her. She gets away with killing Billy, whose mauled body is never connected to her, and she has the potential to harm those who disrespect her like Fat Joey, who keeps "crowding [her] in science lab, trying to get a feel" (Charnas 491). Because Kelsey can use her lycanthropic body to protect her, she no longer feels impotent in her human female form when she feels anger.

Maris and Vivian, who have had more negative conditioning about female anger, come to reconsider their feelings about this emotion after they are put into situations where its expression is a consequence of their emerging feelings of self-respect. Maris begins to see the flaws in her negative judgment of women's anger after Barb's death thrusts her into the role of wife and mother in the Forrest household. Suddenly, Maris sees "things through Barb's eyes" (Windsor 228). After Derrick changes Maris into a werewolf, she realizes that he has put her in a position where he has complete control of her. Maris's ignorance about lycanthropy combined with her lack of legal standing in a foreign country mean that "she had no power over [Derrick]. He could send her away with the snap of his fingers. He controlled her destiny completely" (Windsor 238). This realization gives way to anger, a catalyst enabling Maris to develop the required self-respect to fight Derrick's attempts to manipulate her. Anger prompts Maris to rummage around the house in Derrick's absence for information that might help her understand her lycanthropy. The search unearths Barb's diary, which reveals how terrified she was of her husband, and how dangerous Derrick might be. Reading and writing are powerful tools that connect women to one another, even through time. After Maris reads Barb's diary, she has a better appreciation of what provoked her deceased employer's angry outbursts.

When Maris can see Barb's anger as justified rather than an irrational response, she can begin to understand her mother's point of view as well, a perspective that puts her on her way becoming an autonomous adult. Modleski observes that Gothic fiction serves to "convince women that they are not their mothers" through enabling them to develop "an understanding of the mother's difficulties" (71). This is precisely Maris's situation. Maris's anger towards Derrick leads her to realize that her mother might be right about some things, such as how "crazy people are unreliable" (Windsor 250), and that her father's own unreliability, as revealed through his failure to make more of an effort to contact her after the divorce, supports her mother's claim that he was manic depressive and too difficult to live with (Windsor 70). Once Maris can begin to appreciate some of her mother's difficulties, she can begin the process of separation that permits her to see that she is *not* her mother, nor must she become her as she matures.

Anger is similarly tied to Vivian's emerging sense of self respect, which prompts her to fight injustice. This emotion causes Vivian to take the swift action required to save her mother's life and lets her find "the mate of her flesh." In Klause's werewolf culture, both males and females are encouraged to engage in physical confrontations with one another to settle differences. Pack leaders are chosen through violence rather than through acclimation. During the Ordeal, all willing adult male pack members fight in their wolf skins to determine the new pack leader. The Bitches' Match is a similar method for settling who has the right to become Queen Bitch, the leader's mate and the female head of the pack. When Astrid badly injures Esmé during the Bitches' Match, Vivian jumps into the fray without thinking and saves her mother's life by savaging her opponent. As a result, Vivian wins the contest that she has not even entered and accidentally becomes Queen Bitch.

But this is not the end of the fight for Astrid, who sets up Vivian so that she appears to be guilty of a recent string of murders that law enforcement believes have been caused by a wild animal that is mauling the victims. The pack, however, knows that the murders were committed by one of their own. Gabriel, the new leader, will be obligated to execute the perpetrator because his or her actions endanger the pack by threatening to reveal their existence to humans. Vivian eventually discovers that she did not murder the woman whose body was found on the night that she blacked out. Instead, Astrid engineered the whole scenario to make it appear as if Vivian were the responsible party. She did this by arranging for one of the male teen werewolves to console Vivian after she was rejected by Aiden, getting her drunk enough to forget her whereabouts that night. Vivian can only embrace her anger as a natural aspect of herself after learning that it did not send her into a blind rage and cause her to kill someone. After this realization, Vivian can appreciate her anger as something positive that leads her to protect those she loves rather than an emotion that permits "the animal to reign supreme." The novel concludes with Vivian's learning that anger does not have to be a quality necessarily repellant to men, or at least, other male werewolves. Gabriel, Vivian's eventual romantic partner, is attracted by Vivian's anger, which he sees as evidence of her fierce ability "to care" for those she loves. In this way, Vivian's anger makes her *more* feminine in that it is linked to that stereotypical feminine affinity for caring and connection. Thus, the text sadly reinforces as many stereotypes as it challenges.

## Monstrous Bodies

### *The Werewolf as a Powerful Hybrid of Human and Animal*

Finally, as werewolves, Kelsey, Maris, and Vivian are more than animals in drag in human skin. Kelsey, Maris, and Vivian are unlike Ginger, Bridgette, or Tara in that they are true hybrids who can *continuously* pass between the boundaries separating human and animal, male and female, and even adult and child, thereby revealing the permeability of these borders. As Butler notes, if "an illusion of the unity of gender is maintained through the constant repetition of stylized acts" (*Gender* 141), acts that reinforce difference, then the female werewolf's hybridity undermines this illusion. Ultimately, this hybridity endows Kelsey, Vivian and Maris with agency that Ginger, Bridgette, Tara, and their normatively human sisters lack.

Kelsey's lycanthropy does not just give her the ability to change bodies, but empowers her because she can combine the strength of both forms. Like Ginger, Kelsey's lycanthropy is linked to her menstrual cycle. Both view menstruation negatively: Ginger quips of the experience that the words "just and cramps don't go together," while Kelsey describes menstruation as "messy and disgusting" (Charnas 474). But for the werewolf Kelsey, menstruation is just a minor bother: instead of bleeding when it is time for her period, she just gets cramps and sore breasts and more acne prior to changing into her wolf form. As a consequence, Kelsey has the confidence to enjoy her human female form because she knows that she has monthly access to her more powerful wolf form. Thus, when Kelsey goes on her first date, she no longer has to feel "self-conscious, even if the guy stares" (Charnas 492) at her breasts because she always has the ability to deal with him or anyone else who might decide to harass her. We never learn if Kelsey will retain her power to change into her wolf form when she goes into menopause, but perhaps several decades of switching forms will let her become an older woman whose strength lies in her confidence and wisdom more than her ability to change forms in order to mete out violence to those who would harm her.

Klause' werewolves derive their power not from their animalistic natures, but due to the flexibility afforded to them by lycanthropy, their ability to recognize themselves as being more than just one thing or another. Like Ginger and Bridgette, Vivian is also a monster because she crosses boundaries. However, this mutability gives Vivian more agency than she would

## 2. Blood and Bitches

have if she were a human girl. At the end of the novel, when Aiden shoots Vivian, she momentarily becomes stuck between forms. The resulting body is a chimera depriving her of agency because her mismatched parts do not permit her to live comfortably as either a wolf or a human. Vivian can only regain her autonomy after Gabriel helps her understand that her hybridity is empowering. Humans too have "a beast within," Gabriel tells her, yet they are weaker than werewolves because this beast will "break out in evil ways" (Klause 261) if it is suppressed too fiercely. Werewolves, with their ability to cross the boundaries between human and animal, can give this beast a voice and make use of the strengths it affords them without necessarily losing touch with their own humanity. After remembering the strength inherent in her changeable body, Vivian regains her ability to transform along with the agency that this ability gives her.

Maris's ability to shapeshift is a metaphor for another, greater type of malleability that gives her agency. "Could anyone or anything keep her now," Maris ponders. "If she could change herself, she could change her life" (Windsor 233). The conclusion subtly hints that Maris is on track to change her life, despite the humiliating circumstances in which she finds herself. When Derrick in his wolf form attempts to kill someone out of malice, Maris transforms to stop him. Both are shot before Derrick can murder his intended victim, and the injury causes them to revert to their nude human forms. Derrick dies and Maris is found unconscious in what seems to be an ignominious tableaux indicating that she and her employer were engaged in deviant sex. After a spate of humiliating questions, Maris is deported, and she dreads returning to her mother, who will see this experience as further confirmation of her daughter's inability to take care of herself. Yet there is hope for Maris, for whom "everything had changed" (Windsor 280). She is returning home much stronger than when she left, so much so that she wonders "how she was going to live two lives in the same body, how she was going to keep pretending she was only Maris Pelham when the gray wolf was alive inside of her" (Windsor 280). For the time being at least, Maris will have to perform the sort of drag that Vivian performs daily. Maris "had to appear weak and ordinary, when inside she was fierce, strong, and cunning, perhaps even vicious" (Windsor 280). Yet Maris also realizes that it is not possible to completely repress this side of herself that is wholly incompatible with conventional femininity. She knows that "there might be times when she would let the gray wolf out, when it would be necessary to do so" (Windsor 280–81).

Letting out that side of herself that is "fierce, strong and cunning" will not lead Maris into danger the way it did Derrick; rather it will augment her human personality. It was not Derrick's lycanthropy that got him killed, but his rigidity. For Derrick, lycanthropy is an extension of the worst traits of conventional masculinity, rather than a contradiction of them. If normative masculinity is characterized by violence (Kimmel 150), then Derrick is stereotypically masculine both in his pelt and in his skin. In his human form, Derrick is bullying and manipulative, characteristics that both Barb and Maris have been preconditioned to view in men as falling within an acceptable range of masculine behavior. As a wolf, Derrick is better able to express his more violent impulses that highlight the difference between himself and Maris, a difference that is demonstrated when he kills animals for reasons other than food or self defense and when he tries to murder a human. Not surprisingly Derrick speculates that a time will come when he and Maris "cannot resume human shapes" (Windsor 260). Certainly that time was near for Derrick, whose behavior grows less civilized with each passing day, and who has lupine traits even when he is in his human form.

Barb too is unable to survive because she is not a hybrid. While Derrick believes that he will eventually be unable to change back to his human form, Barb is too human to fully transform into a wolf. When Barb hunts with Derrick in spite of her limitations, she cannot kill her own prey, or even consume the flesh of the animals that Derrick brings to her. Barb's humanity is connected with the most negative characteristics of conventional femininity, and she lacks the physical and emotional resources to counter her husband's manipulative and abusive treatment of her. Because Barb too is limited by her femininity, she cannot survive.

Maris, on the other hand, is a hybrid, and her past actions hint at how the animal part of her will never erase the human part, nor will the normatively masculine part erase the normatively feminine part. Maris in her wolf form retains human sensibilities that permit her to consider the feelings of others. In her wolf form, she has stopped Derrick from wantonly killing another human, and she has also declined to eat the Forrest children's caged pet rabbit in spite of her hunger. As a hybrid, Maris has multiple strategies for dealing with the world. As a result, she is stronger than either Barb or Derrick.

## Conclusion

The young adult female werewolf offers more powerful and vivid, even visceral versions of the dangers of traditional femininity. However, the works I examine differ greatly in how they represent the consequences of girls "refusing what they are." Ginger, Bridgette and Tara demonstrate how threatening a girl is to the dominant culture when she will not, or cannot, perform as conventionally feminine. Ginger ultimately becomes something so monstrous that she must be destroyed, while Bridgette continues to have the potential to menace others if her keeper unleashes her. Tara outwardly conforms so well to normative femininity that it is difficult for others to see that she does not behave in other conventionally human ways, such as wearing clothing, or speaking, or walking erect. Ultimately all three are locked into a type of stereotypical femininity: Tara is trapped in the body of a beauty whereas Ginger and Bridgette are confined to the body of a beast that is both connected to the natural world due to its animal form and a complete Otherness in that it is not like anything found in nature. As a consequence, each girl is deprived of the flexibility that hybridity might afford her.

Kelsey, Vivian, and Maris, on the other hand, have rejected stereotypical femininity, and so more fully understand the dangerous consequences of repressing feelings and desires that are incompatible with this subject position. While the haunted girls in Chapter 1 were able to refuse what they are, Kelsey, Vivian and Maris are able to go a step further and accept what they are. As a result, Kelsey, Vivian and Maris are hybrids of human and animal, a state that gives each girl the resources to develop strategies that permit her to express these supposedly unacceptable parts of herself without provoking the wrath of members of the dominant culture. In this way, Kelsey, Vivian and Maris are hopeful monsters.

Still, both the haunted girls of Chapter 1 and the teen female werewolves of this chapter are not completely autonomous. Because these characters are not legal adults, each must conceal her strengths from those who might be threatened by them until she is older and in a position where she has more autonomy.

Nevertheless, like the haunted girl, the female werewolf presents specific and unique qualities that can be used to expose and critique the situation of adolescent females. Through the female werewolf's transformation, the young woman's transformation is shown to be both empowering and traumatic, an event to be controlled. Portraying anger and sexuality as legitimate and powerful forces, these texts expose how young women are placed in the role of monstrous Other. If the appeal of the ghost is that the haunted girl is not fully responsible for her resistance to traditional femininity, so too the female werewolf is not responsible for her monstrous side. But while this side empowers her, it also limits her. The teen witches of Chapter 3, on the other hand, will not, and cannot, conceal their strengths. For the teen witch, magic is an expression of her ability to enact her will.

CHAPTER 3

# *"An ye harm none, do as ye will"*[1]*: Magic, Gender and Agency in Young Adult Narratives of Witchcraft*

LIKE THE GHOST AND THE WEREWOLF, the witch uses fantasy elements to expose the dangers of restrictive female gender roles. However, the witch is the most powerful of these three figures because she not only reveals the particular features of oppression, but also presents an alternative feminist worldview. The figure of the witch is thousands of years old and common to many cultures. However, while the ghost and the werewolf have easily recognizable forms as monsters, the witch is difficult to define as it always has a human appearance (even if it has shapeshifting capabilities) and can be any age or sex, though the figure we are most familiar with is usually female. Today the witch is stereotypically depicted as a loathsome crone with the potential to harm others. This characterization is seen in fairy tales (and Disney's interpretations of them), and reproduced in Halloween decorations. However, the witch is increasingly represented in fictional accounts as a "young and beautiful sexual temptress" (Ringel 1221) who may use her powers for good or evil.

While the ghost and the werewolf are wholly fictional creations, the witch has many real-life counterparts that inform contemporary representations of her. Some of these counterparts include shamans and cunning women, traditional healers who used their knowledge of herbs and folklore to cure ailments, deliver babies, tell fortunes, make love spells and even protect others against black magic. Other real-life analogues are people who were persecuted for sorcery in Europe and North America between the fifteenth and eighteenth centuries during the Early Modern witch trials. Still other correlates include Wiccans, practitioners of a neo–Pagan, nature-based religion who describe themselves as witches and whose spiritual practices draw upon the idea of the witch as both historical and mythic figure. Wicca, in turn, has influenced many contemporary fictional narratives of witchcraft that are set during the Burning Times, a Wiccan term for the Early Modern witch trials. These narratives re-imagine those accused of sorcery as proto-Wiccans in possession of supernatural abilities. Many of these fictional representations are mediated by feminist scholarship about those who were tried for witchcraft, such as Barbara Ehrenreich and Deidre English's influential work *Witches, Midwives and Nurses: A History of Women Healers* (1973), which connects the persecution of women healers as witches to the rise of a male-dominated medical profession.

In this chapter, I examine six YA novels and one film: Julie Hearn's *The Minister's Daughter* (2005), Libba Bray's Gemma Doyle Trilogy (2003, 2005, 2007), Celia Rees' Witch Child series (2000, 2002), and the film *The Craft* (1996). Collectively, these works offer a representative sampling of the figure of the witch in her various modern incarnations as cunning woman, shaman, victim of the witch hunts and practitioner of Wicca. Common to all of these works, however, is a portrayal of the witch as the embodiment of female freedom and power nurtured by sisterhood. Most of the teen witches I examine in this chapter are white, a consequence of the YA texts about witches that were available to me in 2013. However, while these teen witches are predominantly white, they are not all uniformly middle class, which *is* the case with the haunted girls I examined in Chapter 1. The two protagonists in novels set during the Early Modern witch hunts are members of the peasantry. During this historical period, poor women were more likely to be charged with witchcraft than were women from more privileged backgrounds.[2]

Like the werewolf and the haunted girl, the witch is also a gendered monster. Though witches can be either sex, the figure that we are most familiar with is female since "the witch often represents female freedom and power, which is itself often the cause of ambivalent responses" (Bosky 699). The witch's Otherness is grounded in her female body and connection to the natural world, representing all that patriarchal culture negatively associates with women and femininity. She is an aging crone whose withered flesh recalls men to their own fearful mortality, or she is a beautiful young woman whose relatively free sexuality makes men anxious: they desire her, yet they also fear her because she is outspoken and independent, and so not easily mastered.

Additionally, the witch's Otherness is linked to her affinity with the natural world, which is also connected to her female body in that women's bodies are often perceived as being more closely related to nature than are men's bodies. The witch is at home in the woods, can cure or curse with her knowledge of herbs, and can even control the weather in some instances. Susan Griffin recounts the cultural perception of women as "closer to nature and ... therefore lacking in a spiritual dimension" (26) and this association's implications for how women are represented as dangerous Others in art and literature. From this perspective, nature is not a positive force, but rather, something terrifying and chaotic that must be mastered, as "nature can make [men] want. Nature can cause [men] to cry in loneliness, to feel a terrible hunger, or a thirst. Nature can even cause [men] to die" (Griffin 28). As a result, the witch's body, through its association with the natural world, is viewed by male characters as evidence of her monstrous Otherness because it represents all that men fear about themselves.

The teen witch who appears in YA literature also has a deep and abiding connection to the natural world, a place that is viewed with mistrust by other characters. Moreover, she is young, outspoken and independent. And the defining feature of the witch — that she has supernatural powers — is represented in a number of YA texts as a positive quality that can be used for good. The fictional teen witches I examine do not exhibit stereotypically feminine behavior. They have overt sexual desires, sometimes for men of different races; they revel in their physical abilities; or they are unconcerned with being beauties who compete for the attention of men. However, what is most important to a feminist critic is how these fictional teen witches' epistemological perspective enables them to resist a subordinate feminine subjectivity. The teen witch's constructivist perspective leads her to question authority and to help other women, which encourages sisterhood and collaboration. This epistemological position can be viewed as feminine[3] in how it enables the witch to become more fully connected to the natural world and to others. As a result, the teen witch is subversive of patriarchal order, and her example encourages other women to similarly question authority and resist their own subordinate subjectivities.

The teen witch goes from being someone who Mary Belenky and her coauthors in *Women's Ways of Knowing* would describe as a received knower, perceiving all authority as residing outside of the self, to the more mature constructivist who understands that "all knowledge is constructed, and the knower is an intimate part of the known" (Belenky 137). The teen witch's intellectual sea change is not surprising, as most developmental psychologists view this shift in orientation towards authority as one of the hallmarks of the adolescent's transition to adulthood and autonomy (Belenky 54–55). Moreover, this shift in orientation towards authority is also the defining feature of YA fiction (Trites *Disturbing*).

While developing a more sophisticated orientation towards authority is a necessary step in the maturation process, women have more difficulty arriving at this phase than do men because their emerging constructivist perspective is particularly threatening to the stability of traditional gender roles, which uphold patriarchal order. Conventional femininity is predicated on women's subordination, which is most easily achieved by keeping women in the received knowledge phase of development in which they dismiss their own insights in deference to the authority of others, who are most often male. Constructivism, on the other hand, is incompatible with normative femininity because it is an epistemological position from which one questions external authority. This questioning ultimately leads to rejection of a hierarchal way of knowing the world in which one perspective is imposed on others. Constructivist women resist making "premature generalizations about what they would do or what should be done, particularly about matters of right and wrong" (Belenky 149). Instead, they know the world more holistically in that they first insist "on a respectful consideration of the particulars of everyone's needs and frailties" before taking action, "even if that means delaying making decisions or taking action" (Belenky 149).

The teen witch's capacity to mature into a relatively autonomous adult is due to her emerging constructivist perspective, which is linked to her magical ability. Magic gives the teen witch more autonomy because it relies on the accomplishment of the practitioner's will. Magic in these narratives is mediated through a Wiccan/neo–Pagan[4] perspective that connects it "to an understanding of the workings of the mind" (Adler 8). Sociologist and Wiccan Sîan Reid explains that neo–Pagan magical practice is about issues of power and control: magic "is the projection of the Will in the world, in order to cause change" (150). The Wiccan/neo–Pagan conception of magic informs how it is represented in YA texts. As a result, the adolescent female witch's developing magical ability is connected to her own empowerment. Thus, as she comes to understand that the knower "is an intimate part of the known" (Belenky 137), her ability to transform her world through magical and conventional means increases.

In the texts I examine, constructivism is the foundation of the witch's magical abilities, which she employs as much through the strength of her will as due to her own supernatural powers. While the teen witch may have the innate ability to cause a rain shower or tame a tiger, she must develop the strength of her will in order to use these abilities effectively. Moreover, the teen witch does not use her magic to conjure material possessions or manipulate others. Rather, her magic is an extension of her agency in how she uses it to make choices that give her (and sometimes others) greater autonomy. In this way, the teen witch's developing magical abilities are linked to her emerging constructivist perspective, which causes her to consider the needs and frailties of others before taking action rather than using her powers to oppress. Finally, the teen witch offers readers the most realistic model of resistance to feminine subordination. While readers cannot hope to have the teen witch's magical powers, all can cultivate her feminist worldview, which would permit them to see beyond a hierarchal and oppressive model of authority.

All of the texts I analyze have achieved sufficient popularity to be described as influential and widely-known. Each of the literary works I have selected is owned by at least 1000 libraries world-wide. Bray's Gemma Doyle trilogy has spent many weeks on *The New York Times* bestseller lists. Also, the Gemma Doyle trilogy, Julie Hearn's *The Minister's Daughter*, and Celia Rees' Witch Child series have been translated into numerous languages. I have included the 1996 film *The Craft* in my survey of teen witches in Young Adult fiction because it fits into a definition of Young Adult fiction in which adolescent protagonists wrestle with "issues to which teenagers can relate" (Herz 10). *The Craft* is reasonably well-known, and has even garnered a few minor awards. Even more importantly, *The Craft* has influenced adolescents' ideas about witches and witchcraft. Helen A. Berger and Douglas Ezzy's ethnography of Wiccan and neo–Pagan teens found that "mass media provides the cultural background that facilitates cultural orientation toward Witchcraft" (58). Their research singles out films such as *The Craft* as "orienting young people positively" (Berger 58) to witchcraft, as it represents witches in an affirmative way.

The novels I examine are set in distant historical periods where women had few legal rights. Instead, in the eyes of the law during these times, women were perpetual dependents passing from the control of fathers and brothers to husbands and eventually sons. Two of the literary works I examine are set during the Early Modern witch hunts in England and North America respectively. Nell, the adolescent protagonist of Julie Hearn's *The Minister's Daughter,* is a midwife and healer during the English Civil War. Her abilities and independent spirit mark her as a witch in the eyes of the Puritan minister who has recently been assigned to the village church in order to eradicate the old pagan ways. Mary in Celia Rees' Witch Child series also serves as a midwife and a healer. Like Nell, Mary's skills and independence are so intimidating to the Puritan elders of her colonial American village that she is accused of witchcraft and must flee for her life. Libba Bray's Gemma Doyle trilogy is the only historical narrative I examine that is not set during the Early Modern witch hunts. However, Gemma Doyle, an upper-class Victorian girl, lives in a historical period that is also known for its subordination of women. While Bray's heroine does not have to fear being executed for witchcraft, as a woman and a minor in Victorian England, she has few legal rights and can be punished severely for refusing to adhere to her culture's rigid gender roles.

As we have already seen in the female ghost stories I examined in Chapter 1, setting narratives in this historical past allows the author a unique way to illuminate the construction of gender. Setting a work in a place and time that are unfamiliar to the reader denaturalizes recognizable elements of daily life. As a result, the author must explain to the reader how girls in other time periods have limits on their freedom that are unthinkable in the reader's own era. Readers can relate to the frustration these characters experience as a result of these limits, particularly as they are so extreme by contemporary standards. The historical novel in effect invites the reader to compare her own time period to the one being represented, which can eventually show readers how contemporary girls face similar limitations on their freedoms and are coerced into subordinate roles as well.

*The Craft*, the only work that I analyze that is set in contemporary times, depicts the witch as someone who fights a more insidious form of sexism. As modern girls in a first-world country, Sarah and her friends are not in danger of being consigned to a mental institution or executed for practicing witchcraft. Instead, the limits to their autonomy are less visible. In the twentieth and twenty-first centuries, girls are more commonly trained to occupy subordinate gender roles by mass media, which perpetuates impossible norms of femininity that set women up for victimization. This training is constantly reinforced by girls' peers, who police the borders of femininity by ostracizing those who fail to conform to these norms.

One way that girls are ostracized for failing to conform is through being labeled as the "school slut" by their peers. Emily White examines the figure of the school slut in depth, noting that every modern American high school has at least one girl who is cast in this role by her classmates. The school slut is a type of abject Other who is put in this position by peers more due to her inability and sometimes unwillingness to fit into their concept of stereotypical femininity than due to her sexual practices (White 9). Like the witch, the school slut marks the outer limits of conventional femininity, and her treatment by others serves as a warning to every girl of the consequences of stepping outside of her proscribed role. After her first day in her new school, Sarah is labeled a slut by her peers after she refuses to sleep with one of the more popular boys. The school slut as social outcast then is combined with the figure of the witch in *The Craft*, tying this figure in to representations of her as a sexual temptress.

I have broken this chapter into three sections. In the first section, "The Contemporary Witch," I examine how the film *The Craft* represents Wiccan magical practice as something that is empowering to women. This image of the teen witch as a practitioner of Wicca is critical to understanding other representations of her in subsequent sections of this chapter. The second section, "The Witch in the Burning Times," re-imagines the witch as an historical figure with magical powers who practices a sort of proto–Wicca, a modern nature-based religion that emerged in the twentieth century. Early Wicca was based on the writings of scholar Margaret Murray, who claimed that those persecuted for witchcraft were actually the surviving practitioners of a pre–Christian religion that she dubbed "the witch cult."[5] The Witch Child Series and *The Minister's Daughter* are both set in historical periods referred to by some as "The Burning Times," when women accused of witchcraft were burned (or hanged, in some countries). Representing the characters in these novels as our Wiccan foremothers gives Wicca a pedigree that it lacks as a fairly recent faith. "Other Witches," the final section of this chapter, examines a different type of magic represented in The Gemma Doyle trilogy. The Gemma Doyle trilogy is also set in the historical past of Victorian England, a time that is far more romanticized in fiction than Colonial New England or Interregnum England, the settings of The Witch Child series and *The Minister's Daughter* respectively. While Gemma Doyle does not practice Wicca, she is similar to her Wiccan and proto–Wiccan fictional sisters in that her powers are also rooted in nature, and her abilities are nurtured by sisterhood.

## The Contemporary Witch

I begin this chapter with an analysis of the contemporary witch in YA fiction, as she is the figure that is most easily recognizable due to her presence in recent works of popular culture such as television series *Sabrina the Teenage Witch*, *Charmed* and *American Horror Story: Coven*, as well as the film *Beautiful Creatures* and the novel on which it is based.[6] The contemporary witch practices Wicca, a syncretic and nature-based religion that draws upon multiple spiritual traditions. Wicca is similar to American Spiritualism, a religion that flourished from the nineteenth to early twentieth century, in that it is empowering to women. While Spiritualism enabled women to speak publically, both as members of the clergy and as spirit mediums, Wicca is centered on an all-encompassing mother goddess or several goddesses, sometimes in addition to male deities, and positively values the natural world, which is negatively associated with women in most cultures. In the film *The Craft*, the modern teen witch is the embodiment of female empowerment because she positively revalues all that is reviled by patriarchy about nature and women's alleged closer association with it.

The teen witches that I analyze in this chapter are similar to the werewolves I examined in Chapter 2 in how they fall outside the boundaries of their culture's concept of appropriate femininity. Their bodies do not fit ideals of feminine beauty, and they cannot be regulated by the male gaze. Moreover, their paranormal abilities allow them to thwart their peers' attempts to subordinate them. Three of the four protagonists of *The Craft* have been designated as sluts by their classmates at St. Bernadette's because their bodies fall outside of their peers' narrow idea of normative femininity. On Sarah's first day of school, Nancy, Rochelle and Bonnie are pointed out to her by Chris, one of the school's more popular boys, as the "Bitches of Eastwick," an allusion to *The Witches of Eastwick* referring to both their practice of witchcraft and their outsider status in the school. Chris details for Sarah each girl's shortcomings that, within this framework, justify their classification as sluts by their peers. All of the girls are not conventionally feminine because of something about each that cannot easily be changed: Bonnie's body is covered by scars that she conceals with long sleeves and dark tights, Rochelle is the only black girl in the predominantly white school; and Nancy, the leader of the trio, is one of St. Bernadette's few working-class students. So the predominantly white, middle-class student body of St. Bernadette's would never consider girls like Bonnie, Rochelle and Nancy as normatively feminine because their ideal is rooted in a pale skinned and smooth haired model of beauty and middle-class manners and grooming. The girls' outsider status causes each to be classified as a slut by their classmates.

Emily White describes the school slut as an archetype marking the outer limits of appropriate femininity. She is the girl who is different in some way from her female peers — she is non-white in a predominantly white school, she is working-class in a majority middle or upper class student body, she is not conventionally beautiful, she answers back to her tormentors, or she might have even just arrived late in the school year and had difficulty making friends. The school slut is singled out by her more popular peers, and stories about her monstrous sexual appetites circulate, regardless of her actual sexual practices. Nevertheless, her exclusion serves as a warning to others about the dangers of flouting conventions of gender.

Each girl's designation as a slut reveals the workings of the wider category of Other. Chris explains to Sarah that Bonnie, Rochelle and Nancy are sluts because they practice witchcraft. Witchcraft is one way that the three answer back to their tormentors, who are both contemptuous and fearful of the girls' spiritual practices that are so radically different from their own. If we are to accept Chris's explanation at face value, then it would seem that the category of slut is marked by clear boundaries that "normal" people would not dare to cross. In this way, Bonnie, Rochelle and Nancy as Others clearly mark the outer limits of femininity.

However, Sarah's experience on her first day at St. Bernadette's shows that slut is a category with no fixed borders, a revelation that deconstructs the wider category of Other. Soon, she too is labeled as a slut by Chris, one of the school's more popular boys, after she refuses to sleep with him on their first date. The next day, Chris tells his friends that not only did Sarah have sex with him, but she was also an inept partner. His words have the ability to quickly define Sarah as a slut in the eyes of most of her classmates, particularly since she is a newcomer and her peers have no information of their own to counter Chris's negative account of her. Unlike Bonnie, Rochelle and Nancy, Sarah *does* seem to be stereotypically feminine by the standards of St. Bernadette's student body: she is reasonably attractive, upper-middle class, and white. Yet Sarah is quickly designated by Chris as a slut after she refuses to sleep him. If the category of slut was fixed to a girl's sexual practices, then Sarah's refusal to sleep with Chris should ensure that she would never be placed in this category. Yet Chris's popularity gives him the power to brand Sarah as a slut for her refusal. Sarah's rapid slippage into the category of slut exposes how this designation lacks immutable boundaries. Instead, slut is an ephemeral designation that merely reaffirms the normality of those who have not been placed in this category. Sarah's experience of becoming one of the school sluts calls into question the solidity of *all* boundaries separating the normal from the Other. If someone like Sarah can be placed into the category of slut, then perhaps other categories such as those that separate reality from the impossible are equally ill-defined. In this way, the viewer can suspend disbelief in the story's magical elements. Eventually, once the category of the Other has been deconstructed, Sarah is free to "refuse what she is"[7] and re-imagine her subjectivity as someone who can transcend how her peers see her.

So, like the werewolf, the teen witch unsettles others because she exceeds the limits of her restrictive gender role. However, the teen witch is uniquely threatening because her body is not regulated by the male gaze.

## 3. "An ye harm none, do as ye will"

Laura Mulvey defines the male gaze as the overweening perspective of patriarchal culture whereby "woman displayed as sexual object is the leitmotif of erotic spectacle ... she holds the look, plays to and signifies male desire" (33). But the teen witch does not connote the quality of "to-be-looked-at-ness" that Mulvey describes (33). Instead, she returns the male gaze. Stephen Heath sums up the threat implicit in the female gaze in film: "if the woman looks, the spectacle provokes, castration is in the air" (92).

The menace of the female gaze in film is a modern day version of one of the abilities to do supernatural harm that women accused of witchcraft were purported to possess. Women accused of witchcraft were often reputed to be able to cast a spell with a glance, visualizing what they wished to achieve and sometimes giving the "evil eye" to the target of their magic. Alternately, they were accused of being able to cast glamours on others, a type of magic performed by looking directly at the victim and altering his or her perception of reality. Nancy inverts the male gaze when she casts a glamour over Chris as punishment for his scorning her and attempting to rape Sarah. Chris is so disoriented by what he sees after Nancy casts a glamour over him that he falls to his death. Nancy and Sarah both use this ability in the film's conclusion: when the two fight for dominance of the group, they have a magical battle where they disorient one another in order to gain a momentary advantage by casting glamours.

The teen witch's body is also unsettling because it is a *female* body, which connects her to nature and to traits that are negatively associated with femininity. However, this connection is particularly threatening in the body of the contemporary teen witch because these associations are positively revalued in Wicca, a religion rooted in a respect for and understanding of the natural world. In fact, many Wiccans hide their faith from others because of widespread misconceptions that they worship Satan. Sarah's affiliation with nature is emphasized through the circumstances of her birth. She is described as a "natural witch," meaning that she inherited a set of special powers from her mother, also a witch, that her friends do not have. Both Nancy and Sarah can control the weather. Sarah can make it rain, and she is constantly attracting snakes, spiders, rodents and insects, animals viewed as inherently evil in Western culture and often associated with witches as a result. In antiquity, however, serpents were associated with various goddesses, representing their power to heal and prophesize (Eisler 86–69), while spiders are sacred beings in some Native American religions. These ancient associations are recalled in some Wiccan practices in which all creatures are sacred, including those that even many animal lovers find loathsome. Because *The Craft* is about Wicca, the writers are aware of this ancient positive association of serpents with various goddesses as well as more contemporary and better-known associations of snakes with evil.

Nancy's powers are connected to the natural world in a more sinister way where she abuses nature rather than respects it. In order to increase their supernatural abilities, the four perform a ritual near the ocean in which they implore Mano, the male deity worshiped by the coven, to gift them with power. This ritual involves the use of dark magic, and the girls have been warned by Lirio, the older witch who runs the new age book store that they frequent, that their request to Mano is dangerous, particularly since they are novices who will have difficulty controlling what they invoke. Lirio's warning is prophetic: the girls' ritual unleashes so much powerful dark magic that all four are knocked unconscious after they complete their invocation to Mano. Nancy, the first to awaken, is gratified to see that their supplication to Mano has beached several dolphins and even a whale.

The coven's worship of a male deity also merits examination. Wiccans generally venerate a mother goddess, or a combined god and goddess in one or several forms, who personifies the natural world. However, Nancy, the coven's leader, has decided that they will worship the male deity Mano, which foreshadows how she will misuse the magical powers she receives from him. Nancy's abuse of her power is rooted in her underdeveloped way of understanding the world and her role in it. Or put another way, Nancy's paranormal abilities are patriarchal in that she receives them from a male deity, and she uses them to give her power over others, while Sarah's abilities are matriarchal because she inherited them from her mother and uses these gifts to give herself more agency in her life rather than to deprive others of agency. However, when Sarah is momentarily under Nancy's influence, she too will abuse the additional abilities she receives from Mano before she realizes that this use of power is unethical, and ultimately not empowering.

While the teen witch's body is disturbing because it is stubbornly resistant to being trained into a restrictive gender role, her epistemological perspective or "way of knowing," which is intimately connected to her magical powers, is her most empowering quality. Knowing is more than the neutral acquisition of facts from authoritative sources. Rather, it is a dynamic process whereby the knower negotiates her subjectivity. Belenky and her co-authors explore the way that gender mediates how subjects answer questions such as "What is truth? What is authority? To whom do I listen? What counts ... as evidence? How do I know what I know?" (3). Each woman's answers reveal her "basic assumptions about the nature of truth and reality and the origins of knowledge" (Belenky 3), which shape her definition of herself, how she interacts with others, and most importantly, her sense of control over her life.

Belenky and her co-authors identify several ascending ways of knowing and their relationship to subjectivity. These epistemological perspectives range from received knowing, a position where subjects are nearly passive agents for whom knowledge is something situated outside of the self; to subjectivism, where all knowledge is subjective; to constructivism, a position in which subjects are active participants in the formation of knowledge. Developmental psychologists view the shift to constructivism as integral to maturity and autonomy (Belenky 54–55). The subjectivist is similar to the received knower in that both are still rooted in a dualistic way of seeing the world where there are still "right" and "wrong" answers. Instead, what has changed for the subjectivist is the source of these answers: authority is now internal rather than external, a shift that merely reverses the order of the hierarchal structure of knowledge rather than transforms it.

The transition from childhood to adulthood is characterized by the individual's shift from received knowing to constructivism, and teens frequently demonstrate their immaturity whey they persist in viewing the world subjectively. Women's subordinate subjectivity, however, is an impediment to their making this shift at all, or as early as men do. They are encouraged to see themselves as lacking authority due to their sex, which necessitates that they look outside of themselves for knowledge rather than actively participate in its formation.

In the teen witch narrative, the protagonist's developing magical abilities are tied to her transition from subjectivism to constructivism, which gives her a feminist worldview. Constructivism necessitates that the knower abandon a dualistic way of thinking of the world in favor of a more holistic way of seeing it, which makes it a feminist way of viewing the world in that it is anti-hierarchal. Through the constructivist perspective, both women and men can offer useful advice for deciding what is right and true, and both are deserving of equal consideration when deciding on a course of action. The subjectivist perspective, on the other hand, is oppressive for women (and men) in that it is more about controlling others than being aware of one's own agency.

The most emphatic example of how subjectivism oppresses women appears in *The Craft*. At the beginning of the film, Sarah, Bonnie, Rochelle and Nancy are all subjectivists. The girls' practice of Wicca shows how authority has been defrocked in their eyes and supplanted by their own way of knowing the world. Their spellwork, guided by directions found in tomes from the local occult bookstore, is derived from their own intuition, and they do not even seek advice from those more practiced in Wicca such as Lirio. The girls' subjectivism is partially in keeping in Wiccan practice, where there is no central authority: Wiccans are encouraged by one another to rely on their own instincts more than they have been trained to do through their formal educations.[8] Also, because women often come to subjectivism after a crisis of faith in male authorities, they begin to mistrust logic, which is unfairly conflated with oppressive patriarchal authority and so dismissed without a fair hearing. As a result, "although so-called experts may have done more thinking on a subject, subjectivists feel that they don't have to accept what the experts say." Instead, "subjectivist women's own experience and inner voice are the final arbiters" (Belenky 70) for any situation.

At first, subjectivism seems to be a useful epistemological position for the girls: the results of their magical practice appear to be relatively benign and empowering, allowing them to fight back against peers who are bullying them. During the first ritual that the four perform together, each girl implores Mano to grant her a specific gift which she believes will make her stronger. Bonnie wants her scarred body to be beautiful. Rochelle wants revenge against a racist classmate who taunts her about her "nappy" hair. Sarah wants Chris to be in love with her. And Nancy desires to be more powerful. Soon after, three of the girls' wishes are granted. Bonnie's scars are removed by an experimental treatment she undergoes the next day, Chris is so besotted with Sarah that he follows her everywhere, and Rochelle's tormentor begins to lose her own hair. Only Nancy's wish is not fulfilled immediately. She returns home to her family's squalid trailer, altering her situation momentarily

### 3. *"An ye harm none, do as ye will"*

by causing a power surge that plunges the household into darkness, concealing its ugliness. Nancy's wish to be more powerful is a less specific and larger request than what her friends have asked for, and she will have to perform more rituals in order to get what she wants.

Soon it becomes clear that the girls' wishes are selfish because the results merely give them power *over* others. If feminist power is "more about being aware of one's agency than it is about controlling other people" (Trites *Waking* 8), then we see this principle illustrated in how the granting of each girl's wish for power over others does not make her any happier or give her greater control over her life. Bonnie can now revel in her body by dressing in revealing clothing. Secure in her unscarred flesh, she now openly comments on boys' bodies, treating them as sexual objects in a way that is similar to how several of their sex treat young women. However, Bonnie's "new" body does not open her life to more possibilities, but only serves to reinforce her status as one of the school sluts. Rochelle's life is also not improved when her tormentor begins to lose her hair. Rather, Rochelle is ashamed of what she wished for after she finds the girl in the locker room, weeping over her lost locks. And Chris's newfound infatuation with Sarah does not improve her life. Indeed, Sarah has merely inverted the oppressive patriarchal power structure when she places a love spell on Chris that puts him under her complete control. Eventually, this use of power backfires on Sarah when Chris becomes so obsessed with her that he stalks her and eventually tries to rape her. So the results of each girl's wish are the fruits of subjectivism, which is not a feminist way of viewing the world because it merely reproduces the hierarchal power structure that oppresses them rather than transforming these power relations entirely.

Nancy's experiences, however, provide the most powerful illustration of how subjectivism is not ultimately an empowering epistemological perspective. During a solitary ritual, Nancy invokes Mano again, and is possessed by his spirit, giving her tremendous supernatural abilities. However, Nancy abuses these abilities by manipulating others rather than using them to open her life to new possibilities. With her newfound supernatural abilities, Nancy kills her lecherous stepfather and her mother subsequently inherits $175,000 from a life insurance policy she did not know her partner had. The money gives the mother and daughter the trappings of wealth: they move into an exclusive high-rise apartment building and Nancy gets a sports car. Yet Nancy's new abilities and the trappings that come with them do not make her any happier. Rather, as she begins to use her magical powers to manipulate others, she undermines the coven's sisterhood. Previously, the girls' friendship with one another was as empowering as any magic they could perform. The pain of being the school outcasts was minimized when they could depend on one another for support. Now, however, Mano's power enables Nancy to coerce her friends into doing her bidding. We see how Nancy intimidates her friends as they ride in her new car. Nancy speeds and runs traffic lights that she changes from red to green only seconds before passing through the intersection, causing several cars to crash into one another after their drivers must stop short. Bonnie and Rochelle pretend that this car ride is an exhilarating demonstration of Nancy's power. However, they are secretly as terrified as Sarah is by their friend's recklessness. Afterward, Bonnie and Rochelle obey Nancy because they are afraid to cross her. Only Sarah is not cowed by Nancy's powers, in part because she is a natural witch with her own abilities that she inherited from her mother. So when Nancy goes too far by using her powers to kill Chris, Sarah has the strength to leave the coven because she is able to defend herself in a way that Bonnie and Rochelle cannot.

Ultimately Nancy's power is tenuous because it is not rooted in her own strengths. Nancy's magical abilities, derived from the male spirit who has possessed her, replicate the hierarchal patriarchal power structure in which she is embedded rather than transform it. Furthermore, Nancy's manipulation of others exemplifies the fundamental precept of Wicca, the Rule of Three,[9] a variation of the Wiccan Rede which enjoins practitioners to always be mindful of the consequences of their actions, which will return to them three times stronger. In this way, Wicca is also a feminist faith in that it promotes respect for others. Nancy, on the other hand, is heedless of how her actions affect others, which is her undoing at the film's conclusion when she is completely devoid of agency.

Nancy's power is also tenuous because she uses her subjectivist epistemological perspective when deciding how to deploy it. Because subjectivists replace the authority of others with their own narrow perspective of what they believe to be true and right, they merely invert the hierarchal power structure of patriarchy rather than undermine it. As a result, they are not empowered in a lasting way. Lasting empowerment is only possible through constructivism. Belenky and her coauthors observe that constructivist women "insist on a respectful consideration of the particulars of everyone's needs and frailties, even if that means delaying making decisions or taking action" (149). In this way, constructivism could be described as a feminist way of understanding the world in that the knower values multiplicity.

## Agency Through Sisterhood

The teen witch can only be empowered after transforming her relationship with the institutional forces that shape her life. The alternative perspective of constructivism is fostered by sisterhood, something that the teen witch experiences through mentoring by older women and friendship with girls her own age. Sisterhood gives the teen witch access to multiple perspectives from which to consider a problem, as well as the love and support of other women, which emboldens her to challenge authority. Moreover, sisterhood is linked to the teen witch's magical powers and her emerging constructivist perspective. Reid describes magic as it is practiced by Wiccans as holistic in that it is based upon the idea that "everything is connected to everything else by an assortment of material and non-material 'levels'" (158). This is a particularly feminine perspective, exemplifying what Nancy Chodorow describes as characteristic of the basic feminine sense of self whereby women experience themselves as more connected to the world than do men. The teen witch comes to understand that everything and everyone are connected through sisterhood. This realization is tied to her emerging constructivist perspective through which she views the world holistically, considering others before taking action since everything and everyone are linked. From her constructivist point of view, the teen witch discovers that the most empowering use of magic is not to manipulate others for her own personal gain, but to help others, which engenders sisterhood with other women, thereby perpetuating a cycle of female empowerment. As a result of her constructivist perspective, the teen witch is better able to resist a subordinate feminine subjectivity, and her example encourages other women to do likewise.

Sisterhood empowers women in multiple ways. Through sisterhood, women mentor each other and give and receive emotional support. Sisterhood fosters connections among women, enabling them to compare notes about the particulars of their lives and formulate strategies to resist injustice.

Nancy, Rochelle, Bonnie and later Sarah cannot form bonds of sisterhood outside of their small group because their more popular peers have made them into outcasts by designating them as sluts. The potent threat of becoming the school slut is one way by which women's sisterhood is undermined because women become fearful of forming friendships with anyone that their more powerful peers might see as undesirable lest they too be cast in this role and shunned. Still, the four girls' friendship enables them to develop their inherent magical abilities.

We see how magic fosters sisterhood in the beginning of *The Craft*. If Bonnie's, Rochelle's and Nancy's outsider statuses brought them together, then their mutual interest in Wicca cements their friendship. However, their magical abilities are not terribly strong because their specific practice of Wicca requires four people in order to effectively cast a spell: one to call on the powers governing each of the four directions of the compass. Sarah is this needed fourth person. When she joins the group, the girls' friendship and their magical abilities flourish. The connection between sisterhood and magic is apparent when the girls have a sleepover at Sarah's house and play the childhood game "light as a feather, stiff as a board," where participants place their fingers underneath a prone member of the group and lift her into the air. Supposedly this task can only be accomplished if all participating can convince themselves that the prone person is indeed light as a feather and stiff as a board. But in this instance, the girls' collective efforts become magical: they lift Rochelle, who remains suspended in the air as each girl withdraws her hands. In this instance, Rochelle is literally held aloft by the love of her friends.

However, Sarah and her friends' early use of magic does not lead to feminist power because it is used to harm others. After they are buoyed by their success at levitating Rochelle, the four then cast a spell on Laura, Rochelle's racist tormentor, in fulfillment of the wish that Rochelle made during their first ritual. As part of the spell, Bonnie, Nancy and Sarah weave into Rochelle's locks a strand of Laura's hair. This scene replicates the hair-play that girls often engage in during slumber parties, further emphasizing the connection between their magical abilities and their friendship. Yet this scene also bodes ill for their friendship because the girls' newfound magical abilities come at the expense of others, as we see when Laura is devastated by her baldness.

### 3. "An ye harm none, do as ye will"

The friendship among the four girls rapidly deteriorates after Nancy uses the power she received from Mano to manipulate others. Sisterhood is a relationship that encourages sharing and caring, which mutually benefits the participants. Nancy's use of her abilities to intimidate her friends ultimately destroys their relationship. In the film's denouement, Nancy leads Bonnie and Rochelle in an attack on Sarah in retaliation for her leaving the coven. Sarah's superior magical abilities allow her to defeat Nancy, who ends up in mental institution. Afterwards, Sarah can no longer continue her friendship with Bonnie and Rochelle because they betrayed her when they participated in the attack instead of standing up to Nancy.

Unlike Nancy, Bonnie and Rochelle, Sarah develops spiritually and intellectually so that in the film's conclusion, she has transformed into a skilled witch whose constructivist epistemological position will allow her to use her abilities in ways that are truly liberating. While female friendship fortifies the teen witch in multiple ways, she must develop the strength of her will in order to be able to perform magic. She hones this strength in part by rejecting subjectivism and considering the perspectives of others. When Nancy plans on leading the coven in invoking the presence of Mano, the four venture to Lirio's new age book store to purchase supplies for the ritual. Only Sarah asks for advice, evidence of her emerging constructivism. Lirio encourages the girls to consider the complexity of their actions when she tells them that "true magic is neither black nor white," but "both because nature is both" and that "the only good or bad is in the heart of the witch." Nancy, Bonnie and Rochelle snicker at this advice, while Sarah listens, because she too is beginning to appreciate the complex ramifications of her actions. Sarah turns to Lirio for advice again when she needs help defending herself against her three former friends, who have begun to use magic against her. Lirio encourages Sarah's constructivism by advising her that when she is afraid, she should listen to the voice of her departed mother, who is always with her and telling her daughter to be strong. In this way, Lirio helps Sarah tap into an intergenerational sisterhood that she can come to for advice in order to formulate a holistic course of action.

With the encouragement of Lirio, Sarah is able to confidently tap into the same powerful magic to defend herself that Nancy has misused. Lirio counsels Sarah to invoke the spirit of Mano in order to defend herself against Nancy. When Sarah objects to this plan of action because this invocation claimed Nancy's sanity, Lirio tells her that she will be safe if she does not let the magic take her to a dark place. Presumably, the dark place that Nancy let the magic take her to is one where she is isolated from the perspectives of others, which keeps her mired in subjectivism. When Sarah eventually invokes Mano, she also calls upon the Guardians of the North as she always has in rituals that she has performed with the coven. The Guardians of the North are connected to the element of earth and the mother goddess, and so Sarah's invocation of them gives a feminine balance to the masculine power of Mano that will encourage her to use this power in a holistic way that is more in keeping with the fundamental precepts of Wicca. Once Sarah has invoked Mano, Sarah appeals to the three-fold law, which returns her tormentors' evil actions to them. Bonnie is glamoured into seeing her face covered in the scars that once marred her back and arms, while Rochelle imagines that she has been deformed by the alopecia that she wished on Laura. Sarah then uses the power of Mano to subdue Nancy: she binds her former friend from harming herself or others rather than retaliates.

Because Sarah has carefully considered the needs and frailties of others when deciding on a course of action, she can refuse the subordinate feminine subject position that girls in the twenty-first century are still being groomed to occupy. Sarah's faith in sisterhood causes her to reject the sexual politics of girlfighting, which she demonstrates through her refusal to retaliate against her former friends for trying to kill her. Girlfighting, after all, gets girls to do the work of patriarchy through perpetuating petty quarrels that maintain persistent divisions among women. Unlike Nancy, Sarah still believes in the power of sisterhood (although she can no longer trust her former coven members). As a constructivist, Sarah's magical abilities will continue to strengthen, and she will have bonds of sisterhood with other women in the future given how she has conducted herself with her former friends.

## The Witch in the Burning Times

In this section, I consider representations of the teen witch that are set in what is sometimes called The Burning Times, which roughly refers to the historical period in Early Modern Europe and in Colonial America

## 3. "An ye harm none, do as ye will"

between 1480 and 1750 when women (and sometimes men) accused of witchcraft were burned or hanged. *The Minister's Daughter* and The Witch Child series are both set in this era. In *The Minister's Daughter*, the protagonist Nell is persecuted for sorcery in England five years prior to the Interregnum, just before the regicide of Charles I. In the novel's conclusion, Nell's two accusers, daughters of the intolerant village minister, leave for Salem, Massachusetts, where fifty years later, the younger sister will be charged with being a witch. The Witch Child series also opens in England during the Interregnum: after Mary's grandmother and guardian is hanged for witchcraft, the girl's benefactor sends her to Colonial America, believing that she will be free of persecution in the New World. Instead, Mary is the subject of more intense scrutiny by the Puritan authorities, and she must eventually flee for her life after she is accused of witchcraft by her fellow colonists.

Nell and Mary, the protagonists of *The Minister's Daughter* and the Witch Child series, have more difficulty remaining within the parameters of acceptable femininity than do Sarah and her friends in *The Craft*, in part because their cultures required that they adhere to gender roles that were far more restrictive than modern ones. Mary's and Nell's sexualities are not limited by the bounds of matrimony and monogamy. Mary falls in love with a man of a different race, while Nell is not interested in having a relationship with a man (or a woman). Because her body and her sexuality are not easily mastered, the teen witch is often the focus of what Michel Foucault describes as "correct training," a type of bodily discipline which aims to systematically master her unruly flesh and rebellious spirit. Yet the teen witch, with her magical abilities and constructivist epistemological perspective, can resist the subordinate subject position that correct training attempts to prepare her to occupy.

In *The Minister's Daughter* and the Witch Child series, both Nell's and Mary's lineage suggest that they will not be controlled by their culture's strict rules governing female sexuality. Both girls are born out of wedlock, evidence that their mothers' sexualities could not be contained within the bounds of marriage. In *Sorceress*, the second book in the Witch Child series, Mary weds Jaybird, a Native-American youth. Her relationship with Jaybird runs counter to the Puritan narrative about Native-Americans, whom they viewed as more closely affiliated with nature than whites, and therefore, diabolical. Mary's relationship with Jaybird also contradicts captivity narratives, in which Native Americans are represented as sexually predatory savages looking for opportunities to capture and despoil white women. Mary's love for Jaybird undermines the stereotype of Native Americans as subhuman and hypersexual.

Nell's lineage as a result of her birth is simultaneously unsettling and empowering. Nell is a merrybegot, someone conceived during the village's annual May Day revels, during which men and women freely couple regardless of their marital bonds. As a result, Nell has never really known her mother or her father, as they were not married to one another and both died soon after she was born. Nell is raised by her paternal grandmother, the village cunning woman to whom Nell is now apprenticed. Merrybegots are sacred to the Powers, the amorphous supernatural force revered by those who follow the old pagan ways. Nell's connection to the Powers endows her with unique supernatural abilities that will make her a gifted cunning woman. As a merrybegot, Nell is also the opposite of a bastard, a stigmatized child who is pitiable because she has no claim to her father's wealth. Instead, Nell's parentage makes her even more valued by those villagers who still adhere to the old pagan beliefs in spite of the recent arrival of Puritan clergy in their community; these community members understand that the conditions of her birth give her a superior level of skill as a healer. Nevertheless, both Mary's and Nell's lack of a legal father makes them suspect to their community's Puritan elders for whom the patriarchal family is an indispensible tool used to maintain religious and social order. Nell's unique abilities will enable her to have an independent place in any community that appreciates her skills as a healer and midwife. As a result, the adult Nell will not be easily contained through patriarchal institutions as she has no need to marry in order to be provided for. Instead, Nell can be free of the direct control of a husband, something that the Reverend Madden and his co-religionists in the village find intolerable since she might offer other women a dangerous example of female freedom and independence.

Additionally, Nell and Mary are menacing because they are not contained by the male gaze. Nell cares so little about the male gaze that she expends no effort grooming or displaying herself in ways that men might find pleasing. And Mary, who can cast glamours just as Sarah and Nancy do in *The Craft*, returns the male gaze through this ability. In *Sorceress*, the second novel in the Witch Child series, Mary thwarts a man's attempt to rape her by casting a glamour over him, causing him to see her as a wolf rather than a woman so that he becomes too terrified by what he sees to continue his assault.

While Nell and Mary are perceived as unsettling by others because they are not easily controlled by patriarchal institutions, their relationships with the natural world are also threatening. Hearn and Rees represent Nell and Mary as practicing a type of proto–Wicca where magic is tied to the natural world in the way that it is in *The Craft*. Both girls wander the woods in search of herbs they can use to perform magic and to heal. In *The Minister's Daughter*, the "old ways" that are celebrated in May Day and Twelfth Night rituals that revolved around the worship of nature have been forced underground by the Reverend Madden and his co-religionists who view the natural world as a diabolic force to be mastered by the godly. And in *Witch Child*, Mary is condemned by the Reverend Johnson for walking in the woods, a place he and his fellow Puritans view as teeming with savages who are waiting to murder Christians. Nell's and Mary's affiliations with the natural world are underscored through the circumstances of their births outside of wedlock, and for Nell, as a Merrybegot.

## Correct Training Through Surveillance of the Teen Girls' Body

Because the teen witch's body and sexuality defies proscribed boundaries of normative femininity, it is frequently the focus of correct training, a disciplinary technique whose chief function is "to 'train' [the body] ... to select and levy all the more" (Foucault *Discipline* 170) in order to increase its utility to those who control it. One mechanism by which correct training is accomplished is through surveillance. Disciplinary power functions through a mechanism of "compulsory visibility" in which subjects have to be seen, or more importantly still, know that there is a possibility that they can be seen. "It is the fact of being constantly seen, of being able always to be seen, that maintains the disciplined individual in his subjection" because "[t]heir visibility assures the hold of the power that is exercised over them" (Foucault *Discipline* 187).

As an apprentice midwife, Nell knows that she is always subject to scrutiny by the older women in the community that she calls "the Watchers," who "know best — or think they do" and who "gather, as a matter of course, at every birth and death within walking distance" and who control others through their willingness to be involved in even the most intimate interactions in the village and subsequently spread gossip about what they have seen in order to manipulate public opinion. So because the Watchers are always looking, or can always be looking, Nell knows to carefully regulate her actions so as to avoid scrutiny, since her ability to make a living as a midwife will depend on her reputation in the village, which can be destroyed in the blink of an eye if there are complications during a birth and the Watchers decide that the problems were due to her own incompetence.

The level of scrutiny that Nell is subjected to increases when the Reverend Madden comes to the village. The Reverend Madden has been appointed by the state to serve as the community's spiritual leader, and so he has an authority that the Watchers lack. He can, for example, have villagers whipped for offenses as trifling as insolence. The Reverend Madden controls his parishioners by keeping them under surveillance. When Nell first comes to the Reverend Madden's attention, he warns her that he "has his eye on her," and good to his word, he is constantly observing her for evidence of her sinfulness that requires correction. On Beltane morning, the Reverend Madden patrols the village at dawn in search of frolickers who are in defiance of the Puritans' prohibition of the traditional May first celebrations, which are viewed by the new political order as ungodly. When the Reverend Madden sees Nell gathering herbs on this morning, he assumes that she has been participating in the illegal festivities, so he later singles her out in church as a fornicator.

Mandatory church attendance for all villagers is another way of subjecting them to scrutiny. The Reverend Madden's preaching is calculated to prompt his congregants to see their behaviors through his eyes and regulate them accordingly. So, for example, when the Reverend Madden holds up a looking glass during one of his sermons in which he fulminates about the vanity of women, he is directing his female parishioners to view themselves as spiritually ugly and steeped in sin any time they attempt to view their reflection in a shiny surface with the end goal that they will now only look to authorities such as himself for confirmation of their worth. So in this way, church is a part of the correct training of the body, and the Reverend Madden's scrutiny is a variety of the male gaze through which women's bodies are regulated.

Mary is similarly subjected to the surveillance of religious authorities in *Witch Child*. The Reverend Johnson takes her to task for her ramblings in the woods where she gathers herbs to use for healing others because the forest beyond the village is supposedly a godless space teeming with savages. However, the Reverend Johnson's real objection to her walks seems to be because Mary is more difficult to keep under surveillance when she is in the woods. The Reverend Johnson becomes uncomfortable with Mary's living arrangements for a similar reason. Mary lives in a household with three other people who are unrelated to her: an older woman and an older man and his teenage son. As there are no older male relatives in this household who would presumably have the authority to control her, the Reverend Johnson forces Mary to move in with a more traditional family unit and work as their servant so that they can better coach her in her subordinate gender role.

## *The Perils of Subjectivism*

While the teen witch's comparatively unregulated body is unsettling, the most threatening aspect is her constructivist epistemological perspective, which enables her to resist restrictive gender roles as well as encourage other women to do likewise. As I noted in the previous section of this chapter, the witch's constructivist way of knowing is interwoven with her magical powers. In *The Minister's Daughter* and Witch Child series, Nell and Mary are constructivists before the narratives begin. The perils of subjectivism are illustrated by Nell's and Mary's teen antagonists, Grace Madden, the minister's eldest daughter (*The Minister's Daughter*), and Deborah Vane (*Witch Child*).

Both Grace and Deborah bristle at the restrictive gender roles that they are compelled by law to adhere to in their Puritan communities. Though both girls come from backgrounds of relative privilege, each is required to show her piety through extreme subordination to her male kin and to the clergy, something that they accomplish by pretending to be in the received knowledge stage of development, where all knowledge comes from outside of the self and so the knower always consults with outside authority before deciding on a course of action. Because Grace and Deborah do not openly defy authority, the religious leaders of their respective communities view them as received knowers whose apparent subordination is evidence of their piety and acceptance of their restrictive gender roles. Nevertheless, both Grace and Deborah are subjectivists whose rebellious behavior is a symptom of how authority has been defrocked in their eyes and replaced by their own ideas about what is right and true. Grace rebels by sneaking out of the house at night to tryst with Sam Towser, the blacksmith's son, while Deborah yearns for a life that offers her more interesting possibilities than continually praying, going to church, and performing housework.

Not surprisingly, few women in Grace's and Nell's communities articulate their discontent, since doing so would be viewed as outright rebellion and would bring about severe repercussions. Grace and Deborah rebel against their restrictive gender roles without being punished by pretending to be ensorcelled. Historian Carol Karlsen describes how in the seventeenth century, claiming to be possessed by a witch was simultaneously "a ritual expression of Puritan belief" and "an oblique challenge to both religious and social norms" (244). Pretending to be bewitched is an expression of Puritan belief because the claimant's behavior "proves" the existence of witches, who for Puritans were women who had been granted dangerous supernatural abilities by consorting with the devil. Because the Puritans viewed women as inferior to men in all ways, and therefore more easily tricked by Satan, they were more likely than men to become witches. The existence of witches then justifies the extreme subordination of women by men. But pretending to be bewitched is also an oblique challenge to both religious and social norms in that the alleged victim of black magic can behave in ways that would otherwise be unacceptable. Bewitched girls screamed in church and rolled on the ground, causing a disturbance in a public place where they were normally not permitted to even speak. The girl who claimed ensorcellment was also the center of attention in a way that was contrary to how she was more typically required to recede into the background in order to demonstrate her modesty and piety. In this way, the girl who says that she is possessed by a witch is similar to the haunted girls who are spirit mediums: both bewitchment and mediumship permit the claimant to express what would be prohibited to her sex under other circumstances.

## 3. "An ye harm none, do as ye will"

Grace's and Deborah's claims of bewitchment momentarily liberate them from narrow gender roles while at the same time affirming the tenets of their fathers' faiths. When Grace discovers that the blacksmith's son has gotten her pregnant, she blames Nell for her condition by claiming that the girl has diabolic powers that she has learned as the cunning woman's apprentice, and used these abilities to impregnate her with the Devil's seed. This story positions Grace as a received knower, with a childlike understanding of the world dictated by the truths she has been given by those in authority such as her minister father. So, while Grace's gravid body defies social norms that stigmatize out-of-wedlock pregnancy, her explanation for her condition affirms Puritan beliefs that women are inherently weak: either their flesh is susceptible to being invaded by evil forces or they are so mentally feeble that Satan can easily convince them to do his bidding. Moreover, Grace's explanation for her pregnancy makes it appear that she is well within her subordinate gender role since according to her story, she was not doing anything sinful when she became pregnant. As a result, Grace's improbable explanation for her pregnancy exculpates her.

Deborah Vane's claim of ensorcellment similarly permits her to perform feelings she cannot publicly own while also upholding her community's religious beliefs. Deborah and her friends are frustrated by their powerlessness in their extremely patriarchal Puritan village, where they are permitted virtually no type of self-expression. Dancing and singing are not allowed, clothing must be uniformly bland and functional, and speaking during the community's many religious activities is forbidden to their sex. Desperate to express themselves in some way, Deborah and her friends meet away from prying eyes and pretend to be witches. Their interpretation of the figure of the witch involves dancing in the nude and chanting, something that Mary, who is an actual witch, never does. The girls' characterization of the witch is in keeping with their culture's concept of this figure and also symbolizes a female freedom and power that is demonized by the Puritan elders. Eventually the girls are caught cavorting naked in a neighbor's barn. To avoid punishment, Deborah convinces her friends to assert that they are not witches, but instead, bewitched. They buttress their claim of bewitchment by continuing to behave as if they are possessed while in church, disrupting the services with giggling and screaming fits. Performing as possessed allows Deborah and her friends to appear conventionally feminine while protesting this restrictive subject position. As Karlsen describes, the woman who claimed to be possessed "could assert the witch within [and] rebel against the many restrictions placed upon" (247) her. Such an assertion allowed a woman to express "her *desire for* the independence and power embodied in the symbol of the witch and her rage at the man who taught her that independence and power were the ultimate female evils" (Karlsen 247).

However, claiming to be possessed by a witch is ultimately not an empowering strategy for women in the way that mediumship is. The haunted girls that I examined in Chapter 1 are in subject positions similar to that inhabited by nineteenth century Spiritualist mediums. Ann Braude's history of the American Spiritualist Movement explains how mediumship enabled nineteenth century women to become sources of spiritual truth and assume the authority of religious leaders while the spirits spoke through them (84) without seeming to step outside of their gender role. The medium could speak persuasively in public, something that in the nineteenth century, women were not believed capable of doing. Moreover, the medium could advocate for abolition or women's rights in this pose, because *she* was not really speaking: rather, the spirit was communicating *through* her. Possession by a ghost is similarly empowering for the haunted girl characters I examined in Chapter 1 as the spirit can reacquaint them with knowledge that they have long repressed which they can use to have more agency in their lives. The girl who claims ensorcellment, on the other hand, experiences only a momentary freedom from her restrictive gender role. This is because belief in diabolic possession reinforces rather than challenges her culture's hierarchal power structure, whose linchpin is extreme feminine subordination. As a consequence, the girl who claims ensorcellment must return to her restrictive gender role once those she accuses of possessing her are brought to justice.

Eventually, claiming to be bewitched further imprisons each girl within her very narrow gender role. In *The Minister's Daughter*, Grace's claim that she has been ensorcelled deprives her of what little freedom she had before making her accusation. Pretending to be bewitched does enable Grace to avoid punishment for her out-of-wedlock pregnancy. However, Grace's mobility is further restricted by her story. When the Reverend Madden learns of his daughter's condition, he confines her to her room for the duration of her pregnancy while gathering evidence that Nell has bewitched his child. While the Reverend Madden will publically declare that Grace is the victim of the cunning woman's granddaughter's sorcery, he also understands that even his co-religionists in the village will be hard-pressed to view his daughter's pregnancy as the work of Satan. As a result, he keeps Grace's thickening form out of public view so that it is easier for the villagers to believe his daughter's improbable claim. In *Witch Child*, Deborah Vane's claim of ensorcellment gives her a freedom of expression denied to her under ordinary circumstances. Yet Deborah must eventually name her tormentor. After Deborah identifies Mary as the one who has bewitched her, Mary flees Beulah to avoid being executed. As a result, Deborah can no longer claim that she is under Mary's influence and has to return to her role as a silent and submissive Puritan woman.

Grace's and Deborah's claims that they are bewitched also highlight the wider perils of subjectivism. Neither girl genuinely believes that she has been possessed by a witch. Instead, both accuse others of witchcraft as a way of asserting their own way of viewing the world. One of the ways that subjectivism differs from constructivism is in how the subjectivist does not consider the frailties and needs of others before deciding on a course of action. And in some instances, the subjectivist is indifferent or even hostile to the needs of others. Both Grace and Deborah know that their false accusations will lead to Nell's and Mary's executions. Their callousness derives from their subjective way of viewing the world, where they view their own desire to avoid punishment or to have a little freedom as more important than someone else's life.

The Reverend Madden in *The Minister's Daughter* and the Reverend Johnson in *Witch Child* can also be described as subjectivists in that they interpret scripture in a way that preserves their power over others rather than in a manner that shows genuine concern for their parishioners' salvation. Each man's scriptural justification of witch hunting augments his power over his congregation. To avoid the appearance of lawlessness, witch hunts were conducted under specific rules that included gathering evidence of diabolic influence. As ministers, each man has a unique authority in determining what ordinary events were allegedly infernally engineered. Yet only men of the cloth and witchfinders such as Matthew Hopkins,[10] who is employed by the Reverend Madden, have the authority to adduce whether or not commonplace occurrences such as the sickening of a child or the curdling of a jug of milk are the work of witches. When only a few are qualified to determine what is factual, everyone else is positioned as a received knower who is wholly dependent on outside authority to determine a course of action.

So here too, because subjectivists replace the authority of others with their own narrow perspective of what they believe to be true and right, they merely invert the hierarchal power structure of patriarchy rather than undermine it. As a result, they are not empowered in a lasting way. Lasting empowerment is only possible through constructivism, which is a feminist epistemological perspective because knowledge is formed through considering the needs and frailties of others. This holistic way of knowing the world does not reproduce patriarchal power structures because it is anti-hierarchal.

## *Female Agency Through Literacy*

Constructivism is at the heart of the teen witch's power. Her holistic view of the world is linked to the strength of her will and ability to perform magic. The teen witch hones this strength in part through getting to know herself better. Mary develops some of this self-knowledge through literacy, which she has in common with some of the haunted girls in Chapter 1. Both reading and writing enable the knower to synthesize the perspectives of others along with her own insights. In this way, literacy is also a tool that enables the user to develop a constructivist way of understanding the world. In fact, magic is intimately connected to literacy: spells are most often dependent on precise language, while potions are concocted through strict adherence to recipes. And the words "grammar" and "glamour" once both referred to the power to charm.

Mary comes to know herself better through writing. Mary's story in *Witch Child* is told through her diary, a private space where she can contemplate her baffling magical abilities that, if certain members of her community were to learn about, would be cause to execute her for witchcraft. For this reason, Mary is careful to hide her diary by sewing it in between the layers of a quilt that she makes. But even if Mary had not written about her magical abilities in her diary, she is wise to hide this document anyway because the Reverend Johnson and his congregants are suspicious of female

### 3. "An ye harm none, do as ye will"

literacy. The religious leaders of her village equate female literacy with evil because reading and writing have the potential to encourage independent thinking. Therefore, the Reverend Johnson is wary of Mary after learning that she can read and write both English and Latin. Later, one of the community gossips objects to Mary's living with Jonas and Martha, an elderly couple who are not married or related to her, because Mary is transcribing Jonas's book instead of performing the usual domestic tasks that are relegated to women in their community. The community gossip, an illiterate woman herself, asserts that "inky fingers on a girl are far from natural" (Rees 169). These attitudes prompt Mary to conceal her diary by sewing its pages inside of a quilt that will eventually be found by Alison Ellman, a twentieth century anthropologist who comes into possession of the textile. Literacy is also powerful because it allows for communication through time. Mary will finally have some of the voice she was denied in life when Alison publishes the diary as *The Mary Papers*, the fictional manuscript at the heart of *Witch Child* and *Sorceress*.

*The Mary Papers* encourages its actual and fictional audiences to develop knowledge of themselves through literacy. In *Witch Child*, *The Mary Papers* conclude with a note from Alison asking readers with further information about the people in this account to contact her, as she is desirous of continuing her research (Rees *Witch* 261). Alison receives a reply in *Sorceress*. Agnes Hearn, a Native-American university student, recognizes Mary's story as one her Aunt Miriam has told her about an ancestor. Agnes contacts Alison with the intent of putting her in touch with Aunt Miriam. Instead, when Agnes returns home to broker a meeting between the two women, Miriam, a tribal shaman, puts Agnes in a trance during which she channels Mary to learn what happened to her after she left the Puritan village and married into one of the Native-American cultures. This channeled narrative is the main story in *Sorceress*.

Agnes is similar to the haunted girls I discussed in Chapter 1 because she is also channeling a spirit. Like most adolescents, Agnes is struggling to know herself well enough to understand how she can make a meaningful contribution to the world. After Agnes emerges from her spirit trance, she is initially disappointed because she feels "bereft and even more lost than she did before" (Rees *Sorceress* 309) rather than a sense of closure. Aunt Miriam, however, helps Agnes put her experience into context. She likens

Mary's story to one of the beads on a wampum belt, an article of clothing that does not represent an individual's wealth, as many white people erroneously believed, but instead carries the tribe's history and law. Each bead of the wampum belt is significant, yet meaningless outside of the context of the whole. Miriam sees Mary's story as one bead on a metaphorical wampum belt representing Agnes's life: "Mary, the people in her life, the folk Alison has found out about, Alison herself—we're like the beads on this belt. Look at us apart and you can't tell a lot. But put us together and then you can read the whole story" (Rees *Sorceress* 310). In this way, Mary's spirit has helped Agnes know herself well enough so that she can decide how she will fit into the world. Additionally, the meta-fictional structure of The Witch Child series encourages the reader to contemplate how she too fits into the world.

While the witch must have some innate magical abilities, she can only perform effective transformative magic after she sees the world through a constructivist perspective. This perspective helps her realize that because everything is connected, her actions can have profound unforeseen consequences if they are not carefully considered beforehand.

## *A Constructivist Narrative*

Nell's emerging constructivist perspective is fully explored in *The Minister's Daughter*. The structure of *The Minister's Daughter* emphasizes how this perspective is developed dialogically. Unlike most Young Adult novels, *The Minister's Daughter* is not a first-person narrative. Instead, it is a frame tale told by a now elderly Patience Madden, Grace's dim-witted younger sister who remembers how her father and sibling fabricated evidence against Nell. Patience recounts this story to the court in Salem, Massachusetts fifty years later in order to defend herself against an accusation of witchcraft by levying the charge at her sister Grace. Yet Patience's narrative is not related wholly through her perspective. Instead her story fades into an omniscient third-person voice through which multiple characters view the same events in profoundly different ways — Nell's magical, pagan perspective and Patience's fearful Puritan way of seeing things. For instance, the night that Nell is taken away by a fairy on a black horse to deliver the Fairy Queen's baby is

### 3. "An ye harm none, do as ye will"

narrated through both Nell's pagan way of seeing the world and Patience's Puritan perspective. In Nell's account, the horse and its rider are a wondrous part of the supernatural world as experienced by those who follow the Old Ways, but in Patience's account, the same horse and rider are the devil, who has come to dupe a willing village maid.

Nell's emerging constructivism is also linked to the alternative education she received from her grandmother, who mentored her in the healing arts. When Nell's grandmother is still alive, Nell is called upon with increasing frequency to do the curing and spellwork that allow them to earn a living. Nell can no longer dependably turn to her grandmother for help because the old woman suffers from dementia, so she often forgets the complicated spells and recipes that are part of the healer's art. Neither woman is literate, so Nell's grandmother can only transmit her wisdom orally. Thus, if Nell cannot remember a spell or recipe and is unable to consult her grandmother, she must draw upon multiple perspectives of others in order to decide what to do.

The most powerful example of Nell's emerging constructivism is her handling of Grace Madden's request for an abortion. When Grace realizes that she is pregnant, she visits Nell and her grandmother for a tonic to end her pregnancy so that her father will not learn of her dalliance with the blacksmith's son. Nell and her grandmother are not opposed to abortion on principle and have helped many women end their pregnancies with an abortifacient tonic they concoct. However, because Grace got pregnant during the May Day frolicking, her fetus is a merrybegot who is sacred to the Powers. For this reason, Nell tells Grace she cannot give her an abortion, as doing so would be an affront to the Powers, though she promises to help Grace through her pregnancy and labor. Nell's refusal to help Grace terminate her pregnancy prompts the minister's daughter to publicly accuse the girl of being a witch.

At first, it might appear that Nell's refusal is borne of subjectivism — while Nell may believe that it is wrong to end this pregnancy, Grace does not feel this way, and so it seems like Nell's refusal is rooted in her own subjective way of viewing the world. However, the reader sees Nell carefully considering the perspectives of others, weighing the advice her grandmother would give along with how it must feel to be in Grace's position, before making her decision. While constructivists carefully consider the perspectives of others before arriving at a decision, they do not always choose a course of action that would make others happy.

## *A Constructivist Practice*

Mary's emerging constructivism is implied in *Witch Child* through her becoming an independent thinker while she practices her healing arts. Though Mary's mentor Martha knows a good deal about herbs, she lacks Mary's considerable midwifery skills. Because each pregnancy presents a unique set of challenges that requires the midwife to adapt her technique, when Mary is called upon to help women in childbirth, she must combine what she learned from her deceased grandmother with what others have taught her in order to decide how to approach each birth.

Eventually each girl learns enough about herself to hone the strength of her will in order to perform powerful transformative magic. Yet she initially uses this magic to transform others rather than herself. This use of magic is in keeping with Wiccan spiritual practices. A perusal of neo–Pagan literature indicates that neo–Pagan witchcraft "is usually not directed towards immediate personal material gain" (Reid 157), but is instead worked for the benefit of others. Constructivist women are similar to neo–Pagans in how they too tend to employ their will in the service of empowering and improving the quality of life in others (Belenky 152). Helping others engenders sisterhood (and brotherhood, in some instances), which makes it difficult to keep the teen witch in her subordinate gender role. In this way, the teen witch, with her constructivist epistemological perspective, is especially threatening to the status quo. The strength of her will makes her resistant to patriarchal control, and her example is threatening to patriarchy in that it encourages other women to similarly resist being controlled. Moreover, sisterhood gives the teen witch a social capital she can draw on for help with situations that exceed her magical abilities.

As healers, Mary and Nell both use their magic to help others more than themselves. Nell's selflessness ultimately permits her to be relatively autonomous. When Nell finds a dying soldier who is a stranger to her, she uses her most powerful and valuable magical object, the fairy placenta that she received as payment for delivering the Fairy Queen's baby, to save his life. This object can heal any injury, but can only be used once, so Nell's decision to help a stranger with it reveals the depths of her selflessness. The man that Nell saves is Bonny Prince Charlie in disguise, who has returned to his country in order to assist those who are trying to subdue Oliver Cromwell's soldiers, and who will eventually execute the prince's father King Charles I as part of their revolution. As repayment for her good deed, Prince Charles will later rescue Nell from the gallows just as she is to be hanged for witchcraft, and gift her with a cottage by the sea where she lives out her days healing all who seek her assistance. While Nell is dependent on the king's continued good will in order to live this life, she is more autonomous than she might be if she had married or remained single and had no one to protect her from harassment.

## *The Necessity of Sisterhood*

Both Nell and Mary attempt to nurture their abilities through sisterhood, but each girl's community makes that difficult. For Nell and Mary in *The Minister's Daughter* and *Witch Child*, the persecution of women for witchcraft fosters a hostile climate that similarly works to undermine sisterhood. During the Early Modern Witch Hunts, women accused of witchcraft were often tortured into naming other women as their accomplices. Historian Anne Barstow observes that as a consequence of this practice, women had difficulty trusting "other women, for what woman might not be called up before the judge and start blabbing?" (148). In fact, the climate of distrust between women that pervaded the Early Modern witch hunts fostered girlfighting, the relational aggression between women that ultimately does the work of patriarchy by keeping women separated from one another and "in their place." Grace's and Deborah's accusations of witchcraft against Nell and Mary are a variety of girlfighting in that their claims also serve to police the borders of femininity, marking its outer limits. The witch, after all, is the antithesis of all that is appropriately feminine.

Yet in spite of impediments to sisterhood, the women in these texts have meaningful relationships with members of their sex. These relationships enable the teen witch to develop her inherent magical abilities. All participate in a limited mentoring relationship with older women who help them better understand their paranormal abilities. In *The Minister's Daughter* and the

Witch Child series, the successful healer must do more than merely master a set of skills in order to practice her craft. Instead, to heal she must develop her innate magical ability. For that reason, Nell and Mary are apprenticed to older cunning women who mentor them so that each girl can better understand and control her unique abilities.

Nell's willingness to help others also encourages sisterhood. Mistress Bramlow, a woman who Nell and her grandmother helped through a difficult childbirth, feels so indebted to both that she stands up for each woman as she is accused of witchcraft. When the villagers dunk Nell's grandmother in the pond to ascertain whether or not she is a witch, the old woman dies from the trauma of the trial. Afterwards, Mistress Bramlow shames the villagers into bringing food to the now-orphaned Nell, whose grandmother was proven innocent by her sad death, as she was unable to summon any supernatural forces to save her life when it was in peril. Later, as Nell is led to the gallows, Mistress Bramlow risks punishment to sneak the girl a pack of powerful narcotic herbs that she can ingest so as to be insensible during her execution.

Sisterhood has a powerful transformative effect on Mistress Bramlow, eventually emboldening her to refuse the subordinate position that the Reverend Madden tries to impose on his congregants. When Grace gives birth, the Reverend Madden directs his housekeeper to leave the infant in the snow outside of the village, where it will die of exposure and not be easily connected to his household. However, because the baby is a merrybegot, it is protected by the Powers, who lead Mistress Bramlow to find and rescue it. Mistress Bramlow knew all along that Grace's diabolic pregnancy was a ridiculous ruse, and realizes that the baby she has just found buried in the snow must be the minister's grandchild. Mistress Bramlow visits the minister after finding the infant, ostensibly to make arrangements for the supposedly parentless child's baptism so she can formally adopt him. However, bringing the newborn's attention to the Reverend Madden is also a powerful act of defiance. When Mistress Bramlow asks the minister to baptize the child, she is also confronting him with the evidence of his attempted infanticide without directly accusing him of this crime. Mistress Bramlow's actions question the Reverend Madden's claim of moral superiority that is the foundation of his authority as a minister.

Mary's skills as a witch and a healer also allow her to develop powerful

### 3. "An ye harm none, do as ye will"

bonds of sisterhood with other women. In *Witch Child*, witches have a bond with one another that encourages them to help their sisters, through stealth if necessary. The novel opens in England as Mary's grandmother is seized by the local Puritan authorities, who have accused her of witchcraft and hang her without a trial. As Mary watches the only family she has ever known come to a violent end, a strange woman whisks her away from the crowd before they can turn on the granddaughter of the accused. This woman is actually Mary's mother, who could never openly claim the daughter that she bore out of wedlock. Because in The Witch Child series witchcraft is a hereditary gift passed from mother to daughter, we can assume that Mary's mother is also a witch (thought we never know for sure, as this character only appears in passing). Mary's mother, now married to a prominent member of Cromwell's government, uses her wealth and influence to arrange passage to America for her daughter, where she believes the girl will be safe from the witch hunts of England. There is further evidence of sisterhood among witches as Mary is sailing from England: while her ship passes by the cliffs on the coast of her native land, she sees women standing on the bluffs who seem to be other witches offering her benedictions as she leaves.

Mary's healing powers foster bonds of sisterhood with some of the women of Beulah, Massachusetts. These bonds are important later on, as they save Mary's life. During the journey to America, Mary assists Mistress Rivers during a difficult birth, breathing life into the child that all believed was stillborn. Mary's actions earn her the undying gratitude of Mistress Rivers and her daughter Rebecca, who is close to Mary's age. At the end of the novel, when the Reverend Johnson and a band of witch hunters come to arrest Mary, Rebecca, now a married woman who is in labor with her first child, allows her friend to hide in her birth chamber long enough to escape. Custom dictates that Puritan men cannot enter a place where a woman is giving birth because it is unclean, so they are unable to barge into Rebecca's birth chamber and seize Mary.

The witch is subversive of patriarchy then, not because she can help other women procure abortions, see into the future, or affect the course of events with her spells, but instead, because her way of seeing the world enables her to refuse the subordinate position she is being groomed for because she rejects a hierarchal model of authority.

# Other Witches

In this final section, I examine a representation of the teen witch that is not obviously grounded in Wicca. Gemma in The Gemma Doyle trilogy, however, is *like* her Wiccan and proto-Wiccan sisters in that her powers are also rooted in her body and tied to nature. Moreover, magic in the Trilogy is linked to a syncretic reverence of the old goddesses from many religious traditions. But most importantly, this magic is governed by one of the fundamental principles of Wicca, the three-fold law, which holds that "everything you do comes back to you" (*Great*, Bray 280) three times more powerfully.

Like The Witch Child series and *The Minister's Daughter*, The Gemma Doyle trilogy is set in the historical past. Gemma's Victorian England, however, another era in which women were greatly repressed, is far more romanticized in much fiction than is Colonial New England or Interregnum England, the settings of The Witch Child series and *The Minister's Daughter* respectively. Bray's protagonist and her friends fight against the restrictive gender roles they are being groomed to occupy as young, upper class white Victorian women.

## *The Body as the Site of Magic*

Because The Gemma Doyle trilogy is also a school story, a type of *Bildungsroman* focusing on the protagonist's education, Gemma and her non-magical friends are subjected to correct training. Spence Academy, the finishing school where Gemma is sent to curb her hoydenish behavior, has a curriculum devoted to training students' bodies rather than honing their intellects. Classes prepare students for their debuts, where they will be presented to men seeking wives, by teaching them how to dance and to walk like ladies and how to curtsey before the Queen. Even classes in art and French are more about training students to paint the "right" type of still life or say a few words in French to present the illusion of cultivation rather than encouraging them to ponder the politics of representation. After experiencing nearly a decade of normalizing judgments, graduates of Spence are prepared to be the recipients of the male gaze. As proper young women, they will behave as if everyone is continuously watching them. Foucault

### 3. "An ye harm none, do as ye will"

describes how correct training focuses on the body, which is subjected to micropractices of discipline with the end goal of transforming the whole person, body and mind, making the subject more amenable to control. I have discussed at length in this work how correct training is deployed in order to coerce young women into occupying a restrictive gender role. Gemma's magical abilities make her better able to resist this programming. However, her greatest strength is her feminist constructivist perspective which enables her to question her culture's beliefs that women are inherently inferior to men.

Like the other texts I have examined in this chapter, magic in The Gemma Doyle trilogy is a uniquely female ability that is tied to the body of the witch, a connection that reaffirms how patriarchal control of women is designed to quell anxieties about their bodies. Because women menstruate and give birth, their bodies are commonly thought of as being more closely affiliated to nature. While Gemma's magic does not derive from a religious practice that reveres nature, she does nevertheless have the ability to control the natural world. For example, as a child in India, before she had fully realized her supernatural abilities, Gemma tamed a tiger that had killed several people in the village.

Gemma is also similar to Sarah and Nancy in *The Craft* and Mary in The Witch Child series in how she too can perform magic with a glance, particularly to protect herself or others. For example, in *The Sweet Far Thing*, the last novel of the trilogy, with just a look Gemma makes it appear that she has set a room ablaze with in order to prevent a group of men from overpowering her and appropriating her magic by controlling her body. In fact, most magic in The Gemma Doyle trilogy does not change the fundamental nature of things, but rather, is based on illusion, or the ability to manipulate what others see. So women's magic in the Trilogy is threatening to patriarchy because it inverts the male gaze: instead of Gemma's body being regulated by this gaze, she and other magical women like her look back and can even control what men see.

Because men in Gemma's time are particularly fearful of the bodies of *all* women, parents and suitors want their children and future wives to "behave properly and predictably" (Bray *Great* 207) so that they are not as terrifying. Young women of Gemma's class have this proper and predictable behavior drilled into them via their finishing school educations, a type of correct training during which their bodies and minds are the focus of various micropractices of discipline. The corseted girl on the cover of the American and British volumes[11] of The Gemma Doyle trilogy emphasizes how correct training that Gemma and her friends are subjected to targets both the body and the mind. The corset is a garment that is worn by women to make their bodies fit into their culture's ideal of femininity. Yet it does more than narrow the waist, as is the case with corsets that were popular during the 19th century. Rather, it causes the wearer to move in a way that exaggerates the difference between women's and men's bodies. Indeed, for the English, corsets and stays were "the visible sign of strict morality" (Steele 26). Gemma's training at Spence is calculated to further constrain her body, as well as her mind. At Spence, girls are taught the appropriate way to walk and dance, as well as discouraged from developing their intellects in ways that would cause them to question the whole system that oppresses them. Gemma realizes that the people who have sent their daughters to Spence view them as "hollow vessels ... to be rinsed of [their] own ambitious, wants, and opinions" in order to fill them "with the cool, tepid water of gracious compliance" (Bray *Great* 305).

But in spite of the thoroughness of their training, Gemma and her friends bristle at their confinement within their restrictive gender roles that are about as comfortable as the corsets they are expected to wear at every waking moment. Specifically, each girl's sexuality exceeds the boundaries of her role. Ann's desire transcends class: she is in love for a time with Gemma's priggish brother Tom, who is incapable to seeing her many fine qualities because she is penniless and plain. Pippa's and Felicity's desire for one another is outside of the boundaries of heteronormativity. And Gemma's desire for the Indian Katrick transcends the boundaries of race.

## *The Perils of Subjectivism*

Gemma is like the other witches I have examined in this chapter in that her greatest strength is not her paranormal abilities, but her way of knowing the world, which ultimately enables her to resist subordination and to help other women do the same. The length of The Gemma Doyle Trilogy enables Bray to more fully explore her protagonist's intellectual transition from subjectivism to constructivism in order to show how the later way of thinking makes Gemma better able to control her life. In the first novel of the trilogy, *A Great and Terrible Beauty*, Gemma is in the throes of subjectivism. Soon after the sudden death of her mother, Gemma discovers that she is a powerful witch who can enter the Realms, another dimension filled with magic that she can bring in to our world. But eventually, Gemma comes to understand the limitations of subjectivism as she makes mistakes of her own, and learns about her late mother's mistakes when she was a teen.

In *A Great and Terrible Beauty*, Gemma is in the full-blown rebellion against authority that is characteristic of subjectivism. At this stage in Gemma's life, because she has just realized that adults do not have all of the answers, she believes that they have been misleading her in order to better control her, and so all authority has been defrocked in her eyes. Therefore, when Gemma must make a decision, she no longer defers to the judgment of adults, who were previously viewed as authoritative sources of knowledge. Instead, she is wholly guided by her own perspective. Thus, Gemma will not listen to explanations by adults about why a particular action is inadvisable, but instead, storms off in a huff when she is contradicted. Gemma exhibits this type of behavior in the novel's opening chapter, when her mother attempts to explain why leaving India, where Gemma has lived all of her life, to return to London to have her season as debutant is not the exciting entry into adulthood that she believes it will be. Instead, Gemma would "be paraded around the ballrooms of London society like some prize horse there to have its breeding capabilities evaluated" and find herself "the subject of cruel gossip for the slightest infraction of the rules" (Bray *Great* 5). Because Gemma believes that her mother is merely attempting to thwart her efforts to become autonomous, she runs off rather than continue the discussion. Unfortunately, Gemma's mother dies only moments later in an effort to protect her daughter.

After her mother's death, Gemma gets what she wished for — her grieving father takes her and her brother home to London, and Gemma begins her training as a debutant. But Gemma sees immediately that her mother was correct — her preparation for womanhood in London does not consist of going to museums and attending balls with young men her age, but rather, consists of her learning to suppress all aspects of herself in the interests of being a proper young lady. At Spence, Gemma grows more rebellious in part because the adults in her life are unwilling or unable to give her any meaningful guidance. Gemma's mother is now dead, and her father retreats into a laudanum-induced stupor in order to deal with his grief, so her grandmother and older brother Tom assume the roles of her parents. However, Gemma cannot turn to them for advice because they are merely concerned with forcing her to behave as a proper lady who can be married to a suitable man with his own fortune as soon as possible before she disgraces the family.

Meanwhile, Gemma is beset by disturbing visions where she imagines herself to be in an unfamiliar place. These visions are the harbingers of Gemma's extraordinary magical abilities that begin with her being able to travel to the Realms. However, Gemma has no one to mentor her in the use of these powers, or even reassure her that she is not going mad and explain to her what is happening. Unknown to Gemma at the time, her mother was also an extremely powerful witch who was able to travel to the Realms. Gemma's mother died in order to protect her daughter from one of the dangerous creatures who has been trapped in this dimension and is now threatening to erupt into our world, where it would rip apart the fabric of reality.

While Gemma is extremely rebellious during this phase in her life, she nevertheless longs for a mentor who can show her how to subvert her family's attempts to subordinate her and master her magical abilities while helping her to have the autonomy she longs for. As a consequence, Gemma is particularly susceptible to the machinations of Sarah Reese-Toom, a witch who realizes that Gemma has tremendous supernatural abilities before she fully understands them herself, and who wants to exploit the girl's gifts for her own ends. Sarah is one of Gemma's teachers at Spence, who is living under the assumed name Hester Moore and secretly searching for a girl with Gemma's abilities who will be able to enter the Realms, which have been closed for over two decades in order to contain the dangerous creature there. Miss Moore was once able to access to the Realms on her own, but suddenly lost the ability, which she can only regain if the Realms are opened once more and she can trick another witch into assisting her in a very dangerous ritual. Miss Moore quickly becomes Gemma's favorite teacher because unlike the other faculty at Spence, she shows her students alternatives to the narrow gender roles that they are being groomed to occupy; she encourages her students to read widely in order to expand their minds and takes them on outings to the caves outside of the school, beguiling them with stories about the Order, an ancient group of witches.

Although Miss Moore's pedagogy is calculated to win Gemma's trust so that she can appropriate her student's magical powers, her teaching is also empowering in how it encourages Gemma to view the world holistically. The other teachers at Spence engage in what Paulo Freire terms the banking model of education, whereby pupils are positioned as empty receptacles waiting to be filled with knowledge by their instructors. Most of the teachers at Spence instruct their students in the "right" version of historical events or the "right" way to interpret a poem. This model of education is the opposite of a mentoring relationship, which is necessarily fluid and reciprocal. Rather, the banking model of education is a type of correct training that reinforces the student's subordinate relationship with the teacher while serving the interests of the oppressors "who care neither to have the world revealed nor to see it transformed" (Freire 54). Miss Moore's teaching, on the other hand, is an example of what Freire terms the problem-posing model of education, "which breaks the vertical patterns characteristic of banking education" (61) by making students "critical co-investigators in dialogue with the teacher" (62) rather than docile listeners. The problem-posing model of education fosters a holistic way of viewing the world that "considers neither the abstract man nor the world without people, but people in their relations with the world" (Freire 62). Miss Moore and her students become critical co-investigators when she takes them outside to draw instead of keeping them in the classroom to paint yet another still life. In this unrestricted environment, Miss Moore encourages her students to select something that they feel moved to draw and to use whatever techniques they find appropriate to render the image, inviting her pupils to decide for themselves what constitutes art rather than have the "correct" answer supplied to them. In this way, Miss Moore encourages her students to see themselves as knowers who are an intimate part of the known. Nevertheless, while Miss Moore's teaching is empowering to Gemma and her friends, it is also intended to foster Gemma's budding magical abilities sufficiently to reveal them to her teacher. Inspired by Miss Moore's stories, Gemma and her best friends Pippa, Felicity and Ann steal a bottle of brandy and sneak to the caves in the middle of the night. In this private space where they can experience momentary freedom from the rules of Spence and the greater world, they decide to form their own Order and join hands to perform what they believe would be an appropriate magical ceremony to mark the occasion. Yet the ceremony is more potent than any of the girls imagined it might be. Her powers strengthened by her connection to her new friends, Gemma accidentally opens the door to the Realms, bringing her friends with her into a dimension that she never knew existed. This scene is similar to the one in *The Craft* in which Sarah and her friends have a sleepover and more deeply explore their friendship as well as their magical powers.

As Gemma's supernatural abilities become more powerful, she is less inclined to take the advice of others who are more knowledgeable than she is, and as a result, she uses her powers in a dangerous way. Gemma brings magic from the Realms into our world to share with her friends so that they might have more control over their lives. As graduation draws near, each girl's fate is closing in on her. Gemma's and Felicity's families will expect them to marry soon, while the orphaned Ann is obligated to return to her aunt and uncle, who have paid for her education so that she can become her cousins' governess. But Pippa's fate is the most awful of all: her parents have arranged for her to marry Mr. Bumble, a wealthy barrister who is old enough to be her father, who will pay her father's gambling debts. However, once magic is brought from the Realms into our world, the portal between these two dimensions is permanently open so that others with supernatural powers can access the Realms' magic, which could potentially be used to subordinate the entire human race. Gemma meets her deceased mother in the Realms, who warns her that her actions are dangerous. Yet because Gemma still views the world through a subjectivist perspective and is desperate to help Pippa, she does not take her mother's advice.

Gemma's rash actions quickly show her that subjectivism is not an empowering perspective. Gemma and her friends are not more empowered by the magic that she has brought back from the Realms; instead, it only makes their situations worse. Because the girls lack experience using magic, they employ it to play childish pranks without first considering the consequences of their actions. Indeed, Gemma momentarily frees a gargoyle, who within seconds swells from being the size of her thumb to six feet tall, and it takes all of her wits to put the lecherous creature back into his harmless stone form. But more dangerous still is how their brief use of the Realms'

## 3. "An ye harm none, do as ye will"

magic encourages the four to be rebellious in other ways without adequately considering the consequences of their actions. Their biggest collective act of defiance is when they help Pippa break her engagement to Mr. Bumble. Pippa reveals to her fiancé that she has epilepsy, a condition that the Victorians viewed as a shameful affliction rather than a neurological disorder. However, Pippa's parents will not permit her to break her engagement. Instead, they make plans to take her home and marry her to Mr. Bumble by the end of the week. Mrs. Nightwing, the headmistress of Spence, then punishes Gemma, Felicity and Ann for their part in breaking the engagement and dismisses Miss Moore for giving them "dangerous" ideas that caused them to rebel in the first place. Pippa, desperate to avoid being married against her will, convinces Gemma to take them all to the Realms one more time. While there, Pippa eats a handful of poisonous berries that kill her instantly so that she can live in the Realms indefinitely. But in the Realms, Pippa does not have more control over her life even though she now lives in a dimension filled with magic. Instead, she is transformed into a lonely and jealous creature who, when Gemma brings Ann and Felicity to visit, attempts to trick Felicity into eating a handful of the same berries so that the two can be together forever.

While Gemma's own actions show her that subjectivism is far from an empowering position, her mother's past experiences offer the most powerful evidence about the perils of this way of knowing the world. Gemma learns about her mother as a teen from the diary of Mary Dowd, her mother's assumed name after she and her best friend Sarah Reese-Toom accidentally burned down the east wing of Spence when the two inexperienced girls attempted to manipulate complex magical forces. Sarah convinced Mary to help her summon a dangerous creature from the Winterlands so that they could sacrifice a gypsy child. In exchange, the creature would endow Sarah with supernatural abilities that far surpassed the ones she recently lost. Because Mary and Sarah were emboldened by their previous experiences in the Realms, they were unwilling to take the advice of others more knowledgeable than themselves about the dangerous consequences of summoning this creature, who cannot be easily controlled by even the most experienced witches. But the ritual went wrong when Mary unintentionally suffocated the struggling child, who is useless as a sacrifice once she is dead. But once the creature had been summoned, it could not be sent back. In the ensuing struggle with the creature, a candle was overturned, and the east wing of Spence was set ablaze. When the school's headmistress Eugenia Spence arrived to investigate the fire, she realized what her students had done. Eugenia, also a powerful witch, sealed the Realms indefinitely to keep the creature from entering our world before she died in the raging fire. Sarah and Mary, Gemma's mother, were also presumed dead in the fire, but both escaped and took new names. Gemma's mother married and traveled to India, while Sarah became a teacher who traveled from school to school, searching for the more powerful witch yet to be born who will be able to open the Realms, thus giving her a second chance to recapture her lost abilities. Gemma is that hoped for witch.

Gemma's mother's experience elucidates how subjectivism is not empowering, nor is it a feminist epistemological position because it offers no real alternative to patriarchy. Had the sacrifice been successful, Mary's friend Sarah would not have gained or regained agency, but instead, been empowered through the extreme exploitation of someone else, and used this power to manipulate others rather than to truly transform her own life. Sarah wants the dangerous creature from the Realms to "grant [her] the power that should be [hers]" (Bray *Great* 343). Sarah's use of language here, along with her willingness to sacrifice the child in exchange for this power, reveal how she intends to use this power to manipulate others rather than to give herself more agency. Clearly Sarah would use her gifts while engaging with the world through a subjectivist perspective, merely duplicating patriarchal oppression. Before Sarah's supernatural abilities abandoned her completely as a teen, she adopted the name Circe, revealing her beliefs about the appropriate use of power. Circe was a Greek goddess who used her knowledge of drugs and herbs to transform her enemies into animals. Like Circe, Sarah seeks to have power over others rather than the ability to transform her own life.

### *Constructivism and Sisterhood*

Gemma is only truly empowered after she understands the world through a constructivist perspective in which she views the world holistically. Gemma develops this perspective through sisterhood, something her mother lacked when she eventually came to see the world in this way. Mary's constructivist perspective evolved after her falling out with Sarah in the aftermath of their failed attempt to give her friend access to the Realms' magic once more. Mary's remorse over killing the child and helping to release the creature from the Winterlands caused her to realize that her gifts come with the responsibility to fully consider the needs and frailties of others before taking a significant course of action. Mary demonstrates this understanding in the most extreme way when she takes her own life to protect her daughter, and the world, from the dangerous creature in the realms who is about to escape its bounds now that Gemma is able to enter the formerly sealed realms.

Gemma's sisterhood with Pippa, Felicity and Ann strengthens her magical abilities as well as helps her develop her constructivist perspective. The Realms is a place that nurtures sisterhood. In this dimension, the girls can better explore their friendship with one another in an alternative, non-patriarchal space where they are not divided from one another as beauties competing for the attention of men. Instead, because all in the Realms can partake of its magic, the girls are equal to one another and therefore free to explore their friendship. In this way, the Realms is a place of feminist power. This friendship more than any magic is instrumental in allowing Gemma, Felicity and Ann to discover their strengths throughout the Trilogy. (Pippa, unfortunately, dies before she can discover her strengths in a similar fashion).

Gemma's magical abilities also nurture sisterhood, and are at their strongest when she is helping others, something that further develops her constructivist perspective. Gemma's attempts to assist her friend Ann demonstrate the limits of magic and the power of sisterhood. Unlike the other wealthy girls at Spence, the orphaned Ann lacks a fortune. And because Ann is also plain, there is little chance she will find a wealthy husband who might be willing to overlook her poverty so that she can escape having to become her cousins' governess.

Ann's only hope is that her extraordinary voice can land her a career in the theater. Gemma casts a glamour over Ann, transforming her into a ravishing beauty. In this guise, Ann successfully auditions for a role on stage. Yet because the magic cannot permanently alter her appearance, Ann is fearful that if she takes the role she auditioned for while in this shape, she will be fired after she reverts to her true form. Gemma can only help Ann by enabling her to refuse the subordinate subject position she is being groomed to occupy, a feat accomplished through sisterhood and encouragement rather than through magic. When Gemma can finally convince Ann that she has a right to happiness and autonomy, Ann auditions for a role on stage in her own form. Ann's extraordinary voice earns her the leading role in a musical, establishing her career on stage and subsequent independence. In this way, Gemma has helped Ann see that she has the ability to change her life. As a result, Gemma better understands how her will is strong enough to effect change in the world for her own benefit.

The Gemma Doyle trilogy concludes with the most emphatic example of the connection between sisterhood and magic. Helping Ann teaches Gemma about the possibilities of resisting the attempts of her brother and other men to subordinate her in order to access the Realms' magic in order to oppress others. The Realms, like our world, is made up of many classes of people with varying degrees of access to resources. Some groups such as the Order have historically controlled the lion's share of the Realms' magic, while other groups constitute an oppressed underclass because they have access to precious little magic. As a constructivist, Gemma can weigh the voices of others with her own instincts to dispose of the magic in a way that inverts the Realms' hierarchal power structure. Ultimately, Gemma distributes the magic among all who live there, something that grants agency to members of the most disenfranchised groups rather than permits a minority to manipulate the majority. The results of this decision in turn permit Gemma to process the advice of others along with what she feels to be important and useful in order to decide how to direct her own life.

Gemma's experiences hone the strength of her will and help her understand how she can make a significant contribution to the world, even without the magic that she has returned to the Realms. The trilogy concludes with Gemma standing up to her family to tell them that she has no intention of marrying, ever. As a consequence, she forgoes her debut, the event in her life that would signal to her family's peers that she was ready to marry and assume her subordinate adult female role in society. Gemma then convinces her father to give her the share of her fortune that would have come to her after marriage so she can use it to instead attend university and learn to support herself. In the novel's last scene, Gemma prepares to leave for college in New York, where she hopes to encourage sisterhood on a broader scale by working for women's rights.

## 3. "An ye harm none, do as ye will"

# Conclusion

Of all the types of monstrous Others I have examined in this book, the witch is the most powerful figure. A feminist, she supports other women characters. She benefits from sisterhood and fosters sisterhood among other women. Unlike the figure of the haunted girl, the witch never accepts a subordinate feminine role. Nor has she ever been so potentially out of control and violent that she must be destroyed. Instead, the witch retains control of her body, unlike the ghost and werewolf. And finally, unlike the haunted girls or the female lycanthropes, the teen witch matures into a strong and autonomous adult woman.

At the end of The Gemma Doyle trilogy, *The Minister's Daughter,* and *The Craft*, the protagonists have all matured into strong and autonomous adult women. At the conclusion of *Sorceress*, the final novel of The Witch Child series, we learn that this is also the case for Mary, who has married into a Native-American tribe where her healing and supernatural abilities are valued rather than feared as diabolical. Similarly, we learn that Nell in *The Minister's Daughter* ends her long life in a cottage by the sea, protected by the prince who eventually becomes King Charles II, and healing all who seek her assistance.

On the other hand, we cannot completely assume that Vivian (*Blood and Chocolate*) and Maris (*The Blooding*), or Judith (*Jade Green*), Susan (*A Stir of Bones*), or Molly (*Dreadful Sorry*) will become autonomous. *Blood and Chocolate* and *Jade Green* conclude with a version of the marriage plot, where the heroine is poised to wed in an extremely patriarchal society. One can only hope that Judith and Vivian are strong enough to resist being subordinated by their mates. Susan in *A Stir of Bones* and Maris in *The Blooding* must still live with their controlling parents until each girl is of the age of majority, and so there is a chance that either girl could be browbeaten into submission before she can escape her repressive environment. *Ginger Snaps* and *Blood Moon* end badly for Ginger and Tara — both girls become monstrous Others rather than strong and autonomous young women.

The teen witch then offers the strongest example to readers of how to resist feminine subordination. Her greatest strength is her feminist worldview rather than her magical powers. This perspective encourages the teen witch to view the world holistically and to consider multiple perspectives before taking action. In this way, the teen witch's worldview has the potential to undermine patriarchal order, which is based on a hierarchal way of knowing the world. While readers might not be able to communicate with spirits, change into werewolves, or cast spells, they can change how they look at the world. In this way, the teen witch's example shows how changing one's perspective can be empowering.

# *Conclusion*

YOUNG ADULT FANTASIST URSULA K. LE GUIN describes non-realistic fiction as a valuable tool for helping adolescents understand their world. Non-realistic fiction trains the imagination and opens alternatives to reality (Le Guin 133). As a variety of non-realistic fiction, horror similarly offers alternatives to reality by deconstructing and redrawing the boundaries that perpetuate subjectivity (Creed "Horror" 46). In a world where girls can converse with spirits, change into wolves or cast a glamour with a glance, the solidity of the boundaries separating the living from the dead, human from animal, and the possible from the impossible are called into question. Through the use of fantastical elements, normative masculinity and femininity are similarly revealed as constructed subject positions rather than boundaries that are the "natural" consequence of biological sex. In this way, stories about ghosts, werewolves and witches allow girls to imagine alternatives to the subordinate roles they are being groomed to occupy as adults.

Young Adult horror, like mainstream horror, reveals the existence of the symbolic order and how it is used by those in control in order to oppress others. The monstrous Other, which is the embodiment of the abject, crosses or threatens to cross the border between human and Other, precipitating an encounter between the symbolic order and that which threatens its stability such as those who are not conventionally masculine or feminine. Horror redraws the boundaries between the abject and the subject, between human and nonhuman, through the figure of the monstrous Other. Teen girls have first-hand experience with this Other since in a patriarchal culture, as females they always occupy the position of Other, even when they are

## Conclusion

conventionally feminine. The monstrous Other in the texts I have examined is always a double of the teen girl.

In Young Adult horror fiction, female protagonists reject traditional gender roles. These protagonists discover their voices, explore their sexuality and act independently of male authority. They problematise what is presented to girls as "normal" and "natural" feminine behavior, which can help readers to understand that much of what has been presented to them as reality has actually been made by someone else. Girls are frequently told that their biology makes them inherently physically and intellectually weaker than men, and so their subordination is necessary for men to protect them. In horror, teen girls realize gender roles are constructed rather than natural, and this realization is an important aspect of identifying those roles as restrictive and damaging and ultimately rejecting them.

The monstrous Other is useful in helping other characters, and even the reader, to identify these roles and understand their cost and constructedness because it is a double with a difference. In *The Psychic Life of Power*, Butler argues that resistance to gender roles takes its form not through the repudiation of "what we are," but rather, through varying the iterations of "what we are." The monstrous Other in the texts I examine presents an iteration whose similarity to the original implies the possibility of resistance to that which has been presented as "natural" and unchangeable. Moreover, because in Young Adult horror fiction the monstrous other is nearly always a sympathetic character, it is fairly easy for the reader or viewer to identify with this creature. The monstrous Other then can be a useful tool in helping the reader formulate her own strategies to resisting a restrictive gender role.

In the twenty-first century, girls still need help resisting feminine subordination and "refusing what they are." Perhaps this is because, as Mary Pipher, Peggy Orenstein, Naomi Wolf and Joan Jacobs Brumberg point out, girls are increasingly pressured by the media to embody a doll-like feminine ideal in which they are deprived of voice and agency. Moreover, the more contemporary "together woman" and "riot grrrl" varieties of femininity are not improvements on older more restrictive models, but are instead the same old model in a new package. Therefore, monsters are a girl's best friend in that they "explore and problematise what is considered normal and what troubles us" (Wisker 13) and in some instances, they can foil the effects of discipline.

## Conclusion

Each of the types of monstrous Others examined in this work offers a different model of resistance to feminine subordination. The haunted girls in Chapter 1 are reacquainted with their own strengths through their relationship with a spirit. The haunted girl has originally repressed knowledge of her own strengths and desires in the interests of being conventionally feminine. In fact, she has repressed these qualities so thoroughly that she is in danger of being victimized. However, the ghost who haunts her is not the source of this threat. Instead, the haunted girl is in danger from the family patriarch or his analogue who will exploit her weaknesses in to force her to eradicate her self. The ghost's intervention, however, saves the haunted girl by enabling her to see alternatives to the crippling feminine subject position that she has been forced to occupy. Because the ghost's intervention is subtle, it is able to assist the haunted girl in such a way that she does not appear to be radically departing the boundaries of conventional femininity. The understated nature of the ghost's intervention is particularly important as the girl it haunts is not a legal adult, and so is at great risk of being dominated. The ghost's subtle intervention enables the haunted girl to nurture her strengths in stealth until she is no longer subject to her guardians' intervention.

The teen female werewolves in Chapter 2 expose what happens to girls who are unable to "refuse what they are." Both Ginger (*Ginger Snaps*) and Tara (*Blood Moon*) are trapped within different stereotypes of femininity by the end of each film. As a werewolf, Ginger is all that is negatively associated with femininity: a creature who is completely controlled by her hormones rather than reason. Ultimately Ginger becomes the wild animal that patriarchal culture has always claimed lurks inside of all women and justifies the subordination of their sex. As a consequence, Ginger must be "put to sleep" for the good of other humans. Tara, on the other hand, appears to embody normative femininity: she is silent, seemingly passive, and conventionally beautiful, qualities she has cultivated by actively suppressing parts of herself at odds with this subject position. At the end of each film then, neither girl can "refuse what she is": while werewolves are usually shapeshifters, Ginger and Tara are eternally trapped within their respective bestial and female forms. Kelsey ("Boobs"), Maris (*The Blooding*) and Vivian (*Blood and Chocolate*), on the other hand, can "refuse what they are" by accepting as strong and beautiful the parts of themselves that are at odds with normative femininity rather than succumbing to sexist ideas about woman's alleged inferior

## Conclusion

and dangerous animal nature. As a consequence, each girl has a hybridity that gives her the strength to resist being "put in her place" by others.

The teen witches in Chapter 3 offer the strongest models of resistance. The teen witch "refuses who she is" not by nurturing her strengths in stealth, or even by accepting those parts of herself that are incompatible with stereotypical femininity. Rather, the teen witch resists subordination through her constructivist epistemological perspective. When the teen witch comes to understand that the knower is part of the known, she can reject her culture's hierarchal and oppressive model of knowledge. As constructivist, she also views the world holistically and sees herself connected to others rather than isolated from them. As a result, the teen witch will always consider the needs and frailties of others before deciding on a course of action that might affect them. Also, the teen witch uses her magic to help others more than herself. Moreover, the teen witch's constructivist perspective is not a liability that would keep her perpetually in service to others at the expense of her own independence. Rather, her constructivist perspective is empowering. The teen witch's holistic way of viewing the world nurtures bonds of sisterhood with other women, which empowers all parties. One of the effects of discipline is that those on whom power is exercised "tend to be more strongly individualized" (Foucault *Discipline* 193) and experience themselves as isolated from others whose common condition might encourage them to collaborate in order to resist oppression. Constructivism then has the potential to undo some of the individualizing effects of discipline because it is a position from which the knower experiences herself as connected to others. In this way, the teen female witch presents a positive paradigm of female freedom and power.

In *Learning Curves*, Beth Younger describes Young Adult literature as representing a "feminist continuum of resistance to the discourse of dominant culture" (132). This continuum of resistance is also evident in Young Adult horror fiction. At one end of the continuum are texts that specifically educate readers about feminism as something that empowers women. The Gemma Doyle Trilogy concludes with the heroine rejecting her role as a cosseted beauty who in the normal course of events would land a wealthy husband to protect her. Instead Gemma's emergent constructivist perspective leads her to forgo this role in order to attend university in the United States with the goal of supporting herself and working for women's rights. And in *Dreadful Sorry*, the ghost of Clementine Horn educates Molly about how first- and second-wave feminism have given her possibilities that were never available to Clementine.

At another end of this continuum are texts espousing feminist principles such as the necessity of giving women the social and intellectual freedom afforded their brothers, the value of sisterhood, and the importance of viewing a problem from multiple perspectives. This is the case in *Stir of Bones, Dreadful Sorry, A Certain Slant of Light, Under the Light, Ruined, The Blooding,* "Boobs," *Blood and Chocolate, The Minister's Daughter,* The Gemma Doyle trilogy, The Witch Child series and *The Craft.*

*Stir of Bones, Dreadful Sorry, Ruined, A Certain Slant of Light, Under the Light,* The Gemma Doyle trilogy, and "Boobs" each represent how painful it is for women to lack the freedoms and opportunities given to men. The Creole Lisette helps Rebecca understand how race, class and gender has caused her to be denied opportunities that Rebecca takes for granted. Susan (*Stir of Bones*) is denied so much autonomy by Father that even her flesh does not feel as if it belongs to her. Instead, Susan thinks of herself as a piece of property that Father manages but that she cannot control. Clementine Horn (*Dreadful Sorry*) and Gemma's friend Pippa Worthington (The Gemma Doyle trilogy) are willing to die in order to have the same autonomy and opportunity for intellectual development given to their brothers. When Pippa's family forces her to marry a wealthy man twice her age, she commits suicide to remain forever in the Realms rather than be sold into a loveless marriage. Clementine elopes by sea on a stormy night when sailing is inadvisable so she can have a chance to escape a life of virtual slavery in her uncle's house and instead see the world and continue her education. And Jennifer (*A Certain Slant of Light* and *Under the Light*) dies for all intents and purposes when her parents thwart at every turn her attempts to express herself. Because she cannot even be comfortable in her own flesh, Jennifer's spirit abandons her body. And Kelsey in "Boobs" is terrorized by her classmates for having a female body to the degree that she cannot be comfortable in her own flesh until she develops the ability to change into her wolf form once a month.

The value of sisterhood for promoting women's growth is emphasized in *A Certain Slant of Light, Under the Light, Jade Green, A Stir of Bones, Ruined, The Craft, The Minister's Daughter, Witch Child* (the first book of the Witch Child series) and The Gemma Doyle trilogy. In most of these

## Conclusion

texts, individuals and/or cultural institutions make it difficult for women to partake of sisterhood because when women collaborate and support one another, they are better able to resist subordination. Male religious zealots in *A Certain Slant of Light*, *The Minister' Daughter* and *Witch Child* undermine sisterhood by keeping women isolated in the home. Prevailing discourses of femininity that encourage women to think of themselves as beauties who are in competition with each other for the affections of men make it difficult for Gemma (The Gemma Doyle trilogy) and Sarah (*The Craft*) to have meaningful friendships with other girls. The ghosts in *A Certain Slant of Light*, *Under the Light*, *Ruined*, and *Jade Green*, on the other hand, help the girls they haunt out of a sense of sisterhood. And sisterhood is linked to empowering women individually and collectively, as we see throughout The Gemma Doyle trilogy and in the beginning of *The Craft*.

The protagonists of The Gemma Doyle Trilogy, the Witch Child series, *The Craft* and *The Minister's Daughter* come to view the world more holistically in that they understand the importance of considering how one's actions affect others before making a decision. Gemma, Mary, Sarah and Nell carefully consider the effects of their actions on all parties involved before using their magical powers. Moreover, this holistic way of viewing the world is specifically feminine and feminist in that it encourages women to think of themselves in connection with others rather than isolated from them. Finally, this holistic way of viewing the world promotes sisterhood among women because it encourages them to see one another as friends rather than rivals for male attention.

Young Adult horror fiction uses fantasy to present sympathetically the untenable situation of the adolescent female within society. Young Adult horror fiction does not simply reproduce through the form of the monstrous Other sexist ideas about women. Rather, Young Adult horror fiction uses the tropes of horror to deconstruct sexist ideas about women's supposed essential nature, which have been used to justify feminine subordination. In this way, Young Adult horror fiction differs from mainstream horror fiction, which is as likely to affirm sexist ideas about women (as well as racist ideas about non-whites) as it is to challenge these assumptions. Monsters are a girl's best friend, and they have a lot to teach us.

# Chapter Notes

## Introduction

1. In *Disturbing the Universe: Power and Repression in Adolescent Literature*, Roberta Seelinger Trites defines the genre of Young Adult literature as one that is not just concerned with intellectual growth, but with "what the adolescent has learned about power" (x) during the maturation process.

2. I am basing this assumption on material I have collected over the years while putting together *Hooked on Horror: A Guide to Reading Interests in the Genre*, Volumes 1–3. The volumes, which have been updated every four years, annotate approximately 1000 titles of horror in print that are owned by at least 50 libraries. My survey of the genre over the past 10 years demonstrates that while horror is full of many sympathetic monsters, many more are unsympathetic. Of course, I recognize that "sympathetic" and "unsympathetic" are potentially ambiguous terms, as one person's sympathetic monster is another person's malignant fiend. After all, even Patrick Bateman, the anti-hero of Bret Easton Ellis's notorious novel *American Psycho* (1991), has qualities that can make him momentarily sympathetic.

3. While the monster is always a sympathetic character in Young Adult horror fiction, the same cannot be said for the genre as a whole. Instead, the monster often likely to be someone that the reader or viewer cannot possibly identify with as it is to be represented as someone whose anger is justified, or who is more sinned against than sinning and is so an object of pity.

4. Dark fantasy is loosely defined as fiction with supernatural elements where the overall effect is particularly frightening. Paranormal romance is romance fiction with paranormal elements such as the presence of magic or vampire or ghosts as characters. The paranormal elements in paranormal romance can also produce an overall frightening effect. Contemporary gothic fiction is loosely defined as a type of fiction characterized by mystery and terror.

5. While Young Adult horror is populated exclusively by white protagonists, this is not the case for adult horror fiction over the past 50 years. Some more notable non-white protagonists include Ben in George Romero's 1968 film *Night of the Living Dead* and the revenging revenant Candyman in Bernard Rose's 1992 film of the same name. Horror writers have been predominately white as well until the 1990s. Some better known African-American writers of contemporary horror fiction include Tananarive Due and Brandon Massey, who use the tropes of horror to write about racism. Of course, non-white authors often write about horrific themes and include supernatural elements in their work. However, their work is more accurately characterized as magical realism rather than horror as these supernatural elements are experienced by characters as a normal if disturbing part of the world rather than as something so outside of everyday experience that it must be eradicated.

## Chapter 1

1. For example, Steve Berman's male protagonist in *Vintage* has many things in common with the typical haunted teen female central character: he too is silenced by cultural forces that make it difficult for him to express his feelings as a young gay man. However, Josh, the ghost of a deeply closeted gay teen athlete who died fifty years ago, does not help this protagonist express those feelings. Rather, a bitter Josh nearly kills the protagonist when he touches the living teen, forcing his memories into him. So while a typical haunted teen female protagonist would be empowered by the sisterhood she experiences as a result of sharing the ghost's memories, the protagonist of *Vintage* has to construct a budding narrative of himself as a gay man to free himself of Josh's influence if he is to survive and put this ghost at rest.

2. This is Ann Braude's argument in her book *Radical Spirits: Spiritualism and Women's Rights in the Nineteenth Century*, where she examines the rise and fall of American Spiritualism and the role women played in this faith. According to prevailing beliefs of the period, women were more open to haunting than men in that haunting was an extension of pregnancy whereby the medium provided a hospitable and nurturing temporary environment for the spirit. Moreover, theologians have historically considered women to be more susceptible to possession by a foreign entity than are men in that they were perceived as being too morally weak to throw off a foreign influence or to know when they were being tricked, as is the case with Eve and the serpent. These ideas about women's supposed greater susceptibility to haunting and demonic possession are reproduced in contemporary popular culture, where there is a preponderance of women who are either haunted by spirits or possessed by demons.

3. For more information about how contemporary young women are silenced when they are taught that feminism is no longer relevant to their lives see *Manifesta: Young Women, Feminism, and the Future*, Jennifer Baumgardner and Amy Richards.

4. An alter ego is a specific type of double. A double can be almost any dual, whereas an alter ego is the opposite of the original (Fonseca 188). For example, in Robert Louis Stevenson's story *The Strange Case of Dr. Jekyll and Mr. Hyde*, the good doctor turns into the antithesis of his bourgeois Victorian self when he imbibes his potion and runs amok in the streets of London. The double, on the other hand, retains many salient qualities of the original, as is the case with Helen as a sort of double of Jennifer in *A Certain Slant of Light*.

5. In *Gender Trouble*, Judith Butler describes the pre-discursive subject as an impossibility as culture is such an overarching system that humans are inscribed by it at birth.

## Chapter 2

1. In spite of an explosion of YA horror fiction in the past twenty years, which includes film, there is still a dearth of representations of adolescent female werewolves, particularly of works where they are the primary protagonist. This is one reason that I have opted to not evaluate Maggie Stiefvater's Shiver Trilogy, which focuses on a group of werewolves rather than one female lycanthropic protagonist. Perhaps this lack of YA works with teen female lycanthropic protagonists is because the werewolf is a sexual creature, and authors and directors are uncomfortable with creating an under-age female protagonist whose sexual desires are something that people are uncomfortable with even when expressed by fully adult women.

2. The most prominent of these was the 2002 International Horror Guild Award for Best Film. Successful DVD sales of *Ginger Snaps* lead to the back-to-back filming of a prequel and a sequel in 2003, *Ginger Snaps 2: Unleashed* and *Ginger Snaps Back: The Beginning*. However, neither of these films was as popular as the original: *Ginger Snaps 2: Unleashed* flopped at the box office, and as a result, *Ginger Snaps Back: the Beginning* was released straight to DVD.

3. Because *Blood Moon* was a made-for-television film, it has received little attention from professional film critics. However, it has a following among amateur critics who have posted their reviews on the internet and

whose blogging often persuades horror fans to seek out the film.

4. I am not including the 2007 film version of *Blood and Chocolate* in my study as the director Katja von Garnier transformed Vivian, the novel's teen female protagonist, into a fully adult character. In von Garnier's film, Vivian is nineteen, orphaned and living on her own, whereas in Klause's novel, she is a sixteen-year-old high school student living with her mother. Although Vivian is technically a teenager in von Garnier's version, she has reached the age of majority and is subsequently independent from institutional and familial control, unlike most younger teens represented in Young Adult fiction. von Garnier's Vivian is old enough to patronize bars, for example, and Aiden, her love interest, is a graphic artist who is old enough to be traveling alone through Romania (the film's setting). As a consequence, von Garnier's film lacks some of the typical elements of Young Adult fiction such as protagonists wrestling with institutional control in order to become fully adult.

5. Fantasy fiction is defined as literature taking "place in another realm, with rules, characteristics, and often inhabitants ... different from those of our world and reality, or in what appears to be our world but with magical or paranormal elements" (Tixier-Herald and Kunzel, xii). Fantasy differs from horror in its effect — its primary purpose is to create awe and wonder more than dread and terror — though that effect is in the eyes of the reader as much as it is in the intent of the author.

6. See *Femininity*, Susan Brownmiller and *The Beauty Myth*, Naomi Wolf.

7. See *The Frailty Myth*, Colette Dowling.

8. *Ginger Snaps 2: Unleashed* and *Ginger Snaps: The Beginning*, however, do not similarly represent the transformation from human to werewolf as gendered.

9. "The Mirror Stage As Formative of the I Function As Revealed in Psychoanalytic Experience," Jacques Lacan, *Ecrits: The First Complete Edition in English*. New York: W.W. Norton, 2006.

10. Emily White. *Fast Girls: Teenage Tribes and the Myth of the Slut* (New York: Scribner, 2002).

11. Lynn Phillips discusses how discourses of normative masculinity and femininity are perpetuated by romance fiction, as well as though other forms of mass media such as women's magazines.

## Chapter 3

1. The Wiccan Rede, which expresses the core belief of Wicca.

2. In her history of the European witch hunts, Anne Barstow remarks on how mostly impoverished women were accused of witchcraft: "In most areas of Europe, the accused was very poor, and their accusers were better off than they. Even though most accusers were neighbors who also lived in poverty, still they possessed more goods than their victims" (26). Historian Carol Karlsen makes a similar claim about those accused of witchcraft in Colonial New England: "poor women, both the destitute and those with access to some resources, were surely represented, and very probably overrepresented, among the New England accused" (78).

3. In *The Reproduction of Mothering*, Nancy Chodorow describes how women tend to experience themselves as connected to the world, whereas men tend to experience themselves as separate from the world. "Because [girls] are parented by a person of the same gender (a person who has already internalized a set of unconscious meanings, fantasies and self-images about this gender and brings to her own experience her own internalized early relationship to her own mother), girls come to experience themselves as less differentiated than boys, as more continuous with and related to the external-object world" (Chodorow 167).

4. The term "neo-Pagan" describes any adherent of a new-age spirituality that is a loose interpretation of older religious traditions. Wicca is one of these neo-Pagan religions.

5. For a more thorough history of Wicca, consult Margo Adler's excellent book *Drawing Down the Moon: Witches, Druids, Goddess-Worshippers, and Other Pagans in America Today* (Boston: Beacon Press, 1986).

6. I have not included *Sabrina the Teenage Witch* in my analysis because the show lacks sufficient horror elements to be part of my study. I excluded the television series *Charmed* as well because the protagonists are too old to fit into the parameters of my study — while the principals are all young, by the standards of the twenty-first century, they are more adult than teen as they live independently of parents. I similarly excluded *American Horror Story: Coven* as the teen characters of the show are not its primary focus, but rather, part of the show's ensemble cast. Finally, I excluded both film and novel of *Beautiful Creatures* because both are related through the perspective of a teen boy who recounts his relationship with a teen witch.

7. Judith Butler, *The Psychic Life of Power*, 1979. (Stanford: Stanford University Press, 1997), p. 101.

8. In *Drawing Down the Moon*, Margot Adler describes the anti-authoritarian nature of Wicca and neo–Paganism. While there are other anti-authoritarian religious groups such as the Unitarians and some liberal Christian denominations, "what's unusual about modern Pagans is that they remain anti-authoritarian while retaining rituals and ecstatic techniques that, in our culture, are usually only the province of small and forgotten tribal groups" (ix).

9. The Rule of Three, or the Three-Fold Law, is a variation of the Wiccan Rede: "an ye harm none, do as ye will." The Rule of Three reminds practitioners that whatever good or evil they put into the world will return to them three times stronger.

10. Matthew Hopkins, an unsuccessful lawyer, found his calling as a witchfinder. Between 1645 and 1646, it is estimated that through the confessions he extracted, he caused "more people to be hanged in two years than had been hanged in the previous century" (Russell 97–98).

11. Covers of the Trilogy that were translated into other languages or in English but sold internationally feature the image of a young woman who is not wearing a corset.

# *Bibliography*

Adams, Carol J. *The Sexual Politics of Meat: A Feminist-Vegetarian Critical Theory*. New York: Continuum, 1990. Print.
Adler, Margot. *Drawing Down the Moon: Witches, Druids, Goddess-Worshippers, and Other Pagans in America Today*. 1979. Boston: Beacon Press, 1986. Print.
American Association of University Women. *The AAUW Report: How Schools Shortchange Girls*. Washington, DC: The AAUW Educational Foundation and National Educational Association, 1992. Print.
*American Horror Story*. FX: 2011–2013. Television.
*American Horror Story: Coven*. FX: 2013. Television.
Armstrong, Kelley. *Bitten*. New York: Viking, 2001. Print.
Barstow, Anne L. *Witchcraze: A New History of the European Witch Hunts*. New York: HarperOne, 1995. Print.
Baumgardner, Jennifer, and Amy Richards. *Manifesta: Young Women, Feminism, and the Future*. New York: Farrar, Straus and Giroux, 2000. Print.
*Beautiful Creatures*. Dir. Richard La Gravenesse. Perf. Ethan Wate and Lena Duchannes. Warner Brothers Entertainment, 2013. Film. 12 December 2013.
Belenky, Mary Field, et al. *Women's Ways of Knowing: The Development of Self, Voice and Mind*. New York: Basic Books, 1997. Print.
Berger, Helen A., and Douglas Ezzy. *Teenage Witches: Magical Youth and the Search for Self*. New Brunswick, NJ: Rutgers University Press, 2007. Print.
Berman, Steve. *Vintage: A Ghost Story*. New York: Haworth Positronic Press, 2007. Kindle edition.
Bettelheim, Bruno. *The Uses of Enchantment and Magic: The Meaning and Importance of Fairy Tales*. New York: Knopf, 1976. Print.
Bettis, Pamela J., and Natalie G. Adams. "Landscapes of Girlhood." *Geographies of Girlhood: Identities In-Between*. Mahwah, NJ: Lawrence Erbaum Associates, 2005. pp. 1–18. Print.
Blatty, William Peter. *The Exorcist*. New York: Harper & Row, 1971. Print.
*Blood Moon*. Dir. Thom Fitzgerald. Perf. Tim Curry, Victoria Sanchez and Dov Tiefenbach. Castel Film Romania, 2001. Film.
Bosky, Bernadette Lynn. "The Witch." *Icons of Horror and the Supernatural: An Encyclopedia of Our Worst Nightmares*, vol. 2. Westport, CT: Greenwood Press, 2007. Print.
Braude, Ann. *Radical Spirits: Spiritualism and Women's Rights in Nineteenth Century America*. Boston: Beacon Press, 1989. Print.
Brown, Lyn Mikel, *Girlfighting: Betrayal and Rejection among Girls*. New York: New York University Press, 2003. Print.
_____. *Raising Their Voices: The Politics of Girls Anger*. Cambridge: Harvard University Press, 1998. Print.

# Bibliography

Brown, Lyn Mikel, and Carol Gilligan. *Meeting at the Crossroads: Women's Psychology and Girl's Development.* Cambridge: Harvard University Press, 1992. Print.

Brownmiller, Susan. *Femininity.* New York: Ballantine, 1984. Print.

Boudreau, Brenda. "The Battleground of the Adolescent Girl's Body." *The Girl: Construction of the Girl in Contemporary Fiction by Women,* Ruth O. Saxton, ed. New York: St. Martin's, 1998. pp. 43–56. Print.

Bray, Libba. *A Great and Terrible Beauty.* New York: Delacourt, 2003. Print.

____. *Rebel Angels.* New York: Delacourt, 2005. Print.

____. *The Sweet Far Thing.* New York: Delacourt, 2007. Print.

Brumberg, Joan, *The Body Project: An Intimate History of American Girls.* New York: Random House, 1997. Print.

Butler, Judith. *Gender Trouble: Feminism and the Subversion of Identity.* New York: Routledge, 1990. Print.

____. *The Psychic Life of Power: Theories in Subjection.* Stanford: Stanford University Press, 1997. Print.

Campbell, Patty. "The Sand in the Oyster: Muddle Middle." *Horn Book* 76 (July-August 2000): 483–85. Print.

Carpenter, Lynette, and Wendy K. Kolmar, eds. *Haunting the House of Fiction: Feminist Perspectives on Ghost Stories by American Women.* Knoxville: University of Tennessee Press, 1991. Print.

____. "The Value of Young Adult Literature." *Young Adult Library Services Organization.* American Library Association, n.d. Web. 24 May 2010. www.ala.org/ala/mgrps/divs/yalsa/profdev/whitepapers.

*Charmed.* WB: 1998–2006. Television.

Charnas, Suzy McKee. "Boobs." *Children of the Night: Stories of Ghosts, Vampires, Werewolves, and "Lost Children."* Martin Harry Greenberg and Elizabeth Ann Scarborough, eds. Nashville: Cumberland House, 1999. 11–35. Print.

Chodorow, Nancy. *The Reproduction of Mothering: Psychoanalysis and the Sociology of Gender.* Berkeley: University of California Press, 1978. Print.

"Chronic Fatigue Syndrome: Who's at Risk?" *Centers for Disease Control and Prevention.* Centers for Disease Control and Prevention, 10 March 2006. Web. 24 May 2010. www.cdc.gov/cfs/cfscausesHCP.htm.

Cixous, Hélène, Keith Cohen, and Paula Cohen. "The Laugh of the Medusa." *Signs* 1 (1976): 875–93. Print.

Clapp, Patricia. *Jane-Emily.* 1969. New York: HarperCollins, 2007. Kindle edition.

Clark, Elizabeth. "'Hairy Thuggish Women': Female Werewolves, Gender and the Hoped-For Monster." MA thesis. Georgetown University, 2008. Web.

Coleridge, Samuel Taylor. "Christabel." *Bartleby.* Bartleby, n.d. Web. 24 May 2010. www.bartleby.com/41/420.html.

*The Craft.* Dir. Andrew Fleming. Perf. Fairuza Balk, Robin Tunney, Neve Campbell, and Rachel True. Columbia Pictures, 1996. Film.

Craig, Zoe. "'Top 10 Longest-Running London Theatre Shows.'" *Londonsit.* 13 April 2011: n.p. Web. 15 May 2013. londonist.com/2011/04/top-10-longest-running-london-theatre-shows.php.

Creed, Barbara. "Dark Desires: Male Masochism in the Horror Film." *Screening the Male: Exploring Masculinities in Hollywood Cinema.* Steven Cohan and Ina Rae Hark, eds. London: Routledge, 1993. pp. 118–133. Print.

____. "Horror and the Monstrous-Feminine: An Imaginary Abjection." *The Dread of Difference: Gender and the Horror Film.* Barry Keith Grant, ed. Austin: University of Texas Press, 1996. 35–65. Print.

*The Curse of the Werewolf.* Dir. Terence Fisher. Perf. Oliver Reed, Catherine Feller, and Clifford Evans. Hammer Film Productions, 1961. Film.

# Bibliography

de Beauvoir, Simone. *The Second Sex.* 1952. New York: Vintage, 1974. Print.
de France, Marie. *French Mediaeval Romances from the Lays of Marie de France.* Eugene Mason, tr. New York: E.P. Dutton, 1911. Print.
Dickens, Charles. *A Christmas Carol.* 1843. New York: Holiday House, 1983. Print.
Dowling, Colette. *The Frailty Myth: Redefining the Physical Potential of Women and Girls.* New York: Random House, 2000. Print.
Driscoll, Catherine. *Girls: Feminine Adolescence in Popular Culture and Cultural Theory.* New York: Columbia University Press, 2002. Print.
du Coudray, Chantal Bourgault. *The Curse of the Werewolf: Fantasy, Horror and the Beast Within.* London: I.B. Tauris, 2006. Print.
Dziemianowicz, Stefan. "The Werewolf." *Icons of Horror and the Supernatural: An Encyclopedia of Our Worst Nightmares,* vol. 2. Westport, CT: Greenwood Press, 2007. Print.
Ehrenreich, Barbara, and Deidre English. *Witches, Midwives and Nurses: A History of Women Healers.* New York: Feminist Press, 1973. Print.
Eisler, Riane. *The Chalice and the Blade: Our History, Our Future.* New York: HarperCollins, 1987. Print.
Ellis, Bret Easton. *American Psycho.* New York: Vintage, 1991. Print.
Endore, Guy. *The Werewolf of Paris.* New York: Farrar and Reinhardt, 1933. Print.
Evans, Walter. "Monster Movies: A Sexual Theory." *Journal of Popular Film* 2 (1973): 353–65. Print.
Fonseca, Anthony. "The Doppelganger." *Icons of Horror and the Supernatural: An Encyclopedia of Our Worst Nightmares,* vol. 1. Westport, CT: Greenwood Press, 2007. 187–214. Print.
Fonseca, Anthony, and June Michele Pulliam. *Hooked on Horror: A Guide to Reading Interests.* Englewood, CO: Libraries Unlimited, 1999. Print.
_____, and _____. *Hooked on Horror: A Guide to Reading Interests,* 2d ed. Englewood, CO: Libraries Unlimited, 2003. Print.
_____, and _____. *Hooked on Horror III: A Guide to Reading Interests.* Westport, CT: Libraries Unlimited, 2009. Print.
Foucault, Michel. *Discipline and Punish: The Birth of the Prison.* Alan Sheridan, trans. New York: Random, 1979. Print.
_____. *The History of Sexuality.* 1977. Robert Hurley, trans. New York: Vintage, 1988. Print.
*Freaks.* Dir. Tod Browning. Perf. Harry Earles, Daisy Earles, and Olga Baclanova. Metro-Goldwyn-Mayer, 1932. Film.
Freud, Sigmund. "The Uncanny." *The Uncanny.* David McLintock, trans. New York: Penguin, 2003. pp. 121–62. Print.
Friere, Paulo. *The Pedagogy of the Oppressed.* 1970. Myra Bergman Ramos, trans. New York: Continuum, 1993. Print.
Gilligan, Carol. *In a Different Voice: Psychological Theory and Women's Development.* Cambridge: Harvard University Press, 1982. Print.
*Ginger Snaps.* Dir. John Fawcett. Perf. Katherine Isabelle, Emily Perkins, and Mimi Rogers. Copperheart Entertainment, 2000. Film.
*Ginger Snaps 2: Unleashed.* Dir. Brett Sullivan, Dir. Perf. Emily Perkins and Katharine Isabelle. 49th Parallel Productions, 2004. Film.
*Ginger Snaps Back: The Beginning.* Dir. Grant Harvey. Perf. Emily Perkins and Katharine Isabelle. 49 Films, 2004. Film.
Grant, Barry Keith, ed. *The Dread of Difference: Gender and the Horror Film.* Austin: University of Texas Press, 1996. Print.
Griffin, Susan. *Pornography and Silence: Culture's Revenge against Nature.* New York: Harper & Row, 1981. Print.
Hahn, Mary Downing. *Wait Till Helen Comes.* 1986. New York: Clarion Books, 2008. Kindle edition.

# Bibliography

Hearn, Julie. *The Minister's Daughter*. New York: Atheneum, 2005. Print.
Heath, Stephen. "Difference." *Screen* 19, vol. 3 (Autumn 1978). Print.
Herald, Diana Tixler, and Bonnie Kunzel. *Fluent in Fantasy*. Westport, CT: Libraries Unlimited, 2007. Print.
Herz, Sarah K., and Donald R. Gallo. *From Hamlet to Hinton: Building Bridges Between Young Adult Literature and the Classics, Second Edition*. Westport, CT: Greenwood Press, 2005. Print.
Herzog, Harold A. "Gender Differences in Human-Animal Interactions: A Review." *Anthrozoos* 20 Issue 1 (2007): 7–21. Print.
Hill, Susan. *The Woman in Black*. 1983. Boston: D.R. Godine, 1986. Print.
Hoeveler, Diane Long. *Gothic Feminism: The Professionalization of Gender from Charlotte Smith to the Brontës*. University Park: Pennsylvania State University Press, 1995. Print.
Hoffman, Nina Kiriki. *A Stir of Bones*. New York: Viking, 2003. Print.
Housel, Rebecca, and J. Jeremy Wisnewski, eds. *Twilight and Philosophy: Vampires, Vegetarians and the Pursuit of Immortality*. The Blackwell Philosophy and Pop Culture Series. Hoboken, NJ: John Wiley and Sons, 2009. Print.
*I Was a Teenage Werewolf*. Dir. Gene Fowler, Jr. Perf. Michael Landon. American International Pictures, 1957. Film.
Kami, Garcia, and Margaret Stohl. *Beautiful Creatures*. New York: Little, Brown, Books for Young Readers, 2009. Print.
Karlsen, Carol F. *The Devil in the Shape of a Woman: Witchcraft in Colonial New England*. New York: Vintage, 1989. Print.
Kimmel, Michael S. "Masculinity as Homophobia: Fear, Shame, Silence in the Construction of Gender Identity." *Theorizing Masculinities*, Harry Brod and Michael Kaufman, eds. Thousand Oaks, CA: Sage, 1994. pp. 119–41. Print.
King, Stephen. *Carrie*. Garden City, NY: Doubleday, 1974. Print.
Kingston, Maxine Hong. *The Woman Warrior: Memoirs of a Girlhood Among Ghosts*. New York: Knopf, 1976. Print.
Klause, Annette Curtis. *Blood and Chocolate*. New York: Delacourt Press, 1997. Print.
Kristeva, Julia. *The Powers of Horror: An Essay on Abjection*. Leon S. Roudiez, trans. New York: Columbia University Press, 1982. Print.
Lacan, Jacques. "The Mirror Stage as Formative of the I Function as Revealed in Psychoanalytic Experience." *Ecrits: The First Complete Edition in English*. New York: W.W. Norton, 2006. pp. 75–81. Print.
Lamb, Sharon, and Lyn Mikel Brown. *Packaging Girlhood: Rescuing Our Daughters from Marketers' Schemes*. New York: St. Martin's Press, 2006. Print.
Le Fanu, Sheridan. *Carmilla. In a Glass Darkly*. 1872. New York: Oxford University Press, 1993. pp. 243–319. Print.
Le Guin, Ursula K. "Why Kids Want Fantasy." *Cheek by Jowl: Talks and Essays on How and Why Fantasy Matters*. Seattle: Aqueduct Press, 2009. pp. 131–35. Print.
Lesko, Nancy. *Act Your Age! A Cultural Construction of Adolescence*. New York: Routledge Falmer, 2001. Print.
Lundie, Katherine A. *Restless Spirits: Ghost Stories by American Women, 1872–1926*. Amherst: University of Massachusetts Press, 1996. Print.
Margolis, Harriet. "A Childe in Love, or Is It Just Fantasy? The Values of Women's Genres." *Paradoxa: Studies in World Literary Genres* 3, 1–2 (1997): 121–44. Print.
Masse, Michelle. *In the Name of Love: Women, Narcissism and the Gothic*. Ithaca: Cornell University Press, 1992. Print.
McCallum, Robyn. *Ideologies of Identity in Adolescent Fiction: The Dialogic Construction of Subjectivity*. New York: Garland, 1999. Print.
\_\_\_\_\_. "Other Selves: Subjectivity and The Doppelganger in Australian Adolescent Fiction."

# Bibliography

*Writing the Australian Child: Text and Contexts in Fictions for Children*. Clair Bradford, ed. Nedlands, Western Australia: University of Western Australia Press, 1996. pp. 17–36. Print.
McNay, Lois. *Gender and Agency: Reconfiguring the Subject in Feminist and Social Theory*. Cambridge: Polity Press, 2000. Print.
*Medium*. CBS: 2005–2010. Television.
Meyer, Stephenie. *Breaking Dawn*. New York: Little, Brown, 2008. Print.
———. *Eclipse*. New York: Little, Brown, 2007. Print.
———. *New Moon*. New York: Little, Brown, 2006. Print.
———. *Twilight*. New York: Little, Brown, 2005. Print.
Modleski, Tania. *Loving with a Vengeance: Mass-produced Fantasies for Women*. New York: Methuen, 1982. Print.
Morris, Paula. *Ruined: A Novel*. New York: Point, 2009. Print.
———. *Unbroken: A Ruined Novel*. New York: Point, 2013. Kindle edition.
Morrison, Toni. *Beloved*. New York: Knopf, 1987. Print.
Mulvey, Laura. "Visual Pleasure and Narrative Cinema." *Issues in Feminist Film Criticism*, Patricia Erens, ed. Bloomington: Indiana University Press, 1990. pp. 28–40. Print.
Naylor, Phyllis Reynolds. *Jade Green: A Ghost Story*. 1999. New York: Simon Pulse, 2002. Print.
O'Farrell, Clare. *Michel Foucault*. London: Sage, 2005. Print.
Orenstein, Peggy. *Schoolgirls: Young Women, Self Esteem and the Confidence Gap*. New York: Doubleday, 1994. Print.
*The Others*. Dir. Alejnandro Amenábar. Perf. Nicole Kidman, Alakina Mann, and James Bentley. Cruise/Wagner Productions, 2001. Film.
Ovid. *Metamorphoses*. Rolfe Humphries, trans. Bloomington: Indiana University Press, 1955. Print.
Phillips, Lynn M. *Flirting with Danger: Young Women's Reflections on Sexuality and Domination*. New York: New York University Press, 2000. Print.
Pinedo, Isabel Cristina. *Recreational Terror: Women and the Pleasures of Horror Film Viewing*. Albany: State University of New York Press, 1997. Print.
Pipher, Mary. *Reviving Ophelia. Saving the Selves of Adolescent Girls*. New York: Ballantine, 1995. Print.
Punday, Daniel. "Narrative Performance in the Contemporary Monster Story," *The Modern Language Review* 97, Issue 4 (2002): 803–20. Print.
Ramsdell, Kristin. *Romance Fiction: A Guide to the Genre*. Englewood, CO: Libraries Unlimited, 1999. Print.
Rees, Celia. *Sorceress*. Cambridge, MA: Candlewick Press, 2002. Print.
———. *Witch Child*. Cambridge, MA: Candlewick Press, 2000. Print.
Reid, Siân. "As I Do Will, So Mote It Be: Magic as Metaphor in Neo-Pagan Witchcraft," in *Magical Religion and Modern Witchcraft*, James R. Lewis, ed. Albany: State University of New York Press, 1996. pp. 141–70. Print.
Reiss, Kathryn. *Dreadful Sorry*. New York: Scholastic, 1996. Print.
Ringel, Faye. "Witchcraft/Sorcery." *Supernatural Literature of the World: An Encyclopedia*, vol. 3. Westport, CT: Greenwood Press, 2005. 1219–22. Print.
Russell, Jeffrey B. *A History of Witchcraft: Sorcerers, Heretics, and Pagans*. London: Thames and Hudson, 1980. Print.
*Sabrina: The Teenage Witch*. ABC: 1996–2003. Television.
Shakira. "She Wolf." 2009. Song.
*The Sixth Sense*. Dir. M. Night Shyamalyn. Perf. Bruce Willis and Haley Joe Osment. Barry Mendel Productions, 1999. Film.
Steele, Valerie. *The Corset: A Cultural History*. New Haven: Yale University Press, 2003. Print.
Stevenson, Robert Louis. *The Strange Case of Dr. Jekyll and Mr. Hyde*. 1886. New York: Dodd Mead, 1961. Print.

# Bibliography

Stiefvater, Maggie. *Forever.* New York: Scholastic, 2012. Print.
\_\_\_\_\_. *Linger.* New York: Scholastic Press, 2010. Print.
\_\_\_\_\_. *Shiver.* New York: Scholastic Press, 2009. Print.
Tobin-McClain, Lee. "Paranormal Romance: Secrets of the Female Fantastic." *Journal of the Fantastic in the Arts* 11, Issue 3 (2000): 294–306. Print.
Trites, Roberta Seelinger. *Disturbing the Universe: Power and Repression in Adolescent Literature.* Iowa City: University of Iowa Press, 2000. Print.
\_\_\_\_\_. *Waking Sleeping Beauty: Feminist Voices in Children's Novels.* Iowa City: University of Iowa Press, 1997. Print.
Updike, John. *The Witches of Eastwick.* New York: Knopf, 1984. Print.
Virgil. "Eighth Eclogue." *Eclogues.* Barbara Hughes Fowler, trans. Chapel Hill: University of North Carolina Press, 1997. 22–25. Print.
*Werewolf of London.* Dir. Stuart Walker. Perf. Henry Hull and Warner Oland. Universal Pictures, 1935. Film.
Whitcomb, Laura. *A Certain Slant of Light.* Boston: Graphia, 2005. Print.
\_\_\_\_\_. *Under the Light.* Boston: Houghton Mifflin Harcourt, 2013. Kindle edition.
White, Emily. *Fast Girls: Teenage Tribes and the Myth of the Slut.* New York: Scribner, 2002. Print.
Windsor, Patricia. *The Blooding.* New York: Scholastic, 1996. Print.
Wisker, Gina. *Horror Fiction: An Introduction.* New York: Continuum, 2005. Print.
*The Witches of Eastwick.* Dir. George Miller. Perf. Jack Nicholson, Cher, Susan Sarandon and Michelle Pfeiffer. 1987. Warner Brothers. Film.
*The Wolf Man.* Dir. George Waggner. Perf. Claude Rains, Bela Lugosi, and Ralph Belamy. Universal Pictures, 1941. Film.
Wolf, Naomi. *The Beauty Myth: How Images of Beauty Are Used Against Women.* 1991. New York: Harper Perennial, 2002. Print.
*The Woman in Black.* Dir. James Watkins. Perf. Daniel Radcliffe, Ciaran Hinds. Hammer Studios, 2012. Film.
Wood, Robin. "An Introduction to the Horror Film." *Planks of Reason: Essays on the Horror Film, Revised Edition.* Barry Keith Grant and Christopher Sherrett, eds. Lanham, MD: Scarecrow Press, 2004. pp. 107–41. Print.
Younger, Beth. *Learning Curves: Body Image and Female Sexuality in Young Adult Literature.* Lanham, MD: Scarecrow Press, 2009. Print.

# Index

The AAUW Report: How Schools Shortchange Girls (American Association of University Women) 13
the abject 15–16, 18, 41, 47, 70, 83, 87–88, 104, 173; see also abject body; the Other
abject body 95
abortion 155
Act Your Age! A Cultural Construction of Adolescence (Nancy Lesko) 75
Adams, Carol (The Sexual Politics of Meat: A Feminist-Vegetarian Critical Theory) 74, 111
Adams, Natalie, and Pamela Bettis (Geographies of Girlhood: Identities In-Between) 57
Adler, Margot (Drawing Down the Moon: Witches, Druids, Goddess-Worshippers, and Other Pagans in America Today) 181–82
adolescent development, theories of 75, 135
alienation from the body see disembodiment
alter ego 40, 180; see also double
American Association of University Women (The AAUW Report: How Schools Shortchange Girls) 13
American Horror Story: Coven (television series) 130, 182
American Horror Story: Murder House (television series) 22
American Spiritualist Movement see Spiritualism
Angel of the House 76
anger, girls see anger, women's
anger, women's 14–15, 28, 66, 74, 77, 79–82, 100–01, 106, 110, 113–117, 122
animal form 87, 89, 92, 96, 103, 109, 118–20, 175
animal nature 73, 76, 86, 96, 111, 175–76; see also nature/culture dichotomy; natural world
animals, attitudes towards 112
anorexia 102–03
Armstrong, Kelley (Women of the Otherworld series) 75
arranged marriage see marriage, arranged
articulateness 28–30, 32, 33, 50, 63, 67, 89, 101, 148–50, 174; see also silencing of women's voices
"As I Do Will, So Mote It Be: Magic as Metaphor in Neo-Pagan Witchcraft" (Sîan Reid) 127, 139, 156
athleticism, women's 77, 84, 102–03

banking model of education 165
Barstow, Anne (Witchcraze: A New History of the European Witch Hunts) 157, 181
"The Battleground of the Adolescent Girl's Body" (Brenda Boudreau) 50, 51, 101
Baumgardner, Jennifer, and Amy Richards (Manifesta: Young Women, Feminism, and the Future) 48, 180
beast within 74–118, 175
Beautiful Creatures (film) 130, 182
Beautiful Creatures (Kami Garcia and Margaret Stohl) 130, 182
beauty culture 14, 80, 83–91, 175, 178
the Beauty Myth 84–91; see also beauty culture
The Beauty Myth: How Images of Beauty Are Used Against Women (Naomi Wolf) 84–85, 89, 174, 181
beauty standards see beauty culture
Belenky, Mary (Women's Ways of Knowing: The Development of Self, Voice and Mind) 126–27, 135–36, 139, 156

# Index

*Beloved* (Toni Morrison) 22
Berger, Helen A., and Douglas Ezzy (*Teenage Witches: Magical Youth and the Search for Self*) 128
Berman, Steve (*Vintage*) 180
Bettelheim, Bruno (*The Uses of Enchantment and Magic: The Meaning and Importance of Fairy Tales*) 20, 100
Bettis, Pamela, and Natalie Adams (*Geographies of Girlhood: Identities In-Between*) 57
bewitchment *see* possession
*Bildungsroman* 12, 160
*Bildungsroman*, female 100–01, 105; *see also* *Bildungsroman*
birth imagery 43–45, 63–67, 68–69
"Bisclavert," Marie de France 74
Blatty, William Peter (*The Exorcist*) 26
blood, menstrual *see* menstruation
*Blood and Chocolate* (Annette Curtis Klause) 78, 80, 99–121, 171, 175
*Blood and Chocolate* (film) 181
*Blood Moon* 78–99, 121, 171, 175, 180–81
*The Blooding* (Patricia Windsor) 78, 80, 99–121, 171, 175, 177
*The Body Project: An Intimate History of American Girls* (Joan Jacobs Brumberg) 14, 85, 174
body, regulation of *see* discipline targeting the body
"Boobs" (Suzy McKee Charnas) 78, 80, 99–121, 175, 177
Bosky, Bernadette ("The Witch") 124
Boudreau, Brenda ("The Battleground of the Adolescent Girl's Body") 50–51, 101
Bray, Libba: Gemma Doyle Trilogy 124, 160–71, 176–78, 182; *A Great and Terrible Beauty* 160–71, 176–78, 182; *Rebel Angels* 160–71, 176–78, 182; *The Sweet Far Thing* 160–71, 176–78, 182
Braude, Ann (*Radical Spirits: Spiritualism and Women's Rights in Nineteenth Century America*) 61, 62, 150, 180
Brown, Lyn Mikel: *Girlfighting: Betrayal and Rejection among Girls* 13–14, 89–91; *Raising Their Voices: The Politics of Girls Anger* 14, 28, 77, 82, 100, 113
Brown, Lyn Mikel, and Carol Gilligan (*Meeting at the Crossroads: Women's Psychology and Girl's Development*) 13, 32
Brown, Lyn Mikel, and Sharon Lamb (*Packaging Girlhood: Rescuing Our Daughters from Marketers' Schemes*) 14
Brownmiller, Susan (*Femininity*) 84, 87, 181

Brumberg, Joan (*The Body Project: An Intimate History of American Girls*) 14, 85, 174
bullying 81, 89–91, 96, 101–04, 132, 177; *see also* relational violence among girls; sexual harassment
the Burning Times 124, 129, 142–59; *see also* Early Modern witch hunts
Butler, Judith: *Gender Trouble: Feminism and the Subversion of Identity* 16, 24, 39–40, 70, 72, 76, 97, 118, 180; *The Psychic Life of Power: Theories in Subjection* 17, 69–70, 77, 81, 131, 174–76, 182

Campbell, Patty ("The Sand in the Oyster: Muddle Middle") 12
captivity narratives 144
carnivory 74, 77, 81, 111–13; *see also* hunting; meat
Carpenter, Lynette, and Wendy K. Kolmar (*Haunting the House of Fiction: Feminist Perspectives on Ghost Stories by American Women*) 22, 27
*Carrie* (Stephen King) 79
Cart, Michael ("The Value of Young Adult Literature") 18, 79
castration fantasy 99
Centers for Disease Control and Prevention 111–12
*A Certain Slant of Light* (Laura Whitcomb) 25, 50–69, 71–72, 177–78, 180
*The Chalice and the Blade: Our History, Our Future* (Raine Eisler) 133
channeling 153–54; *see also* possession
*Charmed* (television series) 130, 182
Charnas, Suzy McKee ("Boobs") 78, 80, 99–121, 177
"A Childe in Love, or Is It Just Fantasy? The Values of Women's Genres" (Harriet Margolis) 105–06
Chodorow, Nancy (*The Reproduction of Mothering: Psychoanalysis and the Sociology of Gender*) 139, 181
Christianity, fundamentalist 25, 27, 51–52, 60, 178; *see also* Puritanism
*A Christmas Carol* (Charles Dickens) 21
Chronic Fatigue Syndrome 111–12
Cixous, Hélène ("Laugh of the Medusa") 32
Clapp, Patricia (*Jane-Emily*) 27
Clark, Elizabeth ("Hairy Thuggish Women": Female Werewolves, Gender and the Hoped-For Monster") 76–77, 81, 83–84

# Index

class 18, 23, 28, 33, 37–38, 45, 78, 91, 124, 132, 160, 162, 177

Clause, Annette Curtis (*Blood and Chocolate*) 78, 80, 99–121, 171, 175, 177

Colonial New England 128, 130, 142, 154

compulsory heterosexuality 27, 103; *see also* heteronormativity

compulsory visibility 145–46; *see also* surveillance and visibility

constructivism 125–27, 135–42, 152–57, 161, 168–70, 176–78; *see also* received knowing; subjectivism

correct training 143, 145–47, 160–62, 165; *see also* discipline targeting the body; overregulation

*The Corset: A Cultural History* (Valerie Steele) 162

*The Craft* (film) 124, 130–42, 161, 166, 171, 177–78

Creed, Barbara: "Dark Desires: Male Masochism in the Horror Film" 95; "Horror and the Monstrous-Feminine: An Imaginary Abjection" 15, 18, 47, 88, 97, 110, 173

Creole characters 34–38

cunning women 123–24, 144, 158–59

curse 35

*The Curse of the Werewolf: Fantasy, Horror and the Beast Within* (Charlotte du Coudray) 74–76, 78, 80

"Dark Desires: Male Masochism in the Horror Film" (Barbara Creed) 95

dark fantasy 18, 80, 179

de Beauvoir, Simone (*The Second Sex*) 13

de France, Marie ("Bisclavert") 74

*The Devil in the Shape of a Woman: Witchcraft in Colonial New England* (Carol Karlsen) 147, 150, 181

the dialogic 15–16, 40, 154

diaries 55, 61, 167–68

Dickens, Charles (*A Christmas Carol*) 21

difference 11–12

"Difference" (Stephen Heath) 133

disavowed knowledge *see* the repressed

disciplinary power *see* discipline; discipline targeting the body; discipline targeting the mind

discipline 16, 17, 26–27, 30–38, 50–56, 145–47, 161–65, 174, 176; *see also* compulsory visibility; correct training; discipline targeting the body; discipline targeting the mind; overregulation; surveillance; visibility

*Discipline and Punish: The Birth of the Prison* (Michel Foucault) 17, 30, 33, 143, 145, 176

discipline targeting the body 17, 27, 30, 33, 36, 50–54, 145–47, 160–62; *see also* correct training; overregulation

discipline targeting the mind 32, 54–56, 160–62, 164–65

discourses of gender 14, 36–37, 70, 87, 105, 178, 181; *see also* Pleasing Woman Discourse

discursive subject 65; *see also* pre-discursive subject

disembodiment 50–52, 55, 101

*Disturbing the Universe: Power and Repression in Adolescent Literature* (Roberta Seelinger Trites) 12, 18, 57, 60, 85, 126, 179

docile subject 51

domestic violence 53; *see also* violence against women

domesticity as prison 25, 27, 31–32, 178

double 15–16, 23, 28–29, 38–42, 59–60, 62, 174, 180; *see also* the Other

Dowling, Colette (*The Frailty Myth: Redefining the Physical Potential of Women and Girls*) 181

drag 16, 76, 96–98, 109

*Drawing Down the Moon: Witches, Druids, Goddess-Worshippers, and Other Pagans in America Today* (Margot Adler) 181–82

*Dread of Difference* (Barry Keith Grant) 12

*Dreadful Sorry* (Kathryn Reiss) 21–49, 71, 171, 176–77

dreams, function of 15

Driscoll, Catherine (*Girls*) 14

drowning 44, 67–69, 158

du Coudray, Charlotte (*The Curse of the Werewolf: Fantasy, Horror and the Beast Within*) 74–76, 78, 80

dunking, trial by 158

Dziemaimowicz, Stefan ("The Werewolf") 74–75

Early Modern witch hunts 124, 128, 142–59; *see also* witchcraft, people accused of

eating disorders *see* anorexia

education of women 30–33, 155, 160–65, 170, 177

Ehrenreich, Barbara, and Deidra English (*Witches, Midwives and Nurses: A History of Women Healers*) 124

Eisler, Riane (*The Chalice and the Blade: Our History, Our Future*) 133

# Index

emotional abuse 58; *see also* domestic violence
Endore, Guy (*The Werewolf of Paris*) 74
English, Deidra, and Barbara Ehrenreich (*Witches, Midwives and Nurses: A History of Women Healers*) 124
English Civil War 128
ensorcellment *see* possession
epilepsy 167
epistemology 125–26, 134–35, 146, 159, 160–72, 176, 178; *see also* knowledge, construction of
Evans, Walter ("Monster Movies: A Sexual Theory") 95
the evil eye 133; *see also* female gaze; glamour
execution for witchcraft 158
exorcism 58, 67
*The Exorcist* (William Peter Blatty) 26
Ezzy, Douglas, and Helen A. Berger (*Teenage Witches: Magical Youth and the Search for Self*) 128

fairy tales, uses of 20, 100
family patriarch, figure of 23–24, 27, 29, 51–53, 175
fantastic fiction, uses of 20, 100, 173, 178; *see also* fantasy fiction
fantasy, dark *see* dark fantasy
fantasy fiction 20, 100, 178–181
*Fast Girls: Teenage Tribes and the Myth of the Slut* (Emily White) 129, 131, 181
female friendship 42, 105, 138–42, 165–69, 178; *see also* sisterhood
female gaze 133, 161; *see also* glamour, casting; male gaze
feminine maternal body 95
feminine mystique 84
feminine sense of self 139, 181
feminine sexuality 60–61, 83, 94–96, 105–06, 110, 112, 122, 143–44, 162, 174, 180; *see also* sexual desire; sexual maturity; sexuality
feminine space *see* space, feminine
*Femininity* (Susan Brownmiller) 84, 87, 181
femininity, conventional *see* femininity, normative
femininity, normative 26, 29–30, 36–37, 61–62, 76–77, 82–86, 90, 106–122, 126, 129, 131, 143–162 174–76
femininity, stereotypical *see* femininity, normative
feminism 36, 47–49, 62, 135–37, 139, 150, 152, 161, 169–71, 176, 178, 180; *see also* first-wave feminism; post-feminism; second-wave feminism; third-wave feminism
femme fatale 82, 95, 97
fiction, non-realistic *see* non-realistic fiction
film as Young Adult fiction *see* Young Adult fiction, film as
fire imagery 44–45
first-wave feminism 40, 50, 61–62, 76, 84, 150, 170, 176–77
*Flirting with Danger: Young Women's Reflections on Sexuality and Domination* (Lynn Phillips) 14, 87, 181
*Fluent in Fantasy* (Diana Tixler Herald and Bonnie Kunzel) 181
Fonseca, Anthony, and June Pulliam (*Hooked on Horror III: A Guide to Reading Interests*) 17, 83
Foucault, Michel: *Discipline and Punish: The Birth of the Prison* 17, 30, 33, 143, 145, 176; feminist interpretations of 17; *The History of Sexuality* 17
*The Frailty Myth: Redefining the Physical Potential of Women and Girls* (Colette Dowling) 181
freak shows 79–80, 87, 97
*Freaks* (film) 80
free people of color 34
Freud, Sigmund ("The Uncanny") 23, 28, 39
Friere, Paolo (*Pedagogy of the Oppressed*) 165
*From Hamlet to Hinton: Building Bridges Between Young Adult Literature and the Classics* (Sarah K. Herz and Donald R. Gallo) 127
full moon *see* lunar cycle
fundamentalist Christianity *see* Christianity, fundamentalist

Gallo, Donald R., and Sarah K. Herz (*From Hamlet to Hinton: Building Bridges between Young Adult Literature and the Classics*) 127
Garcia, Kami, and Margaret Stohl (*Beautiful Creatures*) 130, 182
the Gemma Doyle Trilogy (Libba Bray) 124, 160–71, 176–78, 182
*Gender and Agency: Reconfiguring the Subject in Feminist and Social Theory* (Lois McNay) 17
"Gender Differences in Human-Animal Interactions: A Review" (Harold A. Herzog) 112
*Gender Trouble: Feminism and the Subver-*

# Index

sion of Identity (Judith Butler) 16, 24, 39–40, 70, 72, 76, 81, 97, 118, 180
Geographies of Girlhood: Identities In-Between (Pamela Bettis and Natalie Adams) 57
ghost, figure of 19–72, 150, 171, 175, 178, 180
ghost stories authored by women 22–23
ghost story 19–72, 180
ghost story, definition 22
ghost story, YA definition 22–23, 28
ghosts, definition 21
Gilligan, Carol (In a Different Voice: Psychological Theory and Women's Development) 13
Gilligan, Carol, and Lyn Mikel Brown (Meeting at the Crossroads: Women's Psychology and Girl's Development) 13, 32
Ginger Snaps 78–99, 121, 171, 175, 180; see also The Ginger Snaps trilogy
Ginger Snaps Back: The Beginning 78–99, 121, 180–81; see also The Ginger Snaps trilogy
The Ginger Snaps trilogy 78–99, 121, 175, 180; see also Ginger Snaps; Ginger Snaps Back: The Beginning; Ginger Snaps 2: Unleashed
Ginger Snaps 2: Unleashed 78–99, 121, 180–81; see also The Ginger Snaps trilogy
girlfighting see bullying; relational violence among women; sisterhood
Girlfighting: Betrayal and Rejection among Girls (Lyn Mikel Brown) 13–14, 89–91
Girls: Feminine Adolescence in Popular Culture and Cultural Theory (Catherine Driscoll) 14
glamour, casting a 89, 133, 144–45, 161, 169; see also female gaze
the Gothic 11, 18, 22–25, 27, 31, 46, 49–69, 80, 100, 116, 179; see also ghost story; Gothic romance; the modern Gothic
Gothic feminism 46–47
Gothic Feminism: The Professionalization of Gender from Charlotte Smith to the Brontës (Diane Hoeveler) 31, 46
Gothic hero 107–08
Gothic heroine 31, 46, 107
Gothic romance 82, 106–07, 116; see also paranormal romance; romance
Grant, Barry Keith (The Dread of Difference: Gender and the Horror Film) 12
A Great and Terrible Beauty (Libba Bray) 124, 160–71, 176–78, 182
Griffin, Susan (Pornography and Silence:

Culture's Revenge against Nature) 73, 76, 80, 86, 94–96, 125

Hahn, Mary Dowling (Wait Till Helen Comes) 27
hair 77, 80, 83–87, 140; see also hypertrichosis
"Hairy Thuggish Women": Female Werewolves, Gender and the Hoped-For Monster" (Elizabeth Clark) 76–77, 81, 83–84
Hamlet (William Shakespeare) 21
Harlequin romance 107; see also Gothic romance; paranormal romance; romance fiction
haunted boy, figure of 27, 180
haunted girl, figure of 19–72, 121–22, 150, 171, 175, 178
haunting 19–72, 148, 180
Haunting the House of Fiction: Feminist Perspectives on Ghost Stories by American Women (Lynette Carpenter and Wendy K. Kolmar) 22, 27
healers see traditional healers
Hearn, Julie (The Minister's Daughter) 124, 142–159, 171, 176–78
Heath, Stephen ("Difference") 133
Herald, Diana Tixler, and Bonnie Kunzel (Fluent in Fantasy) 181
Herz, Sarah K., and Donald R. Gallo (From Hamlet to Hinton: Building Bridges between Young Adult Literature and the Classics) 127
Herzog, Harold A. ("Gender Differences in Human-Animal Interactions: A Review") 112
heteronormativity 162; see also compulsory heterosexuality
Hill, Susan (The Woman in Black) 22
hirsutism see hypertrichosis
historical past as setting 24, 26, 36–37, 128–30, 160
history, women's 22, 36, 40, 46
History of Sexuality (Michel Foucault) 17
A History of Witchcraft: Sorcerers, Heretics, and Pagans (Jeffrey B. Russell) 182
Hoeveler, Diane (Gothic Feminism: The Professionalization of Gender from Charlotte Smith to the Brontës) 31, 46
Hoffman, Nina Kiriki (Stir of Bones) 25, 50–72, 171, 177
Hooked on Horror III: A Guide to Reading Interests (Anthony Fonseca and June Pulliam) 17, 83

# Index

hopeful monsters 77–78, 81, 97, 100–01, 121
Hopkins, Matthew 151, 182
hormones *see* sex hormones
"Horror and the Monstrous-Feminine: An Imaginary Abjection" (Barbara Creed) 15, 18, 47, 88, 97, 110, 173
horror fiction 11–12, 15, 18, 100, 173, 178
*Horror Fiction: An Introduction* (Gina Wisker) 174
horror film 12, 18
hunting 111–13
hybridity 81, 95–96, 118–21, 176
hypertrichosis 80, 83, 86–88

*I Was a Teenage Werewolf* (film) 75–76
illegality 33
*In a Different Voice: Psychological Theory and Women's Development* (Carol Gilligan) 13
*In the Name of Love: Women, Narcissism and the Gothic* (Michelle Massé) 51, 107
incest 103; *see also* rape; sexual violence
infanticide 158
institutions, disciplinary *see* disciplinary institutions
"An Introduction to the Horror Film" (Robin Wood) 79, 82–83

*Jade Green* (Phyllis Reynolds Naylor) 21–49, 70–71, 171, 178
*Jane-Emily* (Patricia Clapp) 27
jealousy 92–93, 115, 167
justice 28–29

Karlsen, Carol (*The Devil in the Shape of a Woman: Witchcraft in Colonial New England*) 147, 150, 181
Kimmel, Michael ("Masculinity as Homophobia: Fear, Shame, Silence in the Construction of Gender Identity") 76, 120
King, Stephen (*Carrie*) 79
Kingston, Maxine Hong (*The Woman Warrior*) 22
Klause, Annette Curtis (*Blood and Chocolate*) 78, 80, 99–121, 171, 175, 177, 181
knowing *see* epistemology
knowledge, construction of 126, 135–72, 176; *see also* constructivism; epistemology; received knowing; subjectivism
Kolmar, Wendy K., and Lynette Carpenter (*Haunting the House of Fiction: Feminist Perspectives on Ghost Stories by American Women*) 22, 27
Kristeva, Julia (*The Powers of Horror: An Essay on Abjection*) 15, 18, 88, 95

Kunzel, Bonnie, and Diana Tixler Herald (*Fluent in Fantasy*) 181

Lacan, Jacques ("The Mirror Stage as Formative of the I Function as Revealed in Psychoanalytic Experience") 88, 181
Lamb, Sharon, and Lyn Mikel Brown (*Packaging Girlhood: Rescuing Our Daughters from Marketers' Schemes*) 14
language, power of 54–55, 152; *see also* literacy
"Laugh of the Medusa" (Hélénè Cixous) 32
learned helplessness 82
*Learning Curves: Body Image and Female Sexuality in Young Adult Literature* (Beth Younger) 176
LeGuin, Ursula K. ("Why Kids Want Fantasy") 173
Lesko, Nancy (*Act Your Age! A Cultural Construction of Adolescence*) 75
literacy 32, 54–56, 116, 152–54, 167–68
*Loving with a Vengeance: Mass-produced Fantasies for Women* (Tanya Modleski) 106–07, 116
lunar cycle 79, 86, 95, 103
Lundie, Katherine A. (*Restless Spirits: Ghost Stories by American Women*) 22
lycanthrope *see* werewolf, figure of
lycanthropy 20, 73–122

magic 126–72, 176, 178
male gaze 132–33, 144–45, 147, 160; *see also* female gaze; surveillance
male privilege 55
*Manifesta: Young Women, Feminism, and the Future* (Jennifer Baumgardner and Amy Richards) 48, 180
Margolis, Harriet ("A Childe in Love, or Is It Just Fantasy? The Values of Women's Genres") 105–06
marriage, arranged 166–67, 177
marriage plot 71, 106, 171
"Masculinity as Homophobia: Fear, Shame, Silence in the Construction of Gender Identity" (Michael Kimmel) 76, 120
masculinity, conventional *see* masculinity, normative
masculinity, normative 19, 76, 81, 84, 87, 102, 106–08, 110, 112, 120
masculinity, stereotypical *see* masculinity, normative
mass media and gender identity 14
Massé, Michelle (*In the Name of Love: Women, Narcissism and the Gothic*) 51, 107

194

# Index

McCallum, Robyn: *Ideologies of Identity in Adolescent Fiction: The Dialogic Construction of Subjectivity* 59; "Other Selves: Subjectivity and the Doppelganger in Australian Adolescent Fiction" 15–16, 40

McNay, Lois (*Gender and Agency: Reconfiguring the Subject in Feminist and Social Theory*) 17

meat 81, 111–13; *see also* carnivory; hunting

*Medium* (television series) 22

mediumship 61–62, 148, 150, 180

*Meeting at the Crossroads: Women's Psychology and Girl's Development* (Carol Gilligan and Lyn Mikel Brown) 13, 32

menarche 79, 94, 102; *see also* menstruation

menstruation 79, 86, 94–95, 101–04, 118; *see also* menarche

mentoring relationships among women 157–58, 164–65

merrybegot 144–45, 155, 158; *see also* out of wedlock birth

Meyer, Stephenie (The Twilight Saga) 19

*Michel Foucault* (Claire O'Farrell) 30

micropractices of discipline *see* discipline

midwives 128, 145–46, 156, 158–59

*The Minister's Daughter* (Julie Hearn) 124, 142–159, 171, 176–78

mirror stage 88

"The Mirror Stage as Formative of the I Function as Revealed in Psychoanalytic Experience" (Jacques Lacan) 88, 181

the modern Gothic 49–69

Modleski, Tanya (*Loving with a Vengeance: Mass-produced Fantasies for Women*) 106–07, 116

monster, definition 15–16, 83; *see also* the Other

"Monster Movies: A Sexual Theory" (Walter Evans) 95

monsters, sympathetic 179

monstrous other *see* the Other

Morris, Paula (*Ruined*) 21, 49, 70, 177–78

Morrison, Toni (*Beloved*) 22

mortality, fear of 86

mother-daughter bond 58, 66–67, 71–72, 116–17, 163, 166, 181; *see also* sisterhood

Mulvey, Laura ("Visual Pleasure and Narrative Cinema") 99, 133

Murray, Margaret 129–30

mystery fiction 24

"Narrative Performance in the Contemporary Monster Story" (Daniel Punday) 77, 81, 101

Native Americans 93–94, 143–44, 153–54

nature *see* nature/culture dichotomy; natural world

nature/culture dichotomy 73–76, 80, 85, 93–98, 125, 146, 161, 175; *see also* animal nature; natural world

natural world 86, 93–95, 125, 130, 133–34, 145, 160–61; *see also* animal nature; nature/culture dichotomy

Naylor, Phyllis Reynolds (*Jade Green*) 21–49, 70–71, 171, 178

near-death experience 44, 65

neo-paganism 124, 127, 156, 181–82; *see also* Wicca; paganism

New Orleans, Louisiana 29, 34, 37–38

non-realistic fiction 173

O'Farrell, Claire (*Michel Foucault*) 30

oral tradition 155

Orenstein, Peggy (*Schoolgirls: Young Women, Self Esteem and the Confidence Gap*) 13, 174

the Other 12, 15–17, 18, 41–42, 75, 78–80, 86–88, 97, 98, 104, 122, 124–25, 129, 131–32, 171, 173–75, 178

the Other, definition 15–16, 41–42; *see also* definition; double

"Other Selves: Subjectivity and the Doppelganger in Australian Adolescent Fiction" (Robin McCallum) 15–16, 40

*The Others* (film) 21

out of wedlock birth 143–44, 145, 149, 158

overregulation 23, 50–56, 145–47; *see also* discipline

*Packaging Girlhood: Rescuing Our Daughters from Marketers' Schemes* (Lyn Mikel Brown and Sharon Lamb) 14

Paganism 128, 144–46, 154–55; *see also* neo-paganism; Wicca

paranormal romance 18, 80, 100, 105–06, 179; *see also* Gothic romance; romance

"Paranormal Romance: Secrets of the Female Fantastic" (Lee Tobin-McClain) 106

*pater familias see* family patriarch, figure of

patriarch, figure of *see* family patriarch, figure of

patriarchal culture, origins 15

patriarchal family 144, 146

pedagogy 165

*Pedagogy of the Oppressed* (Paolo Friere) 165

Phillips, Lynn (*Flirting with Danger: Young Women's Reflections on Sexuality and Domination*) 14, 87, 181

# Index

photography 55–56
Pinedo, Isabel (*Recreational Terror: Women and the Pleasures of Horror Film Viewing*) 15, 110
Pipher, Mary (*Reviving Ophelia. Saving the Selves of Adolescent Girls*) 13, 174
Pleasing Woman Discourse 87
pornography 86, 96, 99
*Pornography and Silence: Culture's Revenge against Nature* (Susan Griffin) 73, 76, 80, 86, 94–96, 125
possession 23–26, 62, 67, 148–50, 180; *see also* channeling
possession, diabolic 149–50; *see also* possession
post-feminism 14, 36, 47–48, 84; *see also* girl power
power 12, 17–18, 28, 30, 78, 85, 88, 134, 136–42, 145, 149–54, 166–69, 176, 179
*The Powers of Horror: An Essay on Abjection* (Julia Kristeva) 15, 18, 88, 95
pre-discursive subject 64, 180; *see also* discursive subject
pregnancy 43–44, 149, 155, 180; *see also* abortion; birth imagery; pregnancy outside of marriage
pre-teens 27
problem-posing model of education 165
proto–Wicca 129, 145, 160; *see also* Paganism; Wicca
*The Psychic Life of Power: Theories in Subjection* (Judith Butler) 17, 69–70, 77, 81, 131, 174–76, 182
Pulliam, June, and Anthony Fonseca (*Hooked on Horror III: A Guide to Reading Interests*) 17, 83
Punday, Daniel ("Narrative Performance in the Contemporary Monster Story") 77, 81, 101
Puritanism 128, 142–59, 178; *see also* Christianity, fundamentalism

race 18, 28, 29, 34–35, 37, 41, 78, 93–94, 124, 131, 143–44, 162, 177, 179
*Radical Spirits: Spiritualism and Women's Rights in Nineteenth Century America* (Ann Braude) 61, 62, 150, 180
*Raising Their Voices: The Politics of Girls Anger* (Lyn Mikel Brown) 14, 28, 77, 82, 100, 113
Ramsdell, Kristin (*Romance Fiction: A Guide to the Genre*) 105
rape 33, 95, 133, 136, 145; *see also* incest; rape culture; sexual harassment; sexual violence; violence against women
rape culture 110; *see also* rape; sexual harassment; violence against women
reading *see* literacy
*Rebel Angels* (Libba Bray) 124, 160–71, 176–78, 182
received knowing 126, 135, 148; *see also* constructivism; subjectivism
*Recreational Terror: Women and the Pleasures of Horror Film Viewing* (Isabel Pinedo) 15, 110
Rees, Celia: *Sorceress* 142–159, 171, 177; *Witch Child* 124, 142–159, 161, 171, 177–78; The Witch Child Series 124, 142–159, 161, 171, 177
Reid, Sían ("As I Do Will, So Mote It Be: Magic as Metaphor in Neo-Pagan Witchcraft") 127, 139, 156
Reiss, Kathryn (*Dreadful Sorry*) 21–49, 71, 171, 176–77
relational violence among girls and women 13–14, 37–38, 89–91, 104, 141–42, 157
repetition 16
the repressed 15, 23, 28, 39, 41, 42–43, 63, 67, 77–78, 83, 105, 149–50, 175; *see also* the uncanny
*The Reproduction of Mothering: Psychoanalysis and the Sociology of Gender* (Nancy Chodorow) 139, 181
*Restless Spirits: Ghost Stories by American Women* (Katherine A. Lundie) 22
*Reviving Ophelia. Saving the Selves of Adolescent Girls* (Mary Pipher) 13, 174
Richards, Amy, and Jennifer Baumgardner (*Manifesta: Young Women, Feminism, and the Future*) 48, 180
Ringel, Faye ("Witchcraft/Sorcery") 123
romance fiction 81, 105–08, 110; *see also* Gothic romance; paranormal romance
*Romance Fiction: A Guide to the Genre* (Kristin Ramsdell) 105
Romanticism 80
*Ruined* (Paula Morris) 21–49, 70, 177
Rule of Three *see* The Wiccan Rede
Russell, Jeffrey B. (*A History of Witchcraft: Sorcerers, Heretics, and Pagans*) 182

*Sabrina the Teenage Witch* (television series) 130, 182
Salem, Massachusetts 154
"The Sand in the Oyster: Muddle Middle" (Patty Campbell) 12
school story 160, 164–65

# Index

*Schoolgirls: Young Women, Self Esteem and the Confidence Gap* (Peggy Orenstein) 13, 174
scopophilia 99
*The Second Sex* (Simone de Beauvoir) 13
second-wave feminism 27, 36, 40, 47–48, 50, 84, 176–77; *see also* post-feminism
self-esteem 13
self-expression 55, 56, 149, 177
self-portraits 56–57
sex, biological 16–17
sex hormones 83, 86, 94, 175
sexual abuse 103; *see also* rape
sexual assault *see* rape
sexual desire 77, 79–81, 85–96, 106, 112, 125; *see also* sexuality
sexual difference 11–12, 84, 84, 162
sexual harassment 33, 81, 101–04, 177; *see also* violence against women
sexual maturity 91, 94–96, 101
sexual politics 47, 84, 142
*The Sexual Politics of Meat: A Feminist-Vegetarian Critical Theory* (Carol Adams) 74, 111
sexual violence 33–34, 36–37, 41, 46–47, 103; *see also* incest; rape; sexual harassment; violence against women
sexuality *see* compulsory heterosexuality; feminine sexuality; sexual desire
Shakespeare, William (*Hamlet*) 21
Shakira ("She Wolf") 75
shamans 123–24
shapeshifting 104, 118–22, 175; *see also* hybridity
"She Wolf" (Shakira) 75
Shiver Trilogy (Maggie Stiefvater) 180
silencing of women's voices 13, 15–16, 27–38, 50–56, 72, 89, 96, 105–06, 148–50, 174–75, 180
sisterhood 22, 23, 29, 42, 56, 66–67, 71, 89–94, 105, 116–17, 124, 130, 138–42, 156, 157–59, 165–71, 176 78; *see also* female friendship; mother/daughter relationship
*The Sixth Sense* (film) 21, 22
slut, figure of 104, 129, 131–32, 137, 140
sorcerer *see* witch, figure of
*Sorceress* (Celia Rees) 142–159, 171, 177
sorcery *see* magic and witchcraft
South *see* American South
space, feminine 63, 65–66, 169
speech *see* articulateness, literacy, silencing and voice
spirits *see* ghosts, figure of

Spiritualism 61–62, 130, 150, 180
spirituality 61–62
Steele, Valerie (*The Corset: A Cultural History*) 162
Stevenson, Robert Louis (*The Strange Case of Dr. Jekyll and Mr. Hyde*) 180
Stiefvater, Maggie (Shiver Trilogy) 180
*Stir of Bones* (Nina Kiriki Hoffman) 25, 50–69, 71–72, 171, 177
Stohl, Margaret, and Kami Garcia (*Beautiful Creatures*) 130, 182
*The Strange Case of Dr. Jekyll and Mr. Hyde* (Robert Louis Stevenson) 180
subjectivism 135–39, 142, 147–52, 162–68; *see also* constructivism; received knowing
subjectivity 12, 16–17, 27, 29–31, 39–40, 56–57, 69–70, 78, 85, 126, 135–39, 173
surveillance 30–31, 145–47, 160; *see also* compulsory visibility; male gaze; visibility
*The Sweet Far Thing* (Libba Bray) 124, 160–71, 176–78, 182
symbolic order 41–42, 47, 97, 173

*Teenage Witches: Magical Youth and the Search for Self* (Helen A. Berger and Douglas Ezzy) 128
third-wave feminism 48–49
the three-fold law *see* The Wiccan Rede
Title IX 84
Tobin-McClain, Lee ("Paranormal Romance: Secrets of the Female Fantastic") 106
traditional healers 123–24, 128, 156–59; *see also* cunning women
Trites, Roberta Seelinger: *Disturbing the Universe: Power and Repression in Adolescent Literature* 12, 18, 57, 60, 85, 126, 179; *Waking Sleeping Beauty: Feminist Voices in Children's Novels* 15, 17, 29–30, 32, 63, 71, 89, 100, 137
tweens *see* pre-teens
The Twilight Saga (Stephenie Meyer) 19

the uncanny 28, 39, 41; *see also* the repressed
"The Uncanny" (Sigmund Freud) 23, 28, 39
*Under the Light* (Laura Whitcomb) 25, 50–69, 71–72, 177–78
unrealistic literature *see* fantastic literature
Updike, John (*The Witches of Eastwick*) 131
*The Uses of Enchantment and Magic: The Meaning and Importance of Fairy Tales* (Bruno Bettelheim) 20, 100

197

# Index

"The Value of Young Adult Literature" (Michael Cart) 18, 79
vampire fiction 24
vampires, Young Adult fiction 19
vegetarianism 80, 83, 87
Victorian England 128, 130, 160–72
*Vintage* (Steve Berman) 180
violence against women 22–23, 25, 32–35, 46–47, 53, 81, 101–03, 107, 110; *see also* rape; sexual violence
violence, men's 106, 120
violence, women's 91–93, 104, 115–17
visibility 145–46; *see also* compulsory visibility; surveillance
"Visual Pleasure and Narrative Cinema" (Laura Mulvey) 99, 133
voice *see* articulateness; silencing of women's voices

*Wait Till Helen Comes* (Mary Dowling Hahn) 27
*Waking Sleeping Beauty: Feminist Voices in Children's Novels* (Roberta Seelinger Trites) 15, 17, 29–30, 32, 63, 71, 89, 100, 137
wampum belt 154
water imagery 43–45, 63–69
"The Werewolf" (Stefan Dziemaimowicz) 74–75
werewolf, definition 73–74
werewolf, figure of 20, 73–122, 171, 175, 180; *see also* lycanthropy
*Werewolf of London* (film) 74
*The Werewolf of Paris* (Guy Endore) 74
Whitcomb, Laura: *A Certain Slant of Light* 25, 50–69, 71–72, 177–78, 180; *Under the Light* 25, 50–69, 71–72, 177–78
White, Emily (*Fast Girls: Teenage Tribes and the Myth of the Slut*) 129, 131, 181
"Why Kids Want Fantasy" (Ursula K. LeGuin) 173
Wicca 124, 127, 129–30, 133–34, 138–60, 181–82
the Wiccan Rede 138, 142, 160, 181–82
the will 141, 156, 170
windigo 93
Windsor, Patricia (*The Blooding*) 78, 80, 99–122, 171, 175, 177
Wisker, Gina (*Horror Fiction: An Introduction*) 174
"The Witch" (Bernadette Bosky) 124
*Witch Child* (Celia Rees) 124, 142–159, 171, 177–78
The Witch Child series (Celia Rees) 124, 142–159, 171, 177

The Witch Cult 130; *see also* The Burning Times; Early Modern witch hunts; neopaganism
witch, definition 123
witch, figure of 20, 123–72, 176
witch hunts *see* Early Modern witch hunts
witchcraft 123–72
witchcraft, executions for 157, 159
witchcraft, people accused of 124, 157, 181
"Witchcraft/Sorcery" (Faye Ringel) 123
*Witchcraze: A New History of the European Witch Hunts* (Anne Barstow) 157, 181
*Witches, Midwives and Nurses: A History of Women Healers* (Barbara Ehrenreich and Deidra English) 124
*The Witches of Eastwick* (John Updike) 131
Wolf, Naomi (*The Beauty Myth: How Images of Beauty Are Used Against Women*) 84–85, 89, 174, 181
*Wolf Girl see* Blood Moon
*The Wolf Man* (film) 74, 76, 98
wolves 80
*Woman in Black* (film) 22
*Woman in Black* (Stephen Mallatratt) 22
*Woman in Black* (Susan Hill) 22
*The Woman Warrior* (Maxine Hong Kingston) 22
Women of the Otherworld series (Kelley Armstrong) 75
women's athleticism *see* athleticism, women's
women's education *see* education of women
women's history *see* history, women's
women's silencing *see* silencing
*Women's Ways of Knowing: The Development of Self, Voice and Mind* (Mary Belenky, et al.) 126–27, 135–36, 139, 156
Wood, Robin ("An Introduction to the Horror Film") 79, 82–83
writing *see* literacy

Young Adult fiction, definition 12, 18, 78–79, 85, 176
Young Adult fiction, film as 18, 78–79
Young Adult horror fiction, definition 11–13, 18, 20, 176, 178
Young Adult Library Services Association 18, 79
Younger, Beth (*Learning Curves: Body Image and Female Sexuality in Young Adult Literature*) 176

zombie fiction 24

www.ingramcontent.com/pod-product-compliance
Ingram Content Group UK Ltd.
Pitfield, Milton Keynes, MK11 3LW, UK
UKHW042011140426
5217IPUK00015B/1113